Politics and Economics in the Russian Far East

The dramatic reforms in Russia are affecting all levels of the economy and society as well as the political life of that country. The impact of these changes is also being felt in the Russian Far East and has raised questions as to how that region's relations with other countries in Asia will develop and whether a stable democratic society will evolve.

Politics and Economics in the Russian Far East provides a background to the region's economic development and relations with its neighbors. It surveys the challenges of economic development including fiscal, capital, resource, energy, and environmental problems, highlighting the generally disruptive effects of reform on the region, but also pointing to some areas of potential, including international trade and foreign investment. The book places the Russian Far East in the context of Russia's bilateral relations with the United States, Japan, China and Korea, and examines the political, economic and security significance of the region in Northeast Asia.

This book is a major contribution to the wider debate over Russia's future and its place in the international community. It is a comprehensive, interdisciplinary survey of the region's present situation and future prospects both in terms of its internal, economic, social and political development as well as its changing international role in Northeast Asia.

Tsuneo Akaha is Professor of International Policy Studies and Director of the Center for East Asian Studies at the Monterey Institute of International Studies, California.

Politics and Economics in the Russian Far East

Changing ties with Asia–Pacific

Edited by Tsuneo Akaha

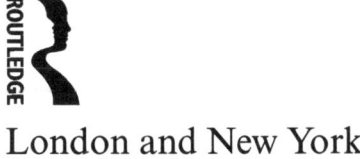

London and New York

First published 1997
by Routledge
11 New Fetter Lane, London EC4P 4EE

Simultaneously published in the USA and Canada
by Routledge
29 West 35th Street, New York, NY 10001

Typeset in Times by M Rules

Printed and bound in Great Britain by Creative Print and
Design (Wales), Ebbw Vale

British Library Cataloguing in Publication Data
A catalogue record for this book is available from the British Library

Library of Congress Cataloguing in Publication Data
Politics and economics in the Russian Far East: changing ties
    with Asia Pacific / edited by Tsuneo Akaha.
    Includes bibliographical references and index.
    1. Russian Far East (Russia) – Economic conditions.   2. Russian
Far East (Russia) – Politics and government.   3. Russian Far East
(Russia) – Foreign economic relations..   I. Akaha, Tsuneo
HC340.12.Z7F2775   1997
338.957 – dc21   96–53636

ISBN 0-415-16029-4 (hbk)
ISBN 0-415-16473-7 (pbk)

Contents

Part III Russia, the Russian Far East and the Asia–Pacific neighbors

Illustrations

Contributors

Tsuneo Akaha is a professor of international policy studies and director of the Center for East Asian Studies, Monterey Institute of International Studies, Monterey, California. He received his MA and PhD in International Relations from the University of Southern California. He has taught at the University of Southern California, Kansas State University, and Bowling Green State University (Ohio). He has been a visiting research fellow or scholar at Hokkaido University's Slavic Research Center, Seikei University (Tokyo), and the University of Tokyo. Among his numerous publications are: *Japan in Global Ocean Politics*; *Japan in the Post-hegemonic World* (co-editor); *International Political Economy: A Reader* (co-editor); *Integrating the Russian Far East into the Asia–Pacific Economy* (editor); 'Soviet/Russian–Japanese Economic Relations' (co-author), in Hasegawa *et al.* (eds), *Russia and Japan: An Unresolved Dilemma between Distant Neighbors*; 'Japanese–Russian Economic Relations and their Implications for Asia–Pacific Security,' in Shirk and Twomey (eds), *Power and Prosperity: Economic and Security Linkages in Asia–Pacific*; and 'Russia and Asia in 1995,' *Asian Survey*, January 1996. He is currently directing an international collaborative project on 'Economic Relations and Regional Order in Northeast Asia.'

Nobuo Arai is the executive director of the Hokkaido Institute for Regional Studies in Sapporo, Japan. He holds a Master's degree from the University of Tokyo and received training in Moscow State University. He is author of several publications and is currently advisor to the Hokkaido Government on the problems of foreign economic relations, a research fellow at Hokkaido University's Slavic Research Center and at the Institute of International Trade and Industry, Ministry of International Trade and Industry, Tokyo. His areas of research include the general developments in the Russian Far East, with a focus on fisheries and other resource developments.

James P. Dorian is a fellow in the Program on Resources, Energy, and Minerals at the East–West Center, Honolulu, Hawaii. He received his PhD in Resource Economics at the University of Hawaii and was a research geologist for the US Geological Survey. His recent works include: *Minerals, Mining and Economic Development in China*; *CIS Energy and Minerals Development: Prospects, Problems and Opportunities for International Cooperation* (co-editor); *Mining in the CIS: Commercial Opportunities*; *International Issues in Energy Policy, Development and Economics* (co-editor); and *USSR–Mongolia: A Minerals Association about to End.* Current projects include 'Central Asia and the Caucasian Republics: A Comprehensive Study of Their Integration into Regional Mineral and Energy Markets' and 'China's Energy Industry: Present and Future Outlook.'

Tsuyoshi Hasegawa is a professor of history at the University of California, Santa Barbara. He received his BA in International Relations from the University of Tokyo, MA in Soviet Area Studies and PhD in History from the University of Washington. Among his numerous publications are: *Russia and Japan: An Unresolved Dilemma between Distant Neighbors* (co-editor); *Between Peace and War: Origins of the Northern Territories Dispute and Russian–Japanese Relations under Gorbachev and Yeltsin* (forthcoming); 'Japan's Policy toward Russia: Principles, Contradictions, and Prospects,' in Ito *et al.* (eds), *Between Disintegration and Reintegration: Former Socialist Countries and the World since 1989*; 'Continuing Stalemate,' in Goodby *et al.* (eds), and *'Northern Territories' and Beyond: Russian, Japanese, and American Perspectives.*

Vladimir I. Ivanov is chairman of the Asia–Pacific Region Studies Department, Institute of World Economics and International Relations, Academy of Sciences, Moscow, and currently a visiting senior researcher at the Economic Research Institute for Northeast Asia, Niigata, Japan. He received his MA in Political Economy from Moscow State University and PhD in Political Economy from the Institute of Oriental Studies, Academy of Sciences of the USSR, Moscow. He has published widely on Soviet/Russian policies in the Asia–Pacific, including *The Northern Territories Issue in the Context of US–Japan–Russia Relations*; *Emerging Asia–Pacific Multilateralism beyond the Cold War*; and *'Northern Territories' and Beyond: Russian, Japanese and American Perspectives.*

Evgenii B. Kovrigin is a professor of international relations at Seinangakuin University, Fukuoka, Japan. He was a department head at the Economic Research Institute, Russian Academy of Sciences Far Eastern Branch until 1992. He received his PhD from the Institute of World Economy and International Relations in Moscow. Past publications include: 'The Prospects of South Korean Investment and Russo–Korean Economic Cooperation in the Russian Far East,' *The Kyungwon Economics and Management Review*, November 1993; 'Problems and Prospects for Japanese Investment in the Soviet Far East' in Drysdale (ed.), *The Soviets and the Pacific Challenge*; and *Prospects and Contradictions of the Formation of the Pacific.* Current projects include 'The Role of Japan in Emerging Asia–Pacific Integration' and 'The Russian Far East in Asia–Pacific Cooperation: Present and Future.'

Vladimir F. Li is director of the Center for Asian–Pacific Research, Diplomatic Academy of Russia, Ministry of Foreign Affairs, Moscow. He received his MA in History of Oriental Societies from Leningrad (St Petersburg) University and his PhD in Modern and Contemporary History from Leningrad Pedagogical University. Among his publications are: *The Intelligentsia and Social Progress in the Developing Countries* (ed.); *The Developing Countries: Studies of Sociological Problems* (ed.); *The Urban Middle Strata in the Developing Countries of the East* (ed.); *The Society, Elite and Bureaucracy in the Newly-free Countries of the East* (ed.); *The Oriental Countries Today – Basic Problems* (Editorial Board member); and *Deportation of Korean National Minority in Russia.*

Robert A. Manning is a senior fellow at the Progressive Policy Institute, Washington, DC, and a research associate at George Washington University's Sigur Center for East Asian Studies. Past positions include Advisor for Policy and Assistant Secretary for East Asian and Pacific Affairs at the US Department of State. Among his publications are: *Back to the Future: Towards a Post-Nuclear Ethic* and *Asian Policy: The New Soviet Challenge in the Pacific.* He has also contributed to *Logic, Bribes, and Threats: Incentives and Disincentives for North Korea in the Korea Nuclear Problem.* Current projects include 'Plutonium Proliferation and Regional Security in NE Asia,' 'US Policy and South Asia,' and 'Clinton and the Korea Questions: A Strategy for the Endgame.'

Pavel A. Minakir is director of the Economic Research Institute, Russian Academy of Sciences Far Eastern Branch, Khabarovsk. He graduated from Moscow State University in 1972 and received his PhD in Economics in Khabarovsk in 1984. His research interests include regional economy, economic development of the Russian Far East, economic forecasting, and economic regulation. His recent publications include: *The Russian Far East: An Economic Review*; *Russian Far East Economy: Reform and Crisis* (ed.); *The Russian Far East: An Economic Handbook*; and 'New Model of the Far Eastern Economic Development,' *Far Eastern Affairs*, 1991.

James Clay Moltz is a research professor and assistant director of the Center for Nonproliferation Studies, Monterey Institute of International Studies, California, and the editor of *The Nonproliferation Review*. He received his MA in Russian and East European Studies from Stanford University and his MA and PhD in Political Science from the University of California, Berkeley. He has received many grants and fellowships, including a Rockefeller Foundation grant, a NATO Science Committee grant, a UC, Berkeley Institute of International Studies research fellowship, a postdoctoral fellowship from the University of California Institute on Global Conflict and Cooperation, and a MacArthur postdoctoral fellowship at Duke University. Among his numerous publications are, most recently: 'Divergent Learning and the Failed Politics of Soviet Economic Reform,' *World Politics*, January 1993; 'Regional Tensions in the Russo–Chinese Rapprochement,' *Asian Survey*, June 1995; and 'The Russian Economic Crisis: Implications for

Asian–Pacific Policy and Security,' in Shirk and Twomey (eds), *Power and Prosperity: Economic and Security Linkages in Asia–Pacific.*

Takashi Murakami is a professor at Hokkaido University's Slavic Research Center, Sapporo, Japan. He is a graduate of Sophia University in Tokyo and has taught at Hitotsubashi University and Osaka City University. Before joining the Slavic Research Center, he was head of the Economic Studies Division, Institute for Russian and East European Economic Research, Tokyo. He is co-author of *Problems of Agriculture and Agriculture–Dairy Trade in the Soviet Union* (in Japanese); *The Awakening Soviet Far East* (in Japanese); and numerous articles on the Russian Far Eastern economy. His areas of specialty include energy problems and the industrial structure in the former Soviet Union, technology transfer and economic developments in Siberia and the Russian Far East.

Kunio Okada is a senior researcher at the Institute for Russian and East European Economic Research, Tokyo, where he has worked since 1989. He did his graduate studies at Soka University's Graduate School of Literature in Tokyo and Moscow State University. Among his many publications (in Japanese) are: *Russia at a Turning Point: The Direction of Marketization and External Economic Policy* (co-author); *The Presence of Former Soviet States in International Commodities Market* (co-author); *The Current Situation and Future Prospects of Economic Cooperation in Northeast Asia* (co-author); *New Economic Relations between Russia and its Neighboring Countries* (co-author); and *The Realities of Private Sector Formation in the Russian Far Eastern Economy* (co-author).

Robert A. Scalapino is Robson Research Professor of Government Emeritus, University of California, Berkeley and founder and former director of the Institute of East Asian Studies at the University of California, Berkeley, where he was also editor of *Asian Survey*. He received his PhD in Government from Harvard University. He has taught at Santa Barbara College, Harvard University, and the University of California, Berkeley. A recipient of numerous honors and awards for his distinguished scholarly achievements, Dr Scalapino serves on the editorial boards of many journals, including *China Studies* (Peking University), *International Security*, *Journal of Northeast Asian Studies*, *Orbis*, *The Washington Quarterly*, and *African Journal of International Affairs and Development*. Among his numerous publications are: *The Last Leninists: The Uncertain Future of Asia's Communist States*; *The Politics of Development: Perspectives on Twentieth-Century Asia*; *Asian Communism: Continuity and Transition* (co-editor); and *Asia and the Major Powers: Domestic Politics and Foreign Policy* (co-editor).

Robert Valliant is director of the Center for Russia in Asia, University of Hawaii at Manoa, Honolulu. Prior to joining the University of Hawaii, he taught at St John's University and West Oahu College. In 1988–94, Dr

Valliant compiled and edited *RA Report*, a semi-annual report on Russian activities in the Asia–Pacific region. He currently teaches a course on contemporary Russia in Asia, including Siberia, Russian Far East, and relations with countries from the Pacific Rim to the Middle East. His most recent publication is 'The Western United States, Hawaii, and the Soviet Union,' in Valencia (ed.), *The Russian Far East and the North Pacific Region: Emerging Issues in International Relations*.

Alexei V. Zagorsky is a section head at the Center for Japanese and Pacific Studies, Institute of World Economy and International Relations, Academy of Sciences of Russia, Moscow. He received his BA and PhD in History from Moscow Institute of International Relations. Among his publications are: *Japan and China: Patterns of Societal Development as Seen by Japanese Historians* (in Russian); *Japanese Leftist Parties on the Eve of the 90s: Social Background of Political Crisis* (in Russian); 'Regional Conflicts in the Context of Soviet–American Relations' and 'Political Aspects of Pacific Security: The Soviet View' in *Beyond the Cold War in the Pacific*; 'Dilemmas of the Soviet Pacific Policy: Japanese and Korean Cases' in *Cooperative Security in the Pacific*; 'Specifics of Japanese Political Evolution' in *Political Changes in Western Nations: Late 70s and 80s* (co-author, in Russian); 'Neo-Conservative Policy in Japan' in *Neo-Conservatism Today*; and 'Soviet–Japanese Relations Under Perestroika: The Territorial Dispute and Its Impact' in Akaha and Langdon (eds), *Japan in the Post-hegemonic World*.

Foreword

Robert A. Scalapino

As the twentieth century comes to a close, the uncertainties concerning the future of Russia remain huge. Here is a people talented and with a highly educated elite, capable of major accomplishments in the scientific-technological realm. Here is a region abundant in natural resources, with a very favorable land–population ratio and a pivotal geopolitical position – astride the Eurasian continent. Yet the economic and political turmoil that has followed the dismemberment of the Soviet empire has not yet ceased.

The euphoria that greeted 'the end of Communism' has recently been decidedly subdued. Many Russians, confronted with the economic hardships of recent times and the seemingly endless wrangling in the political arena, have asked, 'Is this democracy?'

Thus, in Russia as in some other ex-Communist states of East Europe and in the newly independent Central Asian states, Communists of varying political hues have shown increased strength. Frequently, they proclaim themselves social democrats, dedicated to attacking the inequities, lawlessness and corruption of the new order.

At the same time, nationalists of a more strident type have also garnered support, in part a reflection of Russians' historic ambivalence as to whether they are or should be an integral part of the West or whether they should pursue a separate destiny. Heightened nationalist sentiment is also an answer to the humiliation of having lost power and influence, and Russia's perceived exclusion from decision-making on matters important to it.

While political uncertainties continue to abound, there are some signs – as yet not definitive – that Russia's economic crisis may have passed its worst phases. Should this prove to be true, it would encourage the cause of political centrism as well as the continued effort to make the transition from a statist economic strategy to one of greater economic liberalism, albeit with the state retaining an important economic role. Yet, whatever its precise course, the Russian political and economic system will undoubtedly have certain unique features, as has been the case throughout its long history.

It is in this context that the Russian Far East (RFE) must be seen. A part of Russia, and yet apart from the Russian heartland, the RFE faces west politically but with an increasing interest in the east economically. With only 8 million people in the Far Eastern region and close to 1.2 billion Chinese to the south, the advocacy of political independence is likely to remain a minority position. Yet the quest for greater economic autonomy – already amply evidenced – will surely continue.

It has not been easy to break away from the old system whereby this region furnished its natural resources and military supplies for a massive Soviet defense force, a sizeable portion of which was stationed in the region and, in return, received subsidization from the Center. Inter-regional economic intercourse was limited, and economic contact with the rest of East Asia was inhibited by formidable political–ideological barriers.

The old barriers are largely gone, although certain restraints remain including ethnic suspicions and unresolved territorial issues. The greatest barrier to date, however, has been the sorry state of the Russian Far Eastern economy, and the massive costs of the infrastructure requirements if RFE resources are to be more fully exploited.

None the less, the RFE is an eminently logical candidate for growing economic interaction with its close neighbors. It is surely destined to become a part of one or more Natural Economic Territories (NETs) that will grow in years to come: the Tumen River delta, the Sea of Japan (Eastern Sea) rim, and the Sino–Russian border region. NETs, taking advantage of geographic proximity, combine resources, manpower, capital and management to optimal advantage for the parties concerned. They cut across political boundaries, but often include only portions of states. And whatever state support is obtained, NETs depend for their ultimate success upon their attraction to the private sector.

NETs may create new issues or problems. Matters of jurisdiction and control are likely to emerge. Specific problems such as immigration and environmental degradation will require attention. Moreover, certain resources of this region will be increasingly needed within each country. Nevertheless, for the RFE, the pursuit of an export-led strategy that banks on its available resources would seem to be the most logical developmental course. This will lead to the increased involvement of this region – and hence, of the greater Russia of which it is a part – with the political and strategic, as well as economic future, of the surrounding Northeast Asian societies. What happens in China and on the Korean peninsula, for example, will affect the RFE in increasing measure in the years ahead. Russia must thus be a part of the efforts to achieve greater regional cooperation in all fields.

The essays that follow explore many of the issues raised here in greater depth, and with the insights that only those who are scholars well versed in their subject-matter can offer. The mix between Russian and non-Russian specialists is one admirable feature of this volume. We shall revisit the issues set forth here at various points in the future, but now we have an excellent foundation from which to advance.

Robert A. Scalapino
Robson Research Professor of Government Emeritus
Berkeley, California, December 1995

Acknowledgments

On 20–22 October 1994, the Monterey Institute of International Studies' Center for East Asian Studies hosted an international seminar to discuss the possibilities and challenges in integrating the Russian Far East into the Asia–Pacific economy. Earlier drafts of the chapters in this volume were presented at this seminar, except those by Dorian, Moltz, and Zagorsky, which were submitted after the seminar. The funding support for the seminar was provided by the Asia Foundation, Matsushita Electric Corporation of America, Sakaguchi Electric Heaters (Tokyo), Vanderbilt Institute for Public Policy Studies' Center for US–Japan Studies and Cooperation, and the Monterey Institute. Their generous support is acknowledged with great appreciation.

This volume would not have been possible without the editorial and research assistance of graduate assistants at the Center for East Asian Studies, including Marc T. Cryer, Maxine Eber, Patrick Olander, Karen Vogel, and Kevin Zick. Tamara Troyakova of the Institute of History, Archeology, and Ethnology of the Far Eastern Peoples, Vladivostok, who was a visiting fellow of the Center in 1995, also provided valuable assistance with the spelling of numerous Russian names and terms. Special thanks go to these individuals.

Needless to say, the views contained in this volume are those of the individual authors and do not necessarily represent those of the organizations to which they are affiliated or the organizations providing support for the above seminar. Responsibility for editorial work rests with the editor.

Introduction

Tsuneo Akaha

Peaceful relations among countries in any region require stable and mutually beneficial relations at all levels, both governmental and non-governmental, and in all dimensions, including political, economic, security, and social–cultural fields. When countries' ideological orientations pit them against each other and their economic systems are incompatible, there is little or no prospect of cooperative relations among them. This is particularly so if their historical hostilities cloud their contemporary views of each other and their national security establishments see each other as adversaries, potential or real, rather than as partners in cooperative security. Unfortunately, this was largely the case for the former Soviet Union and its capitalist neighbors in Asia–Pacific during the Cold War era.

Within the Cold War geostrategic context, the Soviet Far East had an almost exclusively military significance in Asia–Pacific, and the Soviet Union was seen by its neighbors as a menacing security threat and a source of political instability in the region. Moscow's historical view of the Far East as a vulnerable frontier in perpetual need of military protection did no more to change the hostile international relations in this part of the world than the US forward deployment in the western Pacific as part of its global containment policy against its ideological adversary. Economically, in contrast to the deepening interdependence among the capitalist countries of Asia–Pacific, the Soviet Far East's ties to its regional neighbors were extremely limited. Moreover, any desire among the leaders of the Soviet Far East to develop closer ties with their Asian-Pacific neighbors was subordinated to the Soviet Union's development strategy based on a geographical division of labor, with its Far Eastern region serving almost exclusively as a supplier of natural resources for the country's industrialization and producer of military–industrial products to meet the country's defense needs.

Now that the Cold War is over, the Soviet Union has disappeared, and Russia is attempting to transform itself into a democratic society with a market economy, will the nation be able to forge a stable and peaceful relationship with its Asia–Pacific neighbors, politically, economically, and even in the security realm? What role should and can the Russian Far East and its Northeast Asian neighbors respectively play in bringing Russia and the

Asia–Pacific economies into closer and cooperative relationships? These are the fundamental questions addressed by this collection.

This volume is predicated upon the premise that the peace and stability of Asia–Pacific requires a closer relationship among the countries of Northeast Asia and that this will depend on both Russia's transformation into a democratic society with a market economy and the Russian Far East's integration with the Asia–Pacific economy. The geographical proximity and the unbalanced level of economic development among the Northeast Asian countries, combined with the history of international animosities in this part of the world, are a potential source of conflict and instability that requires serious attention. If the Russian Far East is to be integrated into the Asia–Pacific economy, not only must the region's market forces be allowed to grow, but institutionalized mechanisms of cooperation must be developed to link the fledgling market forces in the Russian Far East to those of the dynamic Asia–Pacific countries, particularly Japan, South Korea, China, and the United States.

Another basic question discussed in this volume relates to the role of government in domestic economic development and international economic cooperation. On the one hand, there is the view that integration among disparate economic units, whether within a nation or among nations, requires market integration which is assisted and sustained by institutionalized cooperation. 'Market integration' refers to the development of a high degree of interdependence among essential factors of production, trade, and consumption, and 'institutionalized cooperation' refers to the development of a 'regime,' or a set of principles, norms, rules, and decision-making procedures, designed to promote the development and linkage of complementary market conditions. The Russian Far East is an underdeveloped region heavily dependent on defense and extractive industries. It borders the two capitalist giants of Japan and the United States with their highly diversified and well integrated economies, the newly industrialized economy of South Korea, and the fast growing economy of China. It also is adjacent to the moribund economy of North Korea and the struggling transition economy of Mongolia. Market forces in these economies are at such disparate levels of development that it would be tempting to suggest that strong policy coordination will be more effective than a *laissez-faire* approach to regional economic cooperation and integration. From this perspective, the central concern is that if left to market principles, the Russian Far East would find itself in an untenable position of permanent dependence, with serious political and security implications. To avoid this, the argument would suggest, the Russian Far Eastern economy needs a 'shot in the arm,' that is, the creation and development of market forces in the region cannot be left entirely to some 'invisible hands,' but rather they must be nurtured and promoted by public and private assistance from outside the region, from Moscow and from international sources. This will require the development of institutional cooperation among all the major actors concerned, including Moscow, the

Russian Far East's separate administrative and territorial units, and the governments of Japan, the United States, China, and Korea. We will return to this issue in the concluding chapter.

On the other hand, others maintain that given the low level of political trust and confidence that characterizes the current relations among the Northeast Asian countries, international policy coordination, even if desirable, is highly unrealistic. It is also problematic in that a state-led strategy of development for Russia would result in a high level of centralization of power that is inimical to market capitalism and stifle or distort the development of a market economy.

There are a number of other important questions which this collection addresses. Should the United States and other neighboring countries of Russia develop an Asia–Pacific policy with an explicit focus on the Russian Far East? If so, what would it look like? Are the growing trade relations between the Russian Far East and the neighboring East Asian economies necessarily conducive to balanced economic development of the region? How should the Far Eastern communities respond to the disintegration of Russia's national economy? Should they welcome it as it would potentially give greater freedom for the regional leaders to forge their own future? How important is the military–civilian conversion in developing a modern market economy in the Russian Far East? What are the regional and international security implications of the growing Russian weapons and weapons technology transfers to Asian countries.

How effective is Russian legislation in establishing the ownership and control of the all-important natural resources in the Far East? What can Russia and the Russian Far East learn from the international community, particularly from the United States, e.g., in the area of conversion, and from Japan, especially in the area of industrial and trade policy development? Should the Russian Far East develop an export-oriented regional economy? Can its exports be competitive enough on the international markets? More fundamentally, what role should government play in the development of industry in Russia? Should Russia follow the developmental state model exemplified by Japan and South Korea?

Is the current pattern of industrial and resource development in the Russian Far East conducive to long-term, environmentally sustainable development? To the extent that ecological awareness is growing in the region, is it being translated into effective policy? What do Moscow, regional governments, and foreign investors need to do to ensure sustainable development? Will the more immediate issues of economic survival prevent the Russian and Far Eastern leaders from developing effective health and welfare programs?

What can the international community do to assist in the development of the Russian Far East? What are the social, political, and security implications of the growing foreign presence in the region, including business joint ventures, foreign laborers and merchants, and foreign goods? What are the outstanding issues between Russia and the neighboring Northeast Asian countries that stand in the way of further cooperation? What incentives do the neighboring countries have for extending cooperative hands? Are their interests purely economic? What political or security concerns do they have? Does the Russian Far East present an opportunity for cooperation or a source of conflict? What confidence-building measures are conceivable in the near future to replace the historical suspicions and animosities that could again flare up with more amicable and mutually beneficial relationships? Is Russia ready to engage the neighboring countries politically, economically, and in the security realm in a way that is also conducive to the economic development of the Russian Far East?

Important as Russia's cooperation with its Asia–Pacific neighbors may be, however, the fundamental course of development for the nation and its Far Eastern territories will be defined by developments within Russia. On the eve of the Russian presidential election in June 1996, many outside observers feared the rise of anti-reform forces among nationalists and Communists throughout the country, some even predicting a sweeping roll-back of reform. After defeating Communist Alexandr Zhuganov in the run-off election in July, President Yeltsin retained Prime Minister Viktor Chernomyrdin and other pro-reform members of his cabinet and added new reform-oriented advisors. The policy of reform survived the pre-election jitter. Following the presidential election, however, Yeltsin underwent heart surgery and his failing health remained a continuing source of uncertainty, prompting many observers to predict further political turmoil in Moscow and throughout the country.

Caught between Russia and the Pacific, will the Russian Far East at last be able to define its own future? It is hoped that our collective effort to answer this question in this volume will contribute to the deepening of our under-standing of the complexity of the issues involved in the development of cooperative relationships between Russia and its Asia–Pacific neighbors.

The sweeping changes in Russia make it very difficult to keep published studies up to date on events and developments. It should be noted that Chapters 1, 2, 4, 6, 7, 8, 9, 11, and 12 in this collection were originally presented at an international conference in Monterey, California on 20–22 October 1994, but they were all subsequently revised for the purpose of this publication. The Foreword, Introduction, Chapters 3, 5, 10 and 13 were prepared after the 1994 conference but before the Russian presidential elections of 1996. The editor revised and updated the Introduction and Conclusion after June 1996. In the end, however, the editor believes that the central issues addressed by the chapter authors remain outstanding and important, and that the authors' analyses and perspectives on those issues remain relevant and valid.

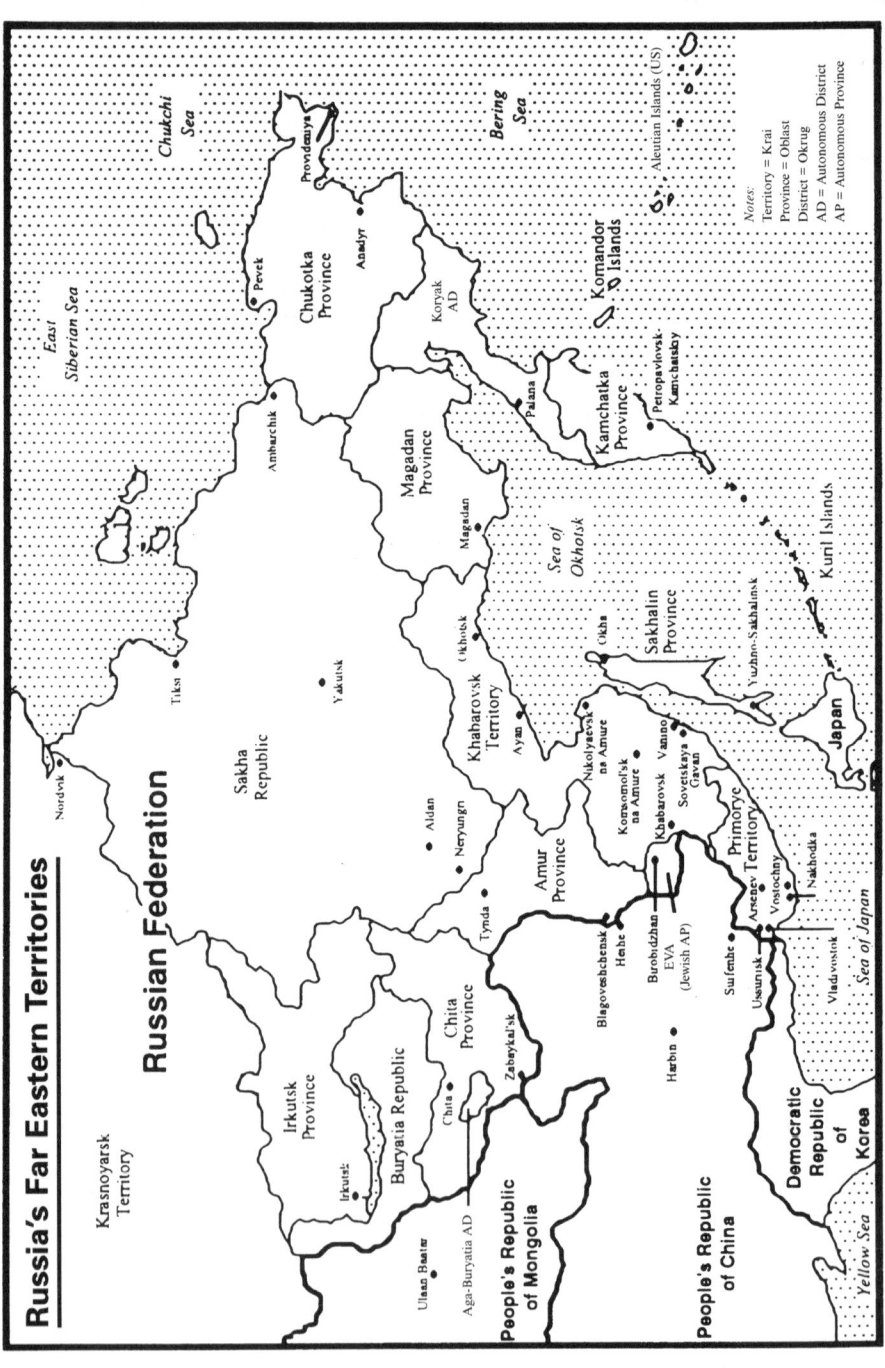

Map of Russia's Far Eastern territories
Source: 1993 University of Alaska, Anchorage. Reproduced with permission of the Center for International Business

Part I

Moscow and the Russian Far East

1   The political dimension

Robert Valliant

INTRODUCTION

The political relationship between Moscow and the Far East is much more than between just those two actors. It is bound up in the way Moscow controls the provinces and the way the provinces, in turn, try to reduce that control through threats and wheedling. If any province achieves anything in the way of autonomy, it will be because all the provinces have worked together. Even as they are trying to cooperate on a larger scale with regional associations, provincial efforts are also being undermined by differences among themselves and within each province. This chapter will attempt to explore some of these factors, and then look at the Far East as a region in its own right.

To head off some confusion an explanation of the terminology is in order. Here the term 'province' is used interchangeably with krai, oblast, republic and okrug. At a more abstract level, the differences among them are only cosmetic. However, when discussing individual provinces, the terms common in Russia will be used. The word 'region' here means a group of provinces. This is in contrast to the Russian tendency to use 'region' for both a 'province' and a group of provinces. Finally, the terms 'governor' and 'head of administration' are used interchangeably. The former is the most common term in the West and in some Russian publications, but the latter is the correct term.

MOSCOW'S CONTROL AT THE PROVINCIAL LEVEL

Yeltsin and the government in Moscow have several means to control the provinces. The most important politically is probably the ability to appoint and dismiss the governors, but this is supplemented by the presence of a presidential representative in each province. Finally, there is the ability to control provincial finances in the broadest sense. That topic will not be touched on in this chapter.

Prior to the attempted *coup* in August 1991, provincial governors, then called chairs of the provincial executive committees, were elected locally. On 22 August 1991, immediately after the suppression of the attempted *coup*,

Russian President Boris Yeltsin changed the electoral system. He issued an edict on the powers of executive authorities, including governors. They were to be appointed by the RSFSR president with the agreement of the corresponding soviet of people's deputies. They would be relieved by the president, who could appoint an acting head for a period of up to six months. These governors could not occupy any other post in state, private, or other public organizations.[1]

The Russian Soviet Federated Socialist Republic (RSFSR) Supreme Soviet followed this up with a law that would again make the position of governor an elected one.[2] It attempted to implement its law by ordering the government to work out a schedule of elections before 1 December 1991. Yeltsin opposed any elections, at least until the following year, in order to prevent a confrontation between the president and the parliament.[3] Finally, on 1 November, the Supreme Soviet issued a resolution canceling, until 1 December 1992, all elections to representative and executive bodies at all levels, except for people's deputies to fill vacancies and previously scheduled elections for the presidents and supreme soviets of RSFSR constituent republics.[4] Immediately after his mini-*coup* in October 1993, Yeltsin assumed authority over the governors. He issued a decree which said that the head of administration of a krai, oblast, autonomous oblast, autonomous okrug or federal city could only be appointed or dismissed by the president upon recommendation of the chairman of the Council of Ministers.

Yeltsin's decree of 22 August 1991 also provided for the establishment of a presidential representative in each of the provinces. These representatives were part of the control staff of the president's administration. Their duties were to fulfill the instructions of the president and to carry out their activity in accordance with local law.[5] The original decree was supplemented with another on 5 February 1992, authorizing the representatives to assist in the implementation of presidential decrees, ordinances, and government decisions; to coordinate the activity of the provincial services of federal agencies; to provide the president with analytical and other information on economic, social and political trends; and to appoint and dismiss the heads of federal bodies in their respective provinces.[6]

In the Far East, the men appointed as representatives, at least in the first round, came from the more 'liberal' part of the Russian political spectrum. In Kamchatka, Yeltsin's first representative was Igor Sidorchuk, one of the leaders of the oblast democratic organization Initsiativ. This organization was created in 1989 for the elections of USSR people's deputies. By training, Sidorchuk was a geologist and a deputy in the oblast soviet.[7] On Sakhalin, Vitalii Gulii, a journalist and a USSR people's deputy, became representative. Gulii was very outspoken and went so far as to say that both the Soviet Union and Japan had a strong legal case to the disputed islands, the so-called 'Northern Territories.' He called for settlement at the negotiating table. He was also one of the first representatives to leave the Communist Party, resigning on 8 May 1990. As a result of his 'liberal' views on the territorial dispute, groups in the Kurile Islands began agitating for Gulii to be Yeltsin's representative in Sakhalin.[8] Vladimir Desyatov was a USSR people's deputy from Khabarovsk Krai when Yeltsin named him representative. He had argued for an economic center to manage the Far East because the Moscow bureaucrats had done such a poor job. Finally, in Primorskii Krai, Yeltsin chose Valerii Butov, a man born in Vladivostok who had worked for Fesco (Far Eastern Shipping Company) and received his law degree from Far Eastern State University. When he was appointed, he had just resigned as chairman of the Yuzhno-Sakhalinsk city soviet.[9]

The allegiance of the representatives came into question in the spring of 1993, before the referendum. They were required to take a loyalty test. The process was referred to as 'attestation,' the same technique the CPSU used to purge its ranks. The aim of the test was to ensure that the representatives would carry out Yeltsin's orders, not those of the Supreme Soviet, and to make sure that they did not become too close to the local authorities.[10] Representatives have proved no more reliable than governors. Yeltsin dismissed the representatives from Amur and Chita provinces in the spring of 1993. The representative in Khabarovsk was fired in November 1993; his departure was followed by those of the governors in Khanty-Mansiisk, Tomsk, Omsk, and Primorskii provinces in the spring of 1994.

In fact, these representatives became a point of conflict between the Supreme Soviet and the president. Early on, the Supreme Soviet must have gotten the upper hand, because in January 1994 Prime Minister Viktor Chernomyrdin said that Yeltsin was going to issue an edict abolishing the post of presidential representative.[11] With no edict forthcoming the Ninth Congress of People's Deputies passed its own decree on 29 March abolishing the institution. It then turned to the provincial leaders and asked them to take measures to 'end the activity of the Russian Federation president's representative.'[12] At least one province tried to abolish the post itself, but the cause was an internal power struggle rather than a dispute with Moscow.

Caught between the Supreme Soviet and the president, life has not been easy for these representatives. By the fall of 1994, newspapers were suggesting that they no longer had any influence over the provincial leadership, and that there were constant clashes between them and the governors.[13] Although the governors had repeatedly petitioned to have the position abolished, Yeltsin did not do so. After all, the governors were his people. Elected governors would not be, and he would have had less control over the provinces.

There is speculation that the power of the representative will be strengthened. A new presidential office is scheduled to be set up in the provinces: the Federal House. The first one will be in St Petersburg. The idea behind it is that all the agencies representing the federal government in the province will be housed under one roof and directed by one person (the representative). In St Petersburg, the Federal House will include offices of the representative, Federation Council deputies and their staffs, the district inspectorate (part of the president's Control Administration), the bankruptcies agency, the anti-monopoly committee, the committee for land resources and land management, and the representative of the Ministry of Foreign Economic Relations. The offices of the Federal Counter-Intelligence Service, the Internal Affairs Main Administration, and the Prosecutor may also end up there. These will all be serviced by a single chancellery, personnel and accounting departments, a car pool, etc.[14] In a counterpoint to the institution of presidential representatives in the provinces, Yeltsin issued decree no. 323 on 23 April 1992 which provided that the provincial administrations could set up missions to the Russian government, provided they paid for them out of their own budgets.[15] Yeltsin has a tendency toward expansive measures: this is easy to see in his trips in the provinces and the promises he makes to local officials in an attempt to win them over or to keep them loyal. For example, in April 1993 he stopped over in Magadan on his way to Vancouver. While there, he promised to create a group to discuss Arctic navigation and to limit the number of people from the North Caucasus and Central Asia coming to Magadan.[16] During his stopover in Yakutsk, he promoted the Republic of Sakha as the model for the management of a multi-ethnic Russia. He chose Sakha because of its natural wealth and because more than 70 per cent of those who voted in the referendum supported him.[17] Finally, during his trip to Tyva, Amur and Novosibirsk provinces, he left a string of promises. He offered Tyva $8 million, Amur 4 trillion rubles over ten years for a space port, and promised Novosibirsk 1,000 combines. Yeltsin said that he has repeatedly heard the criticism that the president takes a bag of money with him on his trips and certain lucky enterprises receive support. He says that he does not like the idea, but he still does it, and he certainly knows that the president cannot solve every problem with money.[18]

ROLE OF THE PROVINCES IN MOSCOW POWER STRUGGLES

A power struggle between Yeltsin and the Supreme Soviet began after the *coup* and continued for almost a year, until the storming of the White House in October 1993. This struggle extended to the provinces as each side sought favor and support and made questionable promises. One of the major skirmishes was over the referendum, over just who would lead the reform, the president or the parliament.

In December 1992 both agreed that a referendum would be held in April. The referendum consisted of four questions. One was a vote on Yeltsin himself, one was on his reform policy, and two were on whether or not early elections were necessary. Participation for Russia as a whole was about 64 per cent; about 59 per cent of the voters approved Yeltsin. In Siberia and the Far East, his support ranged from a high of 82 per cent (in the Yamalo-Nenets Autonomous Okrug (AO)) to a low of 43 per cent (in Chita and Amur Oblasts). Support for his government's policies was shakier from a high of 74 per cent (once again in Yamalo-Nenets Autonomous Okrug) to a low of 40 per cent (in Chita and Amur Oblasts). In any case, voters approved Yeltsin and his policies. They did not favor early elections. In the Far East, except for Amur Oblast, the vote in all provinces 'for' Yeltsin and his policies exceeded 50 per cent.[19]

Hoping to placate the provinces, Chernomyrdin admitted that in 1992 Russia had no regional policy. He also recognized the increasing separatist tendencies in the provinces. However, he refused to concede that strong provinces would mean a strong state, and he would only go as far as calling for harmonious cooperation between federal and provincial authorities. His goal was to make working people feel at home everywhere in Russia.[20] There can be little doubt that Chernomyrdin wanted to maintain a strongly centralized Russia with Moscow in firm control. On the other hand, Ruslan Khasbulatov could go so far as to say, as he did in Novosibirsk, that 'without the serious economic independence of the regions [provinces], the federal center is powerless to implement large-scale reforms.' He went on to add that 'it has become obvious to everyone now that the center of gravity of the reforms must be switched to the regions [provinces].'[21]

The differences between the two sides were sharply etched. Commenting on the parliamentary hearings on regional policy of 22 February 1993, *Kommersant-Daily* wrote that the hearings highlighted the two diametrically-opposed tendencies: the provincial leaders' desire for more authority and the central leaders' desire for them to have less.[22] The attitude of the two sides at the Eighth Extraordinary Congress of People's Deputies in March prompted the independent *Nezavisimaya gazeta* to remark that never had the voices of the provincial leaders sounded so weighty and never had the president and parliament appealed to them so openly.[23]

The president and government did not hesitate to seek support in the provinces. They did this by making numerous trips to show their concern. Most of these trips came in the spring as they sought support for Yeltsin's position in the referendum, but there were also major trips in May, August, and September seeking to persuade provincial authorities to support Yeltsin's version of the draft constitution; no trips were necessary after Yeltsin's mini-*coup* in late September and early October. In April Yeltsin went to the Kuzbass, one of the more liberal provinces, looking for support in the referendum. He got it. At the same time, Deputy Prime Minister Aleksandr Shokhin headed for the Far East, visiting Kamchatka, Sakhalin, Primorskii, and Khabarovsk provinces. Shokhin said his trip was to explain the referendum, to make personal contact with the provincial leaders, and to work out a mechanism for cooperation between central and provincial leadership.[24] The first deputy prime minister, Vladimir Shumeiko, went to the Buryat Republic to explain Yeltsin's position in the referendum. Deputy Prime Minister Sergei Shakhrai visited Irkutsk, Novosibirsk, and Khabarovsk in May seeking support for the draft constitution. Chernomyrdin traveled to Kamchatka, Sakhalin, Primorskii and Khabarovsk provinces in August. He went, he said, because the economic problems of the area merited special attention. He also took with him the message that no province in the Russian Federation could survive autonomously, any leaders who wanted sovereignty were wasting their time and distracting people from the economic work that needed to be done.[25] The last trip was taken by Shakhrai to Novosibirsk, Sakha, Chita and Krasnoyarsk provinces. He also carried a message opposing any kind of separatism.[26]

In contrast, leaders in the Supreme Soviet did not travel all that much to Siberia or the Far East. Ruslan Khasbulatov did go to Novosibirsk in February, and Vice President Aleksandr Rutskoi visited Amur and Khabarovsk provinces in July.

In the course of the struggle, Yeltsin had the advantage because he could appoint his own supporters as provincial leaders. He could also dismiss them, and he did both, although not without mistakes. When Yeltsin dismissed the governor of Irkutsk province, Yurii Abramovich Nozhikov, the soviet rallied to his support, as did Yeltsin's representative. The latter declared, 'There is legal madness going on, primarily in the center.'[27] Even the major business leaders rallied to Nozhikov's side. In the end, Yeltsin was forced to rescind the edict and reinstate Nozhikov. In Novosibirsk, Amur, and Primorskii provinces the governors were not so lucky. They were all replaced. In fact, in Amur province, two successive governors had to be replaced. Two other governors from Krasnoyarsk and Sakhalin provinces were replaced at their own request.

The obvious question is why so many changes at the highest level in the provinces came at roughly the same time. Most were around the time of the referendum or within about two months after it. Yeltsin claimed that the changes were not the result of persecution or a change in personnel policy. He argued that the governors actively supported him. In two cases (Irkutsk and Novosibirsk) he laid the blame on violations of legislation. In other cases (Sakhalin and Krasnoyarsk) he made no comment at all. However, in both Amur and Primorskii provinces there was growing opposition to the governor and, at least in the case of Amur province, the province had voted against Yeltsin in the referendum. When traveling in the provinces, the Moscow politicians found that provincial leaders did not want to take sides in the Moscow power struggle. Neither Yeltsin's nor Khasbulatov's draft constitutions really corresponded to the Federation Treaty that they favored. However, in the end, the leaders signed on with Yeltsin.

After the power struggle was over and Yeltsin had vanquished his opponents, another round of provincial visits began. This time the new politicians were seeking support in the forthcoming elections. At the founding conference of the Party of Russian Unity and Accord (PRES), Deputy Prime Minister Sergei Shakhrai, one of the party founders, said the new party would be the voice of the interests of the provinces. It would be formed from a minimum of Moscow politicians. The party's basis was to be provincial branches.[28] At a conference in Novosibirsk he called for state regulation and protectionism in regional policy. He labeled market mechanisms ineffective in eliminating imbalances in the economic development of provinces.[29] Shakhrai says things the Siberians like.

Yeltsin began traveling again in the late spring to Tatarstan (May), Amur, Tyva and Novosibirsk (June), Krasnoyarsk (July), Volga and Rostov (August). Some saw this as the start of the 1996 election campaign, since he visited provinces trying to pursue an overly autonomous course or provinces that failed to support him in the December 1993 elections.[30]

WHY THE PROVINCES COULD NOT CAPITALIZE ON THEIR POSITION

In spite of the recognition by almost all officials in Moscow that the provinces occupy an increasingly powerful position, they have never been able to capitalize on their good fortune. The reasons are many, but they break down into three broad categories: divisions among the provinces, divisions within the provinces, and lack of broad-based popular support. The provinces are divided into two competing groups: the republics (twenty-one of them) vs. the oblasts, krais, and various autonomous okrugs (sixty-eight of them). The rivalry was focused on the question of the constitution. Early drafts gave the republics more privileges and a larger share of the power by virtue of having more seats in the upper chamber of parliament. The krais and oblasts objected because there were more of them and in most cases they were more populous and wealthier.

The difference between the two types of provinces had been festering since 1991. It had led to a series of precipitant actions: the abortive movement for a Yenisei Republic in the summer of 1991, threats to declare republics (Tomsk and Irkutsk Oblasts), actual declarations of republics (Urals Republic, Amur Republic), postponed declarations of a republic (East Siberian), declaration of intention to declare a republic (Primorskii Republic), discussion of a declaration of a republic (Kamchatka Republic), and even rejection of a republic (Far Eastern Republic).

The differences were more profound than some simple abstract notion of 'equality.' For some republics, the main issue was a Russian pursuit of equal rights in what they considered their own homeland. The republics, usually ethnically based, were receiving special treatment, and the human rights of Russian citizens were being infringed in constitutions and laws. The 'Russian' oblasts and krais wanted their own special recognition. Perhaps more important, however, was the economic struggle. Becoming 'sovereign' meant gaining control over natural resources – oil, diamonds, gold, timber, and fish.

Krai and oblast leaders were very active in seeking a compromise to the problems of the Federation's internal structure. They believed that if the republics' definition of 'sovereign states' was accepted, the Federation would devolve into a confederation. These leaders wanted all members to have equal status, with a few exceptions (e.g., the right to citizenship, state language, constitution, national flag, emblem and anthem).[31]

There were two drafts of the constitution: the president's and the Supreme Soviet's. A constitutional conference met from 5 June to 12 July 1993 to hammer out a single draft. The draft, approved on 12 July, provided for a presidential republic and a two-house parliament and rather strong provincial autonomy. As Deputy Prime Minister Sergei Shakhrai put it, the provincial leaders had finally decided upon a compromise under which the krais, oblasts and republics would be equal in their relations with Moscow, even though they would have a different constitutional status. That this compromise did not satisfy everyone may be seen in the vote: only eight of the twenty-one republics voted for it, as well as about two-thirds of the krais and oblasts. The draft tried to placate the republics, the krais and the oblasts. Each side got equal representation in the upper house (two seats). The krais and oblasts also got the right to draw up their own charters. These were the analogues of the constitutions the republics were to have. The provinces got the rights to pass their own laws and to levy taxes, but no division of tax revenues between the center and the provinces was specified. The republics remained sovereign and able to confer citizenship and have an official language. Both sides got the right to sign treaties with the center.

Yeltsin continued to meet with leaders from both sides in the provincial dispute, and at Petrozavodsk, in August 1993, he finally got the leaders of the republics to go along with the idea of a Federation Council.[32] However, even this compromise proved unnecessary. With Yeltsin's mini-*coup* in September and October and the blizzard of presidential decrees that followed, the balance between the different types of provinces changed again, and in the process Yeltsin expanded both his own powers and those of the executive branch. The new draft constitution published on 9 November granted equal rights to all provinces and made them all subject to Moscow. All provisions in earlier drafts for republic sovereignty, and the right of secession from the Federation were deleted. The provincial leaders approved the changes at a meeting on 3–4 November. This ended the argument among the provinces.

The divisions within the provinces were almost inevitable. The governor served at the pleasure of the president, and the soviet was elected by the people. On the whole, the soviets were probably more conservative than the governors, but that is a very broad generalization.

During the early part of the struggle between Yeltsin and the Supreme Soviet, most soviets did not favor either side. They wanted the constitution obeyed and the argument settled. In many cases the soviets joined with the governors in calling for respect for the constitution and the Federation Treaty. Others proposed a unified draft constitution.

The soviets did not turn against Yeltsin until September 1993 when he began his mini-*coup*, dismissing the congress, suspending the constitution, and calling new elections. By 26 September most of the soviets in Siberia and the Far East had lined up against him. They stayed that way until 9 October, when Yeltsin issued an edict that, in effect, dissolved them.

The independence movement in Siberia and in the Far East has been restricted to the fringes of politics. The Party of Independent Siberia never made much of an impact in either Western or Eastern Siberia. Popular support, such as it has been, has fluctuated with the state of the economy and the popularity of Moscow politicians in the provinces. Meetings generally draw a few hundred people at most.

There are eight regional organizations: Black Earth, Siberian Accord, Central, Northwest, North Caucasus, Urals, Far East and Greater Volga. Of these, two are in Siberia and the Far East. These organizations predominately play an economic role. Indeed, their leaders frequently protest that the organizations are not political and have only economic goals. But just as frequently these same leaders hint that perhaps these regional associations might play a larger political role, and their actions show that this may be true.

The premier regional organization in Siberia is the Siberian Agreement. It was formed in November 1990 for the purpose of stabilizing the region. It has nineteen members, principally the krais, oblasts and republics in Eastern and Western Siberia. Its goals are economic in nature; its leadership has shied away from overt political posturing. However, other leaders in its constituent parts have not. The mayor of Novosibirsk took part in the founding of the Siberian Civic Union which called the center's policies in Siberia 'colonial.'[33] This was neither the first nor the last use of the word 'colonial' in this context. At that time, the city was facing a severe economic downturn and Moscow was not opening its pocketbook to bail out the city.

Political statements have created dissent among the member provinces. Altai Krai suspended its membership in the Agreement in the fall of 1993, claiming excessive politicization and a display of separatist tendencies.[34] Kemerovo Oblast drew up a paper on its official withdrawal from the Agreement. The governor, Mikhail Kislyuk, said that the province had halted practically all involvement in the Agreement in the fall of 1993 when several Agreement leaders called for the creation of a Siberian Republic and blockading of the Trans-Siberian Railroad.[35] However, neither has withdrawn.

Government leaders at the deputy prime minister level attend all meetings of the Agreement. Their rhetoric is usually that the government is doing all it can to help the regions, oblasts, krais or republics, etc., but it can and should do more and faster. These representatives always excoriate attempts to link the regional organizations in any way with independence movements of any kind.

In the power struggle in 1993 between Yeltsin and Khasbulatov, not only were the individual provinces courted by both sides, but the regional associations also began to make demands. Representatives from the Black Earth, Siberian Agreement, Central, Northwest, North Caucasus, and the Urals drafted an agreement that they wanted to sign with the government. It provided a clear delimitation of powers in budget, taxation, and foreign affairs between themselves and the government. Their idea was that they, the regional associations, would replace the separate treaties their members have with the government. Sergei Shakhrai was thought to be the mastermind behind this draft agreement.[36]

By the middle of May the eight regional associations had drafted a cooperation treaty to be signed between themselves and the parliament. They expected that this agreement would be followed by a law on interregional cooperation. In discussing the matter, Vladimir Shumeiko, speaker of the Federation Council, hinted that some kind of state–legal status might be given to the regional associations. However, most of the regional association leaders at the meeting did not want either such a status or federal money.[37]

The two draft agreements bore fruit during the summer. In July the regional associations signed the agreement with the government delimiting the powers between the federal and provincial authorities, placing restrictions on the powers of the federal and provincial executive branches, setting up working groups to coordinate activities, setting up a joint fund to support research, and specifying that the government would issue a decree regulating cooperation between the federal authorities and the regional associations.[38]

Two weeks later a similar agreement with the leaders of the Federation Council and the State Duma was signed. This agreement has interesting implications. It obligates both houses of the Federal Assembly to get preliminary draft resolutions from the regional associations whenever either chamber considers draft laws on the economic development of the provinces. It also gives the associations a certain degree of control over implementation of the Federation Treaty. The associations participate in working out development strategies for leading sectors of the national economy. Their development programs will be integrated into federal development programs. At some time in the future these associations will receive the status of 'state agent' charged with implementing state programs in the provinces, and they will also get the right to consider federal budget and tax laws. These provisions are to be confirmed in a law delimiting powers between the provinces and the center.[39]

It is far too soon to determine what, if anything, these agreements mean. What they do indicate is that both sides, or perhaps all three sides (provinces, associations, center) are trying to work out their relationship. Much will depend on the elections.

In one respect, it is very easy for the regional associations' leaders to meet and do business; most of them are members of the Federation Council. Instances of this in the case of Siberia and the Far East include Mikhail Nikolaev (president of Sakha Republic), Evgenii Nazdratenko (Primorskii), Viktor Ishaev (Khabarovsk), Sergei Leushkin (Koryak AO), Evgenii Krasnoyarsk (Sakhalin), Sherig-ool Oorzhak (president of Tyva), Valerii Zubov (Krasnoyarsk), Yurii Nozhikov (Irkutsk), Vladimir Petrov (president of Altai Republic), Leonid Polezhaev (Omsk), Viktor Kress (Tomsk), Ivan Indinok (Novosibirsk), Leonid Roketskii (Tyumen), Gennadii Nedelin (Taimyr AO) and Aleksandr Filipenko (Khanty-Mansiisk AO). Many of the provincial governors were elected. This makes for easy interchange of opinions among the leaders of the Siberian Agreement and the Far Eastern Association. The same is true for all other regional associations. The provinces that did not elect their head of administration include Buryat Republic, Khakasiya, Altai Krai, Amur Oblast, Kamchatka Oblast, Kemerovo Oblast, Magadan Oblast, Chita Oblast, Aginskii-Buryat AO, Ust-Ordinskii Buryat, and the Evenk AO. This makes for a very high proportion of Yeltsin appointees in the Federation Council.

Leaders of the regional groups meet from time to time, and the associations also send delegates to one another's meetings. For example, the leaders met in March 1994 in Tambov, and they met again in Moscow in the middle of May.

As the federation gropes toward an uncertain future, the provinces and Moscow are trying to work out a new relationship to govern the country. Both sides want decentralization. The question is how much and when. This new relationship will be based on constitutions (charters) in the provinces, treaties between the provinces and the center, and, as has been noted above, agreements between regional associations and the center. However, new players and events may change the equation.

The federation constitution delineates responsibilities and functions, not powers. It gives the provinces limited sovereignty. This means that they are sovereign, except in the areas of federal authority and those of joint federal–provincial authority. Provincial sovereignty or responsibility will be defined in the constitution or charter. (Republics have constitutions; krais, oblasts and autonomous okrugs have charters.) Nine republics have already adopted constitutions. Twelve of the krais, oblasts, and okrugs have either adopted a charter or have drafts, although there appear to be problems with most of them.

The problems stem from the lack of experience on the part of the provincial authorities and from the desires of the provincial elites to retain their privileges and access to money and property. These cravings may be seen in constitutions that represent federal powers as powers granted by the provinces, and indicate that the federation has no powers in and of itself; its authority derives from rights granted to it by sovereign provinces. Other problems are constitutions that make provincial law superior to federal law in case of conflict, or differences in the judicial system on citizenship, or concerning native peoples. Some charters are a problem because they were prepared by the executive branch which blithely infringed on the rights of local self-government.[40]

To head off some of the differences, the president's staff has drawn up a model charter that each province can adapt to its own needs. But even that has not resolved all issues because many deputies see their duty as being in opposition to the executive branch. Thus they add their own provisions that are not always in accordance with Russian law. The presidential representative is responsible for seeing that all charters conform to the constitution. All these charters are supposed to be adopted by the end of 1994.[41]

In addition to the constitutions and charters, treaties will also govern relations between the provinces and the center. There is even a commission to oversee the making of the treaties, the Commission for the Preparation of Treaties on the Delimitation of the Areas of Jurisdiction and Powers between the Federal Organs of State Power and the Organs of State Power of the Components of the Russian Federation. Deputy Prime Minister Sergei Shakhrai is its chairman. The treaties will not be signed until a law has been adopted on the delimitation of powers, a set of procedures for drawing up such treaties has been defined, and until provinces have constitutions (charters) that do not violate the federation constitution. Some restrictions apply. Treaties cannot be copies of the federation constitution. They must lay out the responsibilities of both the federation and the provinces. For example, provinces cannot unilaterally deal with foreign countries; that responsibility falls in the area of joint federal–provincial authority. Moscow is willing to overlook minor deviations from these principles in order to get the work done.[42] The role these treaties will play, and their relationship to the constitutions and charters, is also open to interpretation. In theory, all should present a harmonious whole, but perfection is not easily obtained in a fast moving political environment peopled with actors learning their roles as they go.

The Union of Russian Governors, a new body, is asking Yeltsin to define the status and powers of the governors. They want the government to submit bills on provincial government and civil service to the State Duma. Until laws are passed, the governors want interim regulations specifying that they are accountable only to the president, that they can appoint certain officials, that they can endorse local laws and other legal acts, and that they can only be arrested on warrants from the prosecutor general.[43] The role this Union may play in protecting governors and maintaining their power is unknown, but it is another factor that must be considered.

If the governors have created a supra-provincial organization, the new provincial assemblies are beginning to do the same. The Vologda Oblast parliament is already working to create an association of Northwestern oblasts and republics. The declared aim of the association is to have an information clearing house, so that one province can take advantage of another's work in drafting laws. However, political observers see in such an association some type of regional supra-parliament, followed by an all-Russia assembly of local legislatures which might rival the Federal Assembly.[44]

The Federal Assembly remains an unknown. In the December elections, the party of the provinces, the PRES, did not do particularly well. It won only about nineteen seats, well down on the list from the Liberal Democratic Party of Russia's (LDPR) sixty-four, and Russia's Choice's fifty-eight. That would seem to indicate that the question of regional policy or rights was not much on the minds of the electorate. However, the affiliations of the Assembly members in December did not necessarily last through January. In one of the more surprising moves, a new parliamentary bloc arose, New Regional Policy.

It ended up with sixty-five delegates, second only to Russia's Choice, the liberal group, with seventy-six. The LDPR lost one delegate and as of January had sixty-three. PRES also gained delegates and had thirty. Thus, as of January 1994, there were at least ninety-five delegates supposedly interested in provincial or regional affairs. However, the lesson seems to be that political alignments in the Federal Assembly are fluid. Changes in bloc membership have continued and new blocs have been formed while old ones have become inactive. That makes any predictions of what will happen in the development of provincial or regional policy difficult at best. This could all change with the upcoming elections.

The final unknown are the coming 1996 elections. The first Assembly will serve only two years. As noted above, Yeltsin may already be campaigning. For its part, the Union of Russian Governors is trying to get federal and local elections scheduled simultaneously for 1996. Vladimir Shumeiko, speaker of the Federation Council, proposed the idea to the governors at a meeting in September. The governors don't want to contest elections with the current bad economic conditions; they claim that they haven't been able to do their best because of the crisis, and that they don't think that money spent campaigning would be well spent. Yeltsin has appointed seventy-eight of the eighty-seven governors.[45] The reluctance of the governors to be held accountable is understandable. Many would undoubtedly lose.

Sergei Filatov, head of Yeltsin's staff, has been calling for early elections, but Yeltsin has so far not responded. As noted above, he may be strengthening the position of representative to maintain his control after the elections, should his people not be elected. It is to Yeltsin's benefit to delay the elections as long as possible. Certainly Shakhrai, one of the leaders of the party that is the voice of the provinces, agrees. He feels a decision to hold no elections before 1996 would 'promote economic and political stability.'[46]

THE FAR EAST IN PARTICULAR

The organization around which any independence or regional autonomy movement would have to be based is the Far Eastern Association (FEA). Its name has changed several times, so it is best just to refer to it by its shortened name. It was created in August 1990 by soviets in the provinces of the Far East. Its purpose was to help the soviets to coordinate their activities and allow them to protect the interests of the region.

Like the other regional associations its original main interest was, and remains, economic. It has worked by itself and in cooperation with other regional associations to wring various economic concessions out of Moscow. It has even drawn up a development plan for the Far East as a means of providing a road map for a better, brighter future. However, the FEA has strayed over the line into politics. Indeed, how could it not? When the Sakhalin governor, the ebullient Valentin Fedorov, brought up the question of the Kurile Islands before the group there was little choice. He told the other representatives at a meeting that 'if Moscow cannot defend Russia from national betrayal, then a Far Eastern Republic must save Russia and Moscow itself from a territorial repartition of the Kurile Islands.' The FEA was not willing to go along with his proposal to create a Far Eastern Republic, but it did send an appeal on the Kurile Islands question to Moscow.[47]

Rumors began flying after this that the FEA was going to set up a Far Eastern Republic. The leaders of the FEA denied it, emphasizing that the association's role was economic. Yet the same leaders backed away from that denial by saying the FEA would consider establishing an FER if Moscow sold the Kurile Islands to Japan.[48] This should be seen as more of the posturing that went and goes on between Moscow and regional leaders. It is the domestic equivalent of what the Japanese call 'diplomacy by intimidation.' The siren song of a Far Eastern Republic has proved one of the most seductive visions, particularly in the West.

The single most talked about example of independence in the Far East – at least among Westerners – is the Far Eastern Republic. Since few people know much about it, it has taken on a dimension that is unwarranted at best. What Far Eastern Republic there was existed for a short time in the early 1920s. It was never truly independent, rather it was a creature of Moscow, and when Moscow no longer had need of it, it was liquidated. The chimera reappeared during the elections of 1989–90 and has been talked about ever since. The fact that one can never exist may be easily seen by looking at the domestic and foreign situations

There is not much interest in a Far Eastern Republic or any other type of independent body. There is no real base for such a movement. The vast, overwhelming majority of the population is Russian. They are patriotic. They do not want to see their country dismembered. This helps to account for the lack of sustained popular support for independence or for anything other than more economic freedom. However, Moscow has also seen to it that even the desire for more autonomy is circumscribed by the deadening hand of bureaucratic control from the center.

One of the most attractive bases for an independence movement is ethnic. That base would provide a certain cohesiveness that any multi-ethnic movement would lack. It would also make it possible to distinguish readily between 'we' and 'they.' Unfortunately, in the Far East there is no possibility for such a movement. Excluding the Yakuts, native peoples are 1 per cent or less of the total population. They are scattered across an enormous area, are very poor, and in many cases, are literally dying out. In Eastern Siberia, only the Republic of Tyva [Tuva] provides fertile ground for an anti-Russian ethnic-based movement. In the summer of 1990 Tyvins attacked Russians; several were killed and many chose to leave Tyva even though it meant becoming refugees. In Tyva, native Tyvins outnumber other ethnic groups. Moreover, the republic has a tradition of independence, albeit a weak one. Still, there is no chance that it will become independent. Its president has already made his peace with Moscow. The Republics of Buryatiya and Sakha are the only other provinces with ethnic populations large enough to support movements, but in both cases the native peoples are outnumbered by Russians. Thus, in all of Siberia and the Far East there is simply no basis for an ethnic-based independence or autonomy movement that might succeed.

Talk of an 'independent' Far East began during the elections in 1989 and 1990. When the Vladivostok newspaper *Leninets* published copies of the constitution of the Far Eastern Republic, people snapped up the newspapers off the kiosks. At the Institute of History, Archaeology and Ethnography in Vladivostok scholars held a conference on the seventieth anniversary of the FER. Several candidates in the elections incorporated the idea in their election platforms, and a popular movement 'FER 90' took up the call. Its members covered the spectrum of political views from independence and friendship with the Soviet state to a union republic to a voluntary economic and political association of Far Eastern provinces. However, as the newspaper *Vechernii Vladivostok* was quick to point out, the movement was simply a manifestation of a desire to escape from Moscow's domination. The newspaper went on to note that the Far East's 7 million people were scattered over a vast area, that the idea of an FER had zero influence on political life, and that there was no assurance the West would provide any help.[49] Popular feeling for the idea, at least in one oblast, may be seen in the poll conducted by the Magadan Oblast Center for the Study of Public Opinion in the city of Magadan between 12 and 22 December 1991. Nine hundred and seventy four people took part. They represented all social and demographic groups in the city. When asked, 'Do you support a Far Eastern Republic?' the responses were as follows:

For an FER	57.1%
Unacceptable	26.4%
Difficult to answer	16.5%
Total	100.0%

The high support is understandable when 50 per cent of those polled also said that they thought the process of disintegration had already begun in Russia or that Russia could not escape such a process. Fear of a hard winter undoubtedly colored these gloomy responses.[50]

By the summer of 1990 there was sufficient interest; the constituent congress of the Far Eastern Republic Freedom Party was held in Vladivostok on 8–9 September 1990. According to Anatolii Zabolotnikov, the party had fewer than 100 members but many sympathizers. Zabolotnikov was a former member of Democratic Union. He lived in Vladivostok and was the academic secretary at the basin section of Tikhii Okean. He was also a deputy in the krai soviet but was trounced when he ran for RSFSR people's deputy.[51] The party declared itself to be a republic party opposed to any dictate from the center. It favored freedom of enterprise and private initiative, denationalization of the state sector and de-ideologization of the Army and law-enforcement bodies.[52] It later acquired some notoriety when Zabolotnikov told newspapers that if the party came to power it would shoot the communists.[53] Zabolotnikov subsequently left the party, but his departure did nothing to tone down its posture. Igor Cherevkov, the new leader, sent an ultimatum to Russian President Boris Yeltsin, through Yeltsin's representative in Primorskii Krai, Vladimir Butov. In it he maintained that the territory of the former Far Eastern Republic was not Russian; party members felt the FER had been occupied and seized by Russia. Cherevkov called for a referendum on the reestablishment of the Far Eastern Republic. Butov was not amused. He asked the procurator to call Cherevkov and the author of the declaration, E. Izyurov, to account for stirring up separatism.[54]

The Primorskii Krai branch of the SDPR (Social Democratic Party of Russia) took the idea of a Far Eastern Republic one step further. Its leader, Ilya Grinchenko, felt that the idea of a Far Eastern Republic was too closely associated with the Far Eastern Association, which was nothing but a clear attempt by the pro-communist *nomenklatura* in the Far East to oppose President Boris Yeltsin. As a result, the SDPR constitutional committee began looking into a krai charter that could serve as a transitional document to a Primorskii Republic. The committee's goal was to keep the struggle within legal bounds. Article 70 of the constitution gave subjects the right to change their status through a referendum. Grinchenko said he expected opposition from those with a vested interest in keeping the *status quo* in the ministries and departments in Moscow and even in the krai. However, he hoped to find allies among local industrialists.[55]

There have been other organizations, including the Popular Movement for the Creation of a Far Eastern Republic in Khabarovsk; however, they have never garnered much support, and have been characterized by their shooting star quality.

The governors have played a large role in keeping the Far East under control. There have been two very different kinds of people in the post. The first group, the 'humanists' were clearly transitional figures. The 'industrialists' who followed them were a very different breed of men: not less capable, just different. Yeltsin himself said that in the beginning he and his team favored giving the provinces more autonomy, removing obstacles and letting them solve their own problems. He also admits that the policy did not work.[56] It is easy to see the difference in policy between the two types of people appointed.

A political commentator for one of the newspapers in the Far East took note of the change in governors in the spring of 1993. The governors of Sakhalin (Valentin Fedorov), Amur (Albert Krivchenko), and Primorskii (Vladimir Kuznetsov) provinces were replaced. The commentator, who later became the subject of a law suit for allegedly slandering a politician, lamented the change. He said these three were not politicians (the implication was that this was positive) but that thanks to them the Far East was a freer and more democratic place, that it had a new mentality and the basis for a new economy.

He called them the 'humanists' because they believed in the new ways. In fact, Fedorov and Kuznetsov were academics, and Krivchenko was a journalist. While there can be little doubt that these men were all part of the privileged class, it is also true that they were different from the people they had replaced.

The new group of governors, Evgenii Krasnoyarov (Sakhalin), Evgenii Nazdratenko (Primorskii) and Aleksandr Surat (Amur), were not professional politicians either; they were industrialists. The commentator cited above called them more conservative than their predecessors. They were not humanists but technocrats. Surat, who was eventually replaced by another technocrat, Vladimir Polevanov, was a geologist by background; he spent eighteen years in the Magadan mining industry. The industrialists are seen as getting the economy moving again, getting their provinces back on track. Yet they haven't been so different from their predecessors.

The power brokers in Sakhalin, for example, heaped criticism on Fedorov, the carpet bagger economist from Moscow who went to Sakhalin to carry out a great economic experiment, for failure to perform economic miracles. As things went from bad to worse, criticism grew increasingly bitter. His replacement, Krasnoyarov, has not been able to turn the economy around either.

In Primorskii Krai, Kuznetsov was replaced by the technocrat Nazdratenko. Kuznetsov was criticized for the failures of the economy, for his numerous foreign trips, etc. (in general, for all the things that were wrong in Russia). However, Nazdratenko has not managed to do much better. In many ways he has proved more of a bureaucrat; some of his actions have been more high-handed than anything Kuznetsov ever did – for example, the removal of his chief opponent, the elected mayor of Vladivostok, on a charge of accepting bribes. Some have intimated that Nazdratenko was Moscow's fair haired boy in the Far East. When he scheduled elections for the post of governor at least one paper speculated that he might actually be allowed to hold the elections and be elected, despite presidential edicts to the contrary, because he was so much in favor in Moscow.[57] However, this turned out not to be the case. The election was canceled. Moscow intends to maintain control, and the position of governor is key in its plans.

The major external reason why there was not and will not be any independence movement in the Far East can be summed up in one word: China. In light of the rumors and discontent in the spring of 1994 caused by reports of literally millions of Chinese in Russia, it should be obvious that there can be no true independence in the Far East. The Far East has a long and thinly-populated border with China. It is now becoming less well protected as both sides withdraw troops to make it a border of peace. The Russians are vastly outnumbered by their neighbors across the rivers. There are only about 9 million people in the area that stretches from Lake Baikal to the Pacific. Indeed, there are only about 28 million in the area east of the Ural mountains, but Heilongjiang alone has 36 million inhabitants, Inner Mongolia 22 million, Jilin 25 million and Liaoning 40 million, for a total of 123 million people in just four provinces. This is almost fourteen times more than in the area east of Baikal, and about four times more than are east of the Urals! Yet such comparisons are essentially meaningless. They have been made since the mid-nineteenth century when Russia began settling the Pacific coast. Their chief value comes in playing on fears, on racial prejudice, and on greed.

CONCLUSIONS AND COMMENTS

Many like to warn of the breakup of Russia, Russians not the least among them. Even before the dispute between Yeltsin and Khasbulatov reached its height, Vladimir Berezovskii, a researcher at the Center for Analytical Information of Contemporary Politics in Russia told *The Christian Science Monitor* that there were dozens of scenarios for civil war. The same article noted that other unnamed experts were saying that if the political and economic crisis lasted much longer, neither Yeltsin nor any successor would be able to do much to reverse centrifugal forces. Siberian provinces were singled out as having separatist tendencies in a desire for greater economic autonomy.[58]

Any person who thinks the Far East might one day become independent should look at a map and then ask: if the Russians are unwilling to give several insignificant islands to Japan, why would they be willing to give up this vast expanse of territory? That still leaves the question of a Far Eastern Republic. In this case, a clear misunderstanding of terminology is apparent. To many in the West, a republic means an independent country. That is not the case here. As *Tikhookeanskaya zvezda* noted after a Japanese TV crew did a long report on the possibility of a Far Eastern Republic being formed, even those who are in favor of an FER are unanimous: 'We are for a republic, but we have no intention of separating from Russia.'[59] For Russians, an FER would be the same as, say, the Republic of Sakha. In other words, while it might encompass a large geographical area, little, if any, change in its relationship with the West or Moscow would be noticeable.

Another issue that bears comment is the model for the political relationship between the center and provinces. The language and forms used are those of international affairs: treaties, presidential representatives (ambassadors), provincial representatives to the government (ambassadors). One wonders if this is not because of the sheer distrust of, misuse of, and disbelief in the law. Western businessmen comment frequently about the lack of law in Russia. It makes it very hard to do business. One need not look far to find a law or a potential law that has been countermanded by a presidential edict, and these edicts are sometimes contradictory. On the other hand, treaties are widely regarded in international practice as being higher than domestic law. Could this be a way of overcoming a recognized deficiency in the political environment?

A final conclusion is that Moscow is not going to allow much more autonomy of any kind in the foreseeable future. Yeltsin has borne this out by his actions and by the actions of the government.

NOTES

1 *Selskaya zhizn*, 24 August 1991, p. 1, in FBIS/SOV, 91/165, 26 August 1991, pp. 76–7.
2 *Svobodnyi Sakhalin*, 12 October 1991, p. 1, in *SUPAR Report*, no. 12, January 1992, pp. 140–1.
3 Tans, 25 October 1991, in *SUPAR Report*, no. 12, January 1992, p. 141.
4 *Rossiiskaya gazeta*, 5 November 1991, p. 1, in FBIS/SOV, 91/215, 1 November 1991, p. 46; *Rossiiskaya gazeta*, 6 November 1991, p. 2, in FBIS/SOV, 91/217, 8 November 1991, p. 60.
5 *Selskaya zhizn*, 24 August 1991, p. 1, in FBIS/SOV, 91/165, 26 August 1991, pp. 76–7.
6 Tans, 6 February 1993, in FBIS/SOV, 93/25, 9 February 1993, p. 15, in *RA Report*, no. 15, July 1993, pp. 122–3.
7 *Vostok Rossii*, no. 14, November 1991, p. 11.
8 *Germes*, 5–22 May 1990, pp. 1 and 5.
9 *Svobodnyi Sakhalin*, 2 November 1991, p. 1.
10 AFP, 22 March 1993, in *RA Report*, no. 15, July 1993, p. 123.
11 *Nezavisimaya gazeta*, 15 January 1994, in FBIS/SOV, 94/12, 19 January 1994, pp. 43–4, in *RA Report*, no. 17, July 1994, p. 129.
12 *Izvestiya*, 17 April 1993, pp. 1 and 3, in FBIS/SOV, 94/75, 21 April 1993, p. 49, in *RA Report*, no. 15, 1993, p. 123.
13 *Komsomolskaya pravda*, 7 September 1994, p. 2, in FBIS/SOV, 94/175, 9 September 1994, pp. 37–8.
14 *Komsomolskaya pravda*, 7 September 1994, p. 2, in FBIS/SOV, 94/175, 9 September 1994, pp. 37–8.
15 *Rossiiskaya gazeta*, 7 April 1992, in FBIS/SOV, 92/68, 8 April 1992, p. 24, in *SUPAR Report*, no. 13, July 1992, p. 128.
16 Radio Tikhii Okean, 5 April 1993, in FBIS/SOV, 93/64, 6 April 1993, pp. 58–9, in *RA Report*, no. 15, July 1993, p. 126.
17 *Izvestiya*, 22 June 1993, p. 2, in FBIS/SOV, 93/118, 22 June 1993, pp. 35–6, in *RA Report*, no. 15, July 1993, p. 126.
18 *Trud*, 26 August 1994, pp. 1–2, in FBIS/SOV, 94/166, 26 August 1994, p. 11.
19 *RA Report*, no. 15, July 1993, p. 116.
20 Tans, 13 February 1993, in *RA Report*, no. 15, July 1993, p. 128.
21 *Rossiiskaya gazeta*, 20 February 1993, pp. 1 and 4, in FBIS/SOV, 93/35, 24 February 1993, pp. 44–50, in *RA Report*, no. 15, July 1993, p. 128.
22 *Kommersant-Daily*, 23 February 1993, p. 9, in FBIS/SOV, 93/36, 25 February 1993, p. 46, in *RA Report*, no. 15, July 1993, pp. 128–9.
23 *Nezavisimaya gazeta*, 16 March 1993, p. 1, in FBIS/SOV, 93/50, 17 March 1993, pp. 30–1, in *RA Report*, no. 15, July 1993, p. 129.
24 *RA Report*, no. 15, July 1993, pp. 114–15.
25 *Rossiiskie vesti*, 18 August 1993, p. 1, in FBIS/SOV, 93/159, 19 August 1993, p. 49, in *RA Report*, no. 16, January 1994, p. 103.
26 *RA Report*, no. 16, January 1994, p. 104.
27 *Pravda*, 24 March 1993, p. 1, in FBIS/SOV, 93/57, 26 March 1993, p. 52, in *RA Report*, no. 15, July 1993, p. 118.
28 Tans, 15 October 1993, in FBIS/SOV, 93/198, 15 October 1993, pp. 18–19.
29 Tans, 18 April 1994, in *RA Report*, no. 17, July 1994, p. 140.
30 *Komsomolskaya pravda*, 7 September 1994, p. 2, in FBIS/SOV, 94/175, 9 September 1994, pp. 37–8.
31 *Izvestiya*, 1 July 1993, in FBIS/SOV, 93/132, 13 July 1993, pp. 56–67.
32 Itar-Tans, 14 August 1993, in FBIS/SOV, 93/156, 16 August 1993, pp. 12–13, in *RA Report*, no. 16, January 1994, p. 102.

33 *Seattle Post-Intelligencer*, 30 November 1992, p. A1; *Japan Times*, 30 November 1992, in *RA Report*, no. 14, January 1993, p. 122.
34 *Sibirskaya gazeta*, no. 40, 7 October 1993, p. 1, in *RA Report*, no. 16, January 1994, p. 111.
35 *Izvestiya*, 14 January 1994, p. 1, in *RA Report*, no. 17, July 1994, p. 138.
36 *Segodnya*, 24 March 1994, p. 2, FBIS/SOV, 94/58, 25 March 1994, p. 29, in *RA Report*, no. 17, July 1994, p. 139.
37 *Segodnya*, 17 May 1994, p. 2, in FBIS/SOV, 94/96, 18 May 1994, p. 39, in *RA Report*, no. 17, July 1994, p. 140.
38 *Rossiiskaya gazeta*, 2 July 1994, p. 5, in FBIS/SOV, 94/130, 7 July 1994, pp. 16–17.
39 *Segodnya*, 15 July 1994, p. 2, in FBIS/SOV, 94/137, 18 July 1994, pp. 27–8.
40 *Rossiiskie vesti*, 31 August 1994, pp. 1–2, in FBIS/SOV, 94/171, 2 September 1994, pp. 17–20.
41 *Rossiiskie vesti*, 10 September 1994, p. 1, in FBIS/SOV, 94/176, 12 September 1994, pp. 36–7.
42 *Rossiiskaya gazeta*, 6 September 1994, p. 1, in FBIS/SOV, 94/173, 7 September 1994, p. 16.
43 Interfax, 23 September 1994, in FBIS/SOV, 94/186, 26 September 1994, p. 22.
44 *Obshchaya gazeta*, no. 37/62, pp. 16–22, September 1994, p. 8, in FBIS/SOV, 94/181, 19 September 1994, pp. 33–4.
45 Itar-Tans, 8 September 1994, in FBIS/SOV, 94/174, 8 September 1994, pp. 36–7.
46 Interfax, 8 September 1994, in FBIS/SOV, 94/175, 9 September 1994, p. 19.
47 Tans, 21 October 1991, in FBIS/SOV, 91/203, 21 October 1991, pp. 74–5.
48 Postfaktum, 29 December 1991, in FBIS/SOV, 91/251, 31 December 1991, p. 55.
49 *Vechernii Vladivostok*, 19 May 1990, p. 3.
50 *Magadanskaya pravda*, 9 January 1992, p. 1.
51 *Pravda*, 28 August 1990, p. 1, in FBIS/SOV, 90/168, 29 August 1990, p. 79.
52 *Krasnaya zvezda*, 22 September 1990, p. 1, in FBIS/SOV, 90/188, 27 September 1990, p. 97.
53 *Krasnaya zvezda*, 25 November 1990, p. 1, in FBIS/SOV, 90/230, 29 November 1990, p. 82.
54 *Vostok Rossii*, no. 18, May 1992, p. 1.
55 *Vladivostok*, 6 October 1992, p. 3, in *SUPAR Report*, no. 14, January 1993, p. 120.
56 *Trud*, 26 August 1994, pp. 1–2, FBIS/SOV, 94/166, 26 August 1994, pp. 10–15.
57 *Kommersant-Daily*, 30 July 1994, p. 3, in FBIS/SOV, 94/147, 1 August 1994, p. 30.
58 *Christian Science Monitor*, 12 February 1993, p. 6, in *RA Report*, no. 15, July 1993, p. 128.
59 *Tikhookeanskaya zvezda*, 9 July 1994, p. 2.

2 The security dimension

Alexei V. Zagorsky

INTRODUCTION

Events in the former Soviet Union, ranging from the failure of the *coup* in August 1991 to the break-up of the USSR, the birth of independent states, and the formation of the Commonwealth of Independent States (CIS), have created a new geostrategic and political environment for Russian defense policy. Primarily, geostrategic consequences have moved the Russian defense line eastward.

Although the ramifications of *perestroika* on USSR foreign policy had already led to Russian withdrawal from Central Europe and the establishment of a buffer zone between former USSR and NATO nations, the dismantling of the USSR enlarged the initial zone through recognition of independence for the three Baltic nations and the consequent withdrawal of troops. The birth of independent Belarus and Ukraine with independent armed forces and nationalization of all (in Ukraine) or major (in Belarus) parts of their former USSR military forces, and the Russian loss of direct control over their defense policies, have created a buffer zone to the west of Russia that prevents direct contact with NATO troops and makes useless the former strategy of Soviet force concentration in Europe.

The impact is especially strong because the majority of the elite Russian forces were traditionally deployed in Western (Germany), Central (Poland), and Southern (Hungary) clusters as well as in the Ukrainian, Byelorussian, and Baltic military districts, most of which have now been eliminated. According to General-Lieutenant Leonty Kuznetsov, formerly deputy head of the General Staff of the CIS Unified Armed Forces (CIS UAF), and now head of the General Operative Department of the General Staff, if one compares three military districts in Ukraine (now Ukrainian Armed Forces) and three military districts in Russian European territory (Moscow, Northern Caucasus, and Volga-Ural), Ukrainian power is three times as strong, especially in ground forces.[1] This illustrates the loss of modern weapons by Russia to the Ukraine and Belarus.

The attitude of the Russian military leaders today is that: 'Russia spent so much effort for defense, and now we have practically nothing on European territory. Even beyond the Urals we have only the minimum of what we need.'[2]

The sense of crisis felt by the military command is intensified by the fact that, in addition to troop and weapon losses from Warsaw Treaty quotas, ceilings for USSR conventional arms in Europe are now divided among the newly sovereign states. The Russian military does not have the right to increase its share. As a result of the collapse of the Warsaw Treaty and the disintegration of the USSR, Russia is now allowed to keep 15 per cent of European conventional weapons, as opposed to the 50 to 60 per cent authorized under the Conference on Forces in Europe scheme.[3]

Most worrisome to military leadership are the flank limits set by the CFE, as presented by the head of the General Staff of the Russian Army, General-Colonel Mikhail Kolesnikov:

> after 1995, we may deploy in the Leningrad and Northern Caucasus military districts not more than 700 tanks, 500 armored vehicles and 1,280 artillery systems. Yet these two districts account for more than half of the European territory of Russia. Therefore, that ceiling for weapons does not meet contemporary requirements to create minimally sufficient defense groups, and cannot satisfy us . . . In fact, in the Leningrad and Northern Caucasus districts we need 1,100 tanks, 3,000 armored vehicles and 2,100 artillery systems, with 600 tanks, 2,200 armored vehicles, and 1,000 artillery systems deployed in the south.[4]

Currently, the ideal for the Russian and CIS military remains a common political and security arrangement. This idea was initially presented by Marshall Evgeny Shaposhnikov, then CIS UAF commander-in-chief, who said in 1992:

> In my view we are on the eve of a union of a new type, on the eve of a treaty on collective military security in the area. I am sure such a treaty will be signed because without it, we cannot solve important problems. It may begin as bilateral agreements between Russia and other nations; through it we can achieve a system of collective security.[5]

However, since nations west of Russia demonstrate lack of cooperation on military issues, the most probable partners for Shaposhnikov's idea are in Central Asia. Initial steps to put the idea into practice were taken at the CIS Tashkent summit in May with Russia, Armenia, Kazakhstan, Uzbekistan, Turkmenistan, and Tajikistan signing the treaty on collective security. The nature of the agreement hints for a possible shift of Russian military dominance eastward. In 1993, the framework of the collective security treaty was enlarged by Azerbaijan's membership and the potential participation of Georgia and Belarus. Yet the treaty kept its initial geographical orientation for consolidation of Central Asia and Transcaucasia around Russia as a result of the Russian pull-out from western areas of the former USSR.

The treaty does not deny the strong Russian inclination to enlarge the scope of the CIS Collective Security Treaty westward. Basic new ideas were presented by the Secretary of the Council of CIS Defense Ministers, Lieutenant-General Leonid Ivashov at the CIS conference on Problems of Collective Security at the Staff Meeting for Coordination of Military Cooperation of CIS Nations in July 1994. At present, Russian military leadership proposes three possible options to develop cooperation:

1 a coalition of nations with obligations emerging within specific periods without unified coordinating bodies or unified command;
2 a military or military–political alliance with permanent political and military institutions, unified military structures, and coordinated operation and training planning; or
3 military integration with decision-making by coalition institutions over-ruling national decision-making processes, consolidated military budgets, unified armies, and a unified military command system.

According to Russian experts, CIS is embodying the first option, but the second is most desirable. The third is assessed as politically unrealistic.[6] General Ivashov recognizes that 'not every CIS nation is equally ready to participate in the defense alliance as a full-scope regional military-political organization,' and proposes a 'flexible stage-by-stage approach to permit participation of any nation according to her political, economic and legislative possibilities,' including the chance of close cooperation by some nations (read Russia, Central Asia and Transcaucasia) and case-by-case cooperation by others.[7]

General prospects for CIS military cooperation are regarded as creating regional sub-systems, with every sub-system having its own political, economic, and military institutions and Coalition Defense Forces with corresponding military commands. The third option described above is moved to a sub-regional level in these plans. At present, four sub-regional systems are envisioned:

1 Eastern Europe, including the European territory of Russia, Kalingrad province, and Belarus;
2 a Caucasian region including Russian territories in the Northern Caucasus, Georgia, Armenia, and Azerbaijan;
3 a Central Asian region with two zones: the eastern zone to include Tajikistan and Uzbekistan, and the western zone to include the western Siberian territories of Russia as well as Kazakhstan and Kyrgyzstan; and
4 an East Asian zone, including eastern territories of Russia and eastern provinces of Kazakhstan.

In addition, it is stressed that non-member nations of the CIS Collective Security Treaty (Ukraine, Moldova, and Turkmenistan) are not barred from the regional sub-systems; in fact, their cooperation is assumed.[8] This arrangement presents four distinct geographical areas of current Russian military policy. The Eastern European region is certain to face NATO and its possible expansion to the east; the Caucasian region will have to address various conflicts in this area (the Chechen and Ingush-Osetian on Russian territory, and Abkhazia and South Ossetia issues in Georgia, as well as the Armenian–Azerbaijani conflict over Nagorno-Karabakh). The primary task in the Central Asian region is meeting 'the Islamic challenge from the south,' while the East Asian region seems oriented mostly to possible problems on the Chinese border.

WHENCE THE THREAT?

The new geostrategic realities of Russia pose a problem for the army in regard to possible external threats. Normalization of political relations with the West and the emergence of a chain of buffer states between Russia and NATO nations, as well as the low military potential of Russian neighbors in the Asia–Pacific, eliminates the possibility that Russian territory will be attacked from abroad.

It took from May 1992 to November 1993 to prepare a new vision of threats under these conditions. The Russian military doctrine as adopted at the end of 1993 presents a rather extensive list of possible threats categorized here into five major issues:

1 Local conflicts along the Russian border; an increase in the number of troops stationed along the Russian border reaching levels that disrupt existing balances of power; the training on foreign territory of troops bound for Russian territory or that of her allies; deployment of foreign troops on Russian or adjoining territories unless connected with peace-keeping operations in accordance with UN Security Council resolutions or a decision of a regional organization of collective security with agreement by the Russian Federation.
2 Expansion of military blocks and alliances damaging to the security interests of Russia; border conflicts; territorial claims of nations neighboring Russia; the absence of treaties delineating certain areas of the Russian border; the questionable legal status of Russian troops abroad; assaults on Russian garrisons abroad; infringements on the rights, freedoms, and interests of Russian citizens abroad.
3 Opportunities for use of nuclear as well as other weapons of mass destruction by other nations; proliferation of nuclear and other weapons of mass destruction and their delivery systems; the combination of new military technologies and attempts of certain nations, organizations, and terrorist groups to achieve military and political goals.
4 Undermining of strategic stability as a result of violation of international agreements on arms control and reduction; qualitative and/or quantitative arms increases by other nations; the proliferation of activities by other nations inhibiting the function of Russian systems providing the strategic nuclear force and national military force command (primarily its space component).
5 Domestic sources of instability.[9]

A large portion of the threats indicated are highly hypothetical in nature. The doctrine does not label any nation as a possible enemy. In fact, it states that the 'Russian Federation does not assess any nation as its enemy.' However, a more detailed look at the perceived threats suggests that those which are regarded as probable are concentrated predominantly within the territory of the former USSR.

Among the existing regional and local conflicts along and near the Russian borders, only one is found outside the territory of the former USSR: the situation on the Korean peninsula. Other issues, namely, Georgia, the Armenian–Azerbaijani civil war, the civil war in Tajikistan (numerous statements by Russian leaders stress that they regard the Tajiki–Afghani border as a Russian one), and the conflict in Moldova (although rather remote from Russian territory, there is keen Russian military interest in Transnistria) are all within the former USSR territory. The degree of Russian direct involvement in these regions is much higher than that in Korean affairs.

Border disputes may not seem relevant to CIS problems, but at present Russia is involved in four disputes – one with Japan over the Southern Kuriles, another over the delineation of the Russian–Chinese border (a dispute over islands in the Amur River near Khabarovsk), and two with Baltic nations (Estonia and Latvia) over regions acquired by Russia after the occupation of these nations. None seems likely to provoke armed conflict. In a related issue, the absence of border treaties, the status of Russian troops abroad, and the rights of Russian citizens abroad have exacerbated problems between former Soviet republics. Problems include the absence of Russian border treaties with any of these regions, the assaults on Russian garrisons in Transcaucasia and Baltic nations, and the issue of the rights of ethnic Russians in the Baltic states. The impact of these problems on recent Russian politics seems greater than that of the border disputes with China or Japan. The only issue mentioned here that represents one of the highest priorities of Russian politics outside the CIS is the possibility of expansion by NATO.

While the third and fourth themes of nuclear proliferation and strategic stability seem more generally global, their combination represents a major problem for Russian security planners. Ukrainian nuclear potential followed by North Korean nuclear and missile programs are most important in this area.

The overview of official threats and their implications may be summarized as follows. In the two years following the collapse of the USSR, the majority of major Russian security concerns have shifted to regions within the area of the former USSR. Major issues on the current agenda are Central Asia, Transcaucasia, and Ukraine. In this context, the Asia–Pacific region, Northeast Asia to be more exact, is secondary in Russian threat perceptions; the situation on the Korean peninsula and border disputes with Japan and China predominate.

Proof of this conclusion is apparent in a statement made by Russian

Foreign Minister Andrei Kozyrev, traditionally regarded as an opponent of the Defense Ministry. At the January 1994 meeting of the Russian ambassadors to the CIS and Baltic nations, Kozyrev stated that:

> the near abroad (*blizhneye zarubezhye*, a Russian phrase for the area of the former USSR) represents a major area of Russian interests and a major source of threat to the vital interests of Russia, in connection with the idea of preserving Russian military presence in the region.[10]

The statement by Kozyrev represents a marked departure from the 1992 discussions. At that time, focus centered on the military power component of the great power status visualized through competition with the West. A statement by then Commander-in-Chief of the CIS United Armed Forces, Marshal Evgeny Shaposhnikov, delineated the change: 'The threat of invasion from abroad is drastically decreasing, but we are still far from absolute pacifism. No important state can exist without an army, and the army should be modern.'[11] The logic of this vision was explained in detail in a comment by Valentin Larionov in the daily *Nezavisimaya gazeta* in May 1992.[12] His argument for defense build-up against possible threats from abroad was threefold. First, he maintained, the ability to resist external threats was necessary for Russia to be accepted as an independent state. This is a factor in strategic stability. Second, expenditures for technological modernization of weapons were not reduced in any nation regardless of spending cuts in weapons purchases, military training, etc. Weapons were becoming more sophisticated and more independent of human reaction and, therefore, guarantees of arms control were losing their value and systems for bilateral technological control were required to prevent accidental wars. Third, Larionov asserted, Russia should be wary of and monitor external threats stemming from low level ethnic conflicts that could escalate into international conflicts on Russian borders. In other words, defense strategies targeted outside the CIS would assure Russia's status as a great power, and the nature of the military component should provide a continuing reminder to potential adversaries. This idea is based on the presumption that even after the end of the Cold War, military power would continue to provide Russia with great power status and that regardless of the absence of threat from the West, military competition with it would be inevitable. In other words, the fall of communism in Russia would not change world power relations. Russia was still matched up against Western powers regardless of whether she was communist or democratic.

Several quotations of high ranking military leaders may be cited as examples of this vision. Former Vice-President Alexander Rutskoy has stated:

> Now nobody denies the fact that in general military threat has decreased: in the near future we do not anticipate a world war or a large scale war. But still there is a possibility of so-called limited, local conflicts. Still there is no guarantee that a threat from abroad will not emerge. Therefore we may not drop a balanced and elaborated defense policy.[13]

Russian Defense Minister Pavel Grachev is more sincere, stating:

> If we want to be a powerful nation, if we want to be respected and considered, we should understand that it is not only generals and military who need the army. There are already examples when some nations, feeling our weaker positions, begin approaching us in a different manner. National military prestige is not only a political definition, but an economic and moral one as well. Strong armies increase people's self-respect.[14]

Finally, civilian Deputy Defense Minister Andrei Kokoshin has stated: 'We need strong and effective military might but not a burden for the nation as it has often been in the past.'[15]

In regard to the Far East, specific scenarios still dominate analyses of regional strategic situations. For example, Colonel Sinaysky, in forecasting the shift of the 'continental-Eurasian sector of Russian development to the Pacific coast,' envisages that in the next century the northern part of the Pacific Ocean may become an area of contention between Russia and other major world powers due to decreases in international energy and raw material resources and stronger hegemonic tendencies in the policies of nations.[16] Colonel Viktor Stefashin notes: 'For Russia, the military–strategic importance of the Far East is determined by the presence of large armed forces in neighboring countries, by the unstable situation on the Korean peninsula and other dangerous hot spots.'[17] He foresees five possible scenarios for the region: evolutionary, Korean, Chinese, Taiwanese, and Soviet. The evolutionary, and most welcome, option is based on parallel Russian–American arms reductions in the Far East. Stefashin recognizes that in the case of weaker Russian and American positions in the region, and the formation of regional multipolar structures, one should expect an intensified struggle for spheres of influence. Yet, for him, the reduction of an American regional presence is more important than the prevention of military and political uncertainties.

Stefashin's Korean scenario presumes a Russian–American confrontation with Russia supporting the Democratic Republic of Korea (North Korea), the United States and Japan supporting the Republic of Korea (South Korea), and China remaining neutral. The Chinese scenario is based on a new Russian–Chinese conflict initiated by the political ascent of 'reactionary nationalist forces in China'. In this scenario, the United States, Japan, and China are expected to remain neutral. In the Taiwanese scenario, Russian and American arms reductions occur simultaneously with Chinese increases. In this scenario, China and Russia confront the United States and Japan. The exotic Soviet scenario involves the disintegration of the Russian Federation and the emergence of Far Eastern republics, for example 'Primorye' (Maritime State) and 'Amur State.' Stefashin writes:

> In this situation, Japanese leadership may believe it an opportunity to settle (militarily) the 'Northern Territories' issue. Directly or indirectly, the United

States and China will be eminently involved, claiming themselves friends extending 'international' assistance to prevent Japanese occupation of the Russian Far East. In the end, the United States will annex territories lost by Russia. This kind of event will resurrect the historical 'Slavic' feature of the Russian national character and unify people at the critical moment to meet aggression by the three largest nations of the world.[18]

Formal assessments of potential threats by acting Russian military elite were documented in reports presented by the General Staff and Naval General Staff at the parliamentary hearing on Russian–Japanese relations following the formation of the Russian Defense Ministry. A paper by a Russian General Staff member states:

American and Japanese military and political leadership regard the island of Hokkaido as a basic stronghold to deploy an assault group against the Russian Far East . . . At present American and Japanese armed forces are able to conduct on short notice air and sea assault operations to occupy Southern Kurile islands without additional mobilization through the use of their highly developed infrastructure and superiority in manpower and arms . . . In general the Kurile islands play an important role in the Far Eastern defense system in meeting possible American–Japanese aggression, in ensuring the access of the Pacific Fleet from the Sea of Okhotsk to open seas, and in preventing the entrance of enemy naval forces into the Sea of Okhotsk through the zone of the Southern Kurile straits.[19]

A more detailed document by the Navy General Staff states:

An analysis of direction, scale, and area of US and Japanese military exercises as well as their everyday activities in the Far East indicates that they are probing options of joint action against our troops in the Far East. Targets of joint American and Japanese actions are occupation of the Southern Kuriles, blockade of the La Perouse Strait and Kurile Straits to divide the Pacific fleet into two parts, the disruption of communications between the mainland and Sakhalin and Kamchatka, and destruction of ships, primarily the naval strategic nuclear forces in the Sea of Okhotsk and on Kamchatka . . . Transfer of [the southern Kurile] islands to Japan would give them free passage to the Sea of Okhotsk through the Ekaterina Strait between Kunashir and Iturup islands. Americans will be able to freely deploy their forces in the Sea of Okhotsk (without operations against the Kurile islands or sweeping passages in our mined waters), and the Japanese will extend their ability to close the La Perouse strait and to operate in the southern part of the Sea of Okhotsk, including deployment of fighter aviation on airfields of Iturup Island. Existing and newly built airfields on southern Kuriles will enable them to deploy anti-submarine aviation there to control the entire Sea of Okhotsk and approaches to Kamchatka and Kurile islands. As a result, American and Japanese naval activities to control our strategic submarines in the Sea of Okhotsk and on approaches to Kamchatka and Kurile islands will be more effective and less expensive. In addition, as an analysis of actions by US carrier exercises striking Primorye and Sakhalin indicates, the area west of Sangar Strait is most secure for them. This area is well protected by the Japanese air defense system, and by anti-submarine weapons from the Pacific. To reach carriers in this area our aviation would have to fly around Japan, beyond her zone of air defense (over Sakhalin and the northern part of southern Kuriles), and strike carriers from the Pacific. In the case of transfer of the southern Kuriles to Japan, the Japanese air defense system will expand substantially to the north, and our planes will not have enough of an active radius to bypass it. US and Japanese naval strike forces able to act against Primorye and Sakhalin from the area west of Sangar strait would become invincible.[20]

EURASIANISM

The anti-western sentiment of the Russian military in 1992 may be explained by the inertia of Soviet thinking in the absence of any real threat. To remain focused, an army should be aware of the enemy. The inertia of the old tradition can remain even if external threats are non-existent.

In 1992 local conflicts within the territory of the former USSR did not require military involvement. The army had no significant stakes in the Armenian–Azerbaijani war and welcomed the political decision for Russian withdrawal in summer 1992. The only militarily important conflict areas were Transnistria in Moldova and Abkhazia and Southern Ossetia in Georgia but the majority of military personnel in these conflicts were local residents deeply involved in the political strife. These areas alone were too narrow to be identified as a threat by the new Russian army.

The vacuum of political paradigm was filled in 1993 by two major proposals. One was to enlarge Russian participation in the UN and UN-related peace-keeping operations by increasing Russian peace-keeping personnel in Yugoslavia, expanding Russian–Kuwaiti and Russian–American cohesion in the Persian Gulf, and indicating Russian readiness to join the UN mission in Haiti. The second, and more important, proposal was the increasing Russian claim for a military and peace-keeping leadership role in the post-Soviet era. Russian troops were deployed as peace-keepers to Transnistria, Abkhazia, and Southern Ossetia in 1992. In 1993, in addition to general Russian guarantees against Islamic offensives in Central Asia, CIS joint peace-keeping forces were deployed in Tajikistan. Protection of railroads in Western Georgia was also a dominant role for the Russian army. The next logical step was Russia's willingness to deploy forces in Azerbaijan and Karabakh. Militarily, a large area between Transcaucasia and Central Asia became an area of responsibility for the Russian armed forces.

The 1992 paradigms crystallized the idea of Eurasianism as the philosophical background for Russian responsibility in the post-USSR era.

Initially, the paradigm of Eurasianism was created in the 1920s by Russian emigrants in Sophia, Prague, Belgrade, and Berlin (primarily Nikolai Trubetskoy, Pyotr Savitsky, and Georgy Vernadsky). Their major philosophy emphasized that 'the territory of the former Russian Empire, or USSR, is a specific historical and geographical universe, belonging neither to Europe nor to Asia, being a specific unique phenomenon.'[21] At the same time, Nikolai Trubetskoy stated: 'I deny any possibility of a universal human culture.'[22] Lev Gumilyov, who has developed the paradigm during the 1960–80 period, elaborates further:

> A universal human culture equal to any ethos is impossible as every ethos has a different encompassing landscape and a different past forming its present both in time and space. The culture of every ethos is specific and this mosaic nature of humans as specimens gives them the adaptability due to which Homo sapiens has survived on Earth.[23]

Although this proposal is philosophical in nature, in the Russian circumstances of the 1990s, it has become a paradigmatic argument for a historical definition of Russia as distinct from Western Europe. There are grounds for radical rejection of westernization and westward-oriented foreign and military policy. Lev Gumilyov defines the geographical bounds of Eurasia as follows:

> Eurasia is limited in the south by mountain chains (Caucasus, Kopet-Dag, Pamir, Tyan-Shan), in the north by massive taiga, in the west by negative isotherm in January [east of the boundary, the average temperature in January is negative], in the east the boundary of Eurasia is most distinct as it is marked by the Great Wall of China.[24]

Eurasianism emphasizes specific ways of development for Russia, and the people of the former USSR provide the necessary philosophic ground for Russian claims to a geopolitical zone of influence. Basic ideas are equally acceptable for communists, nationalists, and a large majority of 'democrats.' Today, communist parties in Russia call for restoration of the USSR but do not address the return of Soviet influence over Eastern Europe or the Third World. Even the most radical nationalist branch, represented by Vladimir Zhirinovsky's Liberal Democratic Party, stresses the restoration of only the former Russian Empire in addition to movement south to Afghanistan, Iran, and Turkey.[25] Though Zhirinovsky's statements look astonishingly aggressive, the scope of his claim is narrower than the former territory of the USSR.

On the other hand, numerous claims for a specific Russian role in the post-Soviet era are made in speeches by democrats who support President Boris Yeltsin. Sergei Stankevich, a member of the Presidential Council from 1991–93, is one of the best known ideologues of this Russian form of development. He stresses the importance of the establishment of a Russian zone of influence. In 'Russian Interests: Security, Politics, Economics' appearing in *Krasnaya zvezda*, Stankevich stated:

Instead of the former bipolar, relatively stable equilibrium, several geopolitical blocs are being formed. Look at the North American bloc. The USA, Mexico, and Canada have signed a trade treaty, which means little for their economies, but has a clear geopolitical substance. What about ASEAN? It is a most powerful geopolitical bloc! American experts agree that in ASEAN's case economic substance is very limited. Look at the Asia–Pacific geopolitical bloc and the competition between Japan and China to become region-building nations. Look how intensively Turkey forms her own geopolitical bloc, spreading her activities on the remnants of the USSR. In this situation, a policy of integration with any nation may be dangerous, as we have not yet become ourselves, (and) we don't realize to the full extent our vital interests. And these interests should form the basis to decide with whom, for what, and to what extent we should integrate. Maybe we should think about forming our own geopolitical bloc and building relations with other geopolitical blocs. This is a new configuration formed maybe once in a hundred years. And it is important for us to evade miscalculations (of) strategic option.[26]

Andrei Kozyrev's statement in January 1994, mentioned above, clarifies the scope of possible Russian hegemony and supports the fact that this basic principle is accepted as a framework for Russian foreign policy. Thus far, we have spoken only of hard-line (communists and nationalists calling for the restoration of the USSR or the Russian Empire) and middle-of-the-road (democrats calling for exclusive Russian influence in post-Soviet nations) options of the same Eurasianist policy.

The claim for a special Russian role in the post-USSR republics is repeated by a large spectrum of Russian political forces. Judging from the composition of the State Duma elected in December 1993, the paradigm is shared by the Liberal Democratic (V. Zhirinovsky), Communist (G. Zyuganov), and Agrarian (M. Lapshin) parties, by the Democratic Party of Russia (N. Travkin), the Party of Russian Unity and Progress (S. Shakhrai), the Russian Way faction (S. Baburin and Yu. Vlasov), and in part by the Yavlinsky–Boldyrev–Lukin bloc. Only the most radical factions of democrats: Russia's Choice (Ye. Gaidar), the Union of 12 December (I. Hakamada), and the New Regional Policy faction (V. Medvedev) which represent the interests of local elites, do not seem prone in this way.

With the majority of the political forces in the Duma and the Presidential Administration as well as those in the military leadership accepting the basic ideas of Eurasianism, the general trend of concentrating Russian political and military efforts on problems with former territories of the USSR seems inevitable.

DILEMMAS OF MILITARY REFORM

Another important issue determining the current defence policy in contemporary Russia is the issue of military reform. Initially raised by the democratic opposition in the former USSR, 'the military for democracy group,' a part of the inter-regional parliamentary faction, this issue became a matter of import in April–June 1992 with the establishment of the Russian defense ministry and the Russian armed forces. Elaboration of guidelines for military reform became one of the tasks of the Committee for Establishment of Russian Defense Ministry and Russian Armed Forces, formed in April 1992 under the chairmanship of retired general Dmitri Volkogonov.

The initial composition of the committee, dominated by representatives of the former USSR's General Staff, became the target of harsh criticism by Russian democratic organizations that doubted the ability of the committee members to present a genuine democratic vision for future Russian military policy.[27] The committee failed to produce anything but a decision on the organization of the Defense Ministry and General Staff and, as a result, the issue of military reform fell into the hands of the Afghan faction that monopolized the leadership of the newly established Russian army.

The Russian army, officially created by the 7 May 1992 decree of President Yeltsin, includes all former Soviet troops on Russian territories, Soviet troops deployed outside the territory of the USSR before the December 1991 Minsk declaration, i.e., in Germany, Poland, the Baltic nations, and Mongolia, and troops in territories of former Soviet republics not included in national armies, i.e., troops in Transcaucasia, Central Asia, and the Transnistria region in Moldova, for a total of 2.8 million people.[28] The new Russian army assimilated all troops on Russian territory, including strategic nuclear forces.

The basic idea for military reform was created to adapt to new visions of military threats. First Deputy Head of the General Staff of Russian Armed Forces, General-Lieutenant Victor Barynkin, testifying at the parliamentary hearing on defense legislation, formulated the concept as follows: 'We should stop thinking about a big war (in the future) for which military districts and fronts are needed.'[29] The second pending issue concerns the military budget and personnel cuts demanded by the public.

In general, military reform was divided into two stages (three stages as presented by former Vice-President, Alexander Rutskoy), to be implemented between 1992 and the year 2000. The first stage, defined by Rutskoy, encompasses 1992 and presumes establishment of the Defense Ministry, the General Staff, the integration of troops considered components of the Russian army, and definition of Russian army structure. These tasks were begun during the April–May 1992 time period. The second stage (from 1993 to 1995) includes complete withdrawal of Russian troops from Germany, Poland, and Mongolia, troop reductions to 2.1 million, and introduction of a mixed system of conscription and voluntary service. In this way, the existing structure of the armed forces, i.e., strategic missile forces, ground forces, air defense forces, and air and naval forces will be preserved. Military districts are to be kept intact to ensure the deployment of troops and provision of housing and supplies to those troops on Russian territory that have been withdrawn from abroad. The third stage (from 1995 to 2000) includes complete withdrawal of Russian troops from the Baltic nations, troop reductions to 1.5 million people, arms reductions in accordance with the START and CFE treaties, troop reform, and reorganization.[30]

It should be noted that reform implemented before 1995 does not represent initiatives on the part of the Defense Ministry. The ministry's mission is twofold: control over current troop availability and implementation of international agreements concluded by Mikhail Gorbachev. The proposal to cut troop levels to 2.1 million represents implementation of the January 1992 pledge by Yeltsin to cut troops by 700,000 during the 1992–94 time period.[31]

Major reorganization of the army is scheduled for after 1995, i.e., following the expiration of President Yeltsin's presidential term. It should be noted that during the spring 1993 political crisis, the Defense Ministry stated that troop cuts to 1.5 million could not be implemented by 1995.[32] In December 1993, following the September–October 1993 crisis, Pavel Grachev asserted that a ceiling of 1.5 million personnel was too low to guarantee effective defense. He insisted on a reduction to 2.1 million.[33] Interestingly, Sergei Yushenkov, one of the leaders of the Democratic Choice of Russia movement and chairman of the Duma's Defense Committee, stated: 'I think we will revise the bold statements of our predecessors on the number of troops. We should not cut the army to the scope of the armed forces of a minor nation without thorough consideration.'[34] The issue was raised by President Yeltsin again in June 1994; he stated that (then) current troop levels of 3 million should be reduced to 1.5 million. According to Defense Minister Pavel Grachev and Head of the General Staff Mikhail Kolesnikov, the official number of personnel in June 1994 was 2.2 million; the Defense Ministry planned reductions to 1.9 million. These are official figures; the actual figure is probably around 1.5 million. The Russian army is divided into the Border Guard (200,000 official personnel), Ministry of Internal Affairs troops (350,000 official personnel), troops of the Ministry for Civil Defense, Emergency Situations, and Disaster Control, railroad troops, construction troops, the Kremlin's Presidential Regiment, etc. By expert assessment, units outside the Russian armed forces, while accounting for half of all official military personnel, do not exceed 1 million in number. The basic reorganization of Russian armed forces planned for the 1995–2000 time period consists of a drastic reduction in mechanized infantry divisions, cuts to one-third or one-fourth of existing levels,[35] and the creation of rapid deployment airborne forces to serve as the cornerstone of the Russian army. Rutskoy describes the future structure as including:

1 limited forces (rapid deployment regiments, brigades, and divisions) with constant readiness to operate, located to effectively meet any outside threat and to counter aggressions of local scale;
2 rapid deployment reinforcement troops armed with heavy weapons and able to rapidly deploy in support of rapid deployment forces to any region of the nation;

3 strategic reserves formed from reserve troops for reinforcement in cases where military conflict is not stopped by rapid deployment forces;
4 the strategic missile forces as a major part of strategic nuclear forces, whose role remains as it is;
5 the air defense forces built on the territorial principle (Russian territory divided into air defense zones corresponding to the areas of responsibility of air defense armies);
6 air forces composed of general command aviation, theater aviation, and transport aviation;
7 not less than 80 per cent of the ships and personnel of the Black Sea Fleet, and the Northern and Pacific Fleets as they are currently structured to protect against changes in the political stance of the Baltic nations or in deployment of the Baltic Fleet; and,
8 mixed rapid deployment forces to be set up, and the navy's coastal defense bases strengthened by air defense systems and marines to defend Russian naval zones and coastlines.[36]

Under the new structure of the Russian armed forces, the principle of total border defense is expected to be abandoned and replaced by the deployment of rapid deployment forces, ensuring easy access to any area of national territory.[37] At the same time, deployment of new troops will occur exclusively in Russia's European region, i.e., in the North Caucasus military district as well as in the Moscow, Leningrad, and Volga districts.

A final point to be discussed in connection with Russian military reform is the recent reassessment of the concept of sufficient defense as introduced by Mikhail Gorbachev, which was initially based on the idea of limited military strength.[38] In 1992, discussion of a new understanding of the concept was organized by the monthly *Voyennaya mysl'*. General-Major V. Luzyanin, for example, loosely defined the criteria for minimal sufficient defense in conventional weaponry as the 'organization of troops and weapons in a manner enabling implementation of needed combat tasks at minimum expenditure.'[39] General-Major Yu. Nikolaev stated:

> The upper limit should correspond with the principle of equal security; this consequently suggests equal forces and military opportunities. The lowest level corresponds with minimal composition of armed forces when success in defensive operations against a stronger enemy may be achieved. This composition of the army and navy is characterized as a level of minimal sufficient defense.[40]

General V. Luzyanin and Colonel V. Yelizarov wrote:

> The lowest level of sufficient defense is described by the number of troops able to defeat an enemy, to break his strategy, and to protect the line of defense at maximum acceptable depth with the use of supplementary force. The medium level is the number of forces able to prevent an enemy's breach of defense lines. The highest level is the number of forces able to

prevent an enemy's entrance into defense lines without the use of additional forces.[41]

Compared with the late 1980s, the most fundamental change is that instead of taking into account threat perceptions existing outside Russia, the only factor considered is the minimum force needed to defeat the enemy. This vision is much broader than that of a military threat. Evgeny Shaposhnikov stresses: 'Reasonable sufficiency is the ability of a nation to ensure a loss unacceptable for the offending side.'[42] In accordance with this interpretation, the composition and strength of the Russian armed forces should be limited only by the subjective judgments of the Russian military, not by international complaints and interferences.

Consequently, the essence of military reform as prepared by the Russian Defense Ministry has little to do with understanding the decrease in military threats and the need to downsize the giant army. Troop reductions proposed are based primarily on a shortage in the number of conscripts needed for armed forces of Soviet-era scale. The idea that a stronger military might be achieved with lower levels of manpower and reduced expenditures dominates in military circles. The logic of the USSR Defense Minister, aimed at increasing military potential through more modern weapons of higher quality regardless of troop or arms reductions, has not undergone substantial change. As noted by Alexei Arbatov, the notion of military reform has completely disappeared from the defense doctrine adopted at the end of 1993.[43]

PROSPECTS FOR THE RUSSIAN FORCES IN ASIA–PACIFIC

Russian armed forces in the Asia–Pacific in 1993 consisted of 290,000 personnel, a 25 per cent drop from the 390,000 level in 1989.[44] The forces were classified as follows: a land force deployed along the Chinese border and accounting for nearly 70 per cent of all Russian troops there, and a naval force aimed at the US and Japanese military potential in the Pacific.[45]

Russian military policy in these areas in the 1990s consisted primarily of the implementation of pledges made by the Gorbachev administration. Until now, there was little need to implement larger regional arms control measures. A feature of the late 1980s and early 1990s was 'non-negotiated arms reductions' with active participation by the Soviet Union. Changes are developing in three directions: reduction in the operating tempo (OPTEMPO) of the Soviet Navy, and Soviet withdrawal from overseas military commitments; bilateral arms reduction on the Soviet–Chinese border; and unilateral Soviet and American reductions of their naval facilities.

The first direction is an outcome of the reappraisal of the Soviet political role in Asian regional conflicts, the abandonment of the 'encircle China' strategy, and the gradual disengagement from commitments to Vietnam and other Indochinese nations. This policy limits Soviet Pacific fleet operations to the Japan and Okhotsk seas and the vicinity of the Soviet Pacific coast.

Changing priorities have led to the reduction of Soviet naval assets in Vietnam's Cam Ranh Bay, withdrawal of a squadron of MIG-23 jets and a squadron of TU-16 bombers, and the termination of port calls to Cam Ranh by submarines and large warships.[46]

Changes on Soviet–Chinese borders are the most radical in nature. China cut its armed forces by one million between 1985 and 1987. The USSR cut its forces on the Soviet–Chinese border by 80,000 troops in the 1980s, cut 120,000 troops from the Far Eastern theater by 1991, and completed withdrawal of its military personnel from Mongolia.[47]

An event of lesser military importance took place at the end of 1993 (the eve of President Yeltsin's visit to Japan) in the Southern Kuriles. Territory claimed by Japan was essentially demilitarized (with the exception of border troops) as part of the implementation of Yeltsin's five-stage plan to improve relations with Japan. At the time of presenting this paper [see p.xxi], troops in the Southern Kuriles include a division of coastal surface-to-sea missiles with four launching systems, a unit of coastal artillery (four 100 mm artillery systems), a division (two small ships) for regional maritime defense, a surveillance and communications post and a radio signal tower at Vetrovoye Airfield on Iturup Island, a radio technical platoon and a radio signal tower at Lovsov Cape on Kunashir Island, and a hydrographic service, a navigational service and a radio signal tower at Spanberg Cape on Shikotan Island. There are no facilities or personnel on the Habomai Islands.

How will new trends in the Russian armed forces affect this situation? There are advantages and disadvantages to cutting Russian military presence in the Far East. Foreign Minister Kozyrev had pledged on several occasions to cut Russian troops there. Initially, he indicated during his 1992 visit to Beijing that the Far Eastern military district was included in Yeltsin's scheme to reduce troops by 700,000 during the 1993–94 time period. Later in 1993, during the ASEAN Post-Ministerial Conference, he modified the figure stating that Russia would maintain only half of its forces in the region.

The next factor is related to the first two. After the collapse of the USSR, Russia lost a large number of its conscripts from Central Asia and Western Ukraine. By the end of 1992, Russian armed forces were at only 70 per cent of their previous personnel capacity.[48] Increased Russian involvement in security exercises along borders with former Soviet republics makes it necessary to keep troops there, especially in Northern Caucasus. However, because the Far East does not present a serious threat to Russian security, troop levels of the 1980s are not required there.

On the other hand, a 2.5 million strong army, as supported by Defense Minister Grachev, combined with the severe restrictions on Russian weapons in Europe by the CFE treaty, forces Russia to maintain the majority of its troops beyond the Urals. According to some estimates, the share of weapons allocated to Russia after the collapse of the USSR will enable her to maintain approximately 20–25 divisions.[49] Bearing in mind plans to replace mechanized infantry with rapid deployment troops, it can be assumed that the final number of divisions allowed in Europe will be even less.[50] Troops in the European part of Russia were cut by 75 per cent.

On balance, more than one half of the Russian troops will be deployed beyond the Urals following reform. In 1989, Russian troops outside the Soviet Union were organized into fifty divisions in the Siberian, Transbaikal, and Far Eastern military districts, and in Mongolia; seventeen divisions were organized in the Turkistan (Central Asia) military district.[51] Recent Japanese sources list thirty-eight divisions in Transbaikal, Far Eastern military districts, and Mongolia.[52] Regardless of Russia's close military cooperation with new nations of Central Asia, a large deployment of Russian troops there is unlikely. This model of cooperation does not presume that Russian troops are stationed there, but does assume predominantly local armies using Russian officers and information. Furthermore, the area beyond the Urals where Russian troops are located is very limited. Russian divisions are stationed there in a narrow strip 200 kilometers wide adjacent to the border. They mainly protect vast unpopulated areas in Siberia and the Far East. If the zone where they are stationed is extended by even 100 kilometers, they will cross over into the Siberian taiga, which lacks power supply and has a weak infrastructure.[53] If the present level of forty-six divisions deployed in the three military districts is preserved, allocation of Russian troops will change from 59 per cent in the European part, 31 per cent in Siberia and the Far East, and 10 per cent in Central Asia to 35 per cent in Europe and 65 per cent in Siberia and the Far East. In this sense, it is highly remarkable that initial Soviet–Chinese talks on reductions of border troops and confidence-building measures (CBMs) that started after Gorbachev's visit to China in 1990 have been smoothly transformed into talks on only CBMs.

Reduction of troops and CBMs along the Chinese border was part of Gorbachev's plan to expand the model of East–West relations and part of his 'new political thinking' toward the Asia–Pacific. As understood by the Russian and Chinese military, real security guarantees were based on personal contacts and confidence between elites and did not require legal formulations in treaties, or control measures. When Russian–Chinese contacts were reestablished after the abortive *coup* of 1991, the old elite model of confidence seemed to reemerge. The 1992 draft of the Russian–Chinese agreement on border CBMs, for example, provided for establishment of a 100 kilometer demilitarized zone with a limited number of troops on the Russian side. This agreement was supposed to be signed at Grachev's visit to Beijing in 1993 but was forgotten.[54]

Some points were clarified by Defense Minister Pavel Grachev in 1994. For example, he indicated that during the process of troop reductions, four military districts are considered key districts and will, therefore, retain high capability levels. The key districts are Moscow, Leningrad, the Northern Caucasus and the Far East, but the primary targets of reform are the Northern Caucasus and Transcaucasia.[55] The Far East military district will be the stronghold of a proposed sub-regional system of CIS collective security for East Asia, mainly because Kazakhstan has practically no troops, the official ceiling of the Kazakhstan army set at 150,000, divided between the Eastern and Central Asian zones according to General Ivashov's plan.

Another issue worthy of consideration is the possible reshaping of the military district territories beyond the Urals. Their present composition does not meet the requirements of the CIS sub-regional security scheme. If the territories are redistributed, however, Ural and Western Siberia could be included in the western zone of the Central Asian region, while Eastern Siberia and the Far East could join the East Asian region with the eastern provinces of Kazakhstan. The current Ural and Siberian military districts would be placed in the Central Asian zone and Transbaikal and the Far Eastern military districts would be placed in the East Asian region.

Among the four military districts, the Siberian is the weakest. According to Defense Ministry plans, it will be the first to be integrated with another, stronger, district. Early plans indicate that it will be absorbed into the Transbaikal district. This would be logical, given that the combination of the two units would provide a Russian–Kazakhstani defense line along the Chinese border. However, it will exclude Western Siberia from the Central Asian region. If current plans are not reconsidered, a division of the Siberian military district between the Urals and Transbaikal can be expected.

Mr Grachev has set priorities indicating general future trends for the reduction of Russian armed forces. They are an intensive reduction of the command structure from the top down to the level of military districts; the reduction of rear support structures; and the reduction of personnel in non-priority military districts.

Regarding the Far East, Grachev indicated that only troops in remote northern areas – an infantry regiment at Tiksi and an infantry division at Magadan – are to be reduced.[56] It seems rather improbable, therefore, that the current level of Russian military potential on the ground will be reduced significantly in the near future. Troops may be reallocated, difficult enough under the present economic conditions, but numbers will remain constant.

The real potential of these troops should not be overestimated. In a trend not specific to troops in the Far East, cuts in the military budget and the drastic decrease of financial allocations to the military industrial complex have resulted in the disintegration of training facilities. Additionally, weapons and equipment are outdated. By the assessment of the General Command of Ground Forces, in the near future 70 to 80 per cent of tanks and armored vehicles will be outdated. Finally, the general shortage of fuel affects planned training exercises. The number of training flights, naval exercises, etc. is rapidly declining. This situation affects not only the level of training but also the psychological mood of personnel, especially among officers interested in gaining experience with new weapons and equipment.

The situation may be even worse in the Far East than it is nationally. In the process of European disarmament, despite the health and well-being requirements of the Far East's population, the region became a place to stockpile assets not allowed in European Russia. A prime example of this practice was the explosion that occurred at the Novonezhino naval warehouse near Vladivostok in May 1994. Investigation of the incident revealed that the warehouse was overstocked with ammunition; its inventory far exceeded the requirements of troops in the vicinity. At the time of the explosion, about 2,000 cases of aviation ammunition, 70 per cent of which had been trans-ferred from the Baltic republics, were stockpiled there. A similar example is the scrapping of nuclear submarines. Although missiles are taken off the sub-marines, nuclear reactors remain in place and require constant monitoring. The time required for the queue of submarines waiting for full deactivation is many years; in the meantime, all those in line must be closely monitored.

The issue of Russian naval assets in the Pacific has several aspects worthy of consideration. After reduction of operations in the open sea, the most cru-cial part of Russian naval facilities became the strategic value of SLBM deployment. Although the issue of a closed Sea of Okhotsk functioning as a sanctuary for submarines is often discussed, it is controversial for Russian interests. The issue is closely connected with the provisions of START-II. The ceilings of 1,700–1,750 warheads on SLBMs provided by the treaty force Russia to eliminate about 38 per cent of her SLBM warhead potential of 2,804.[57] Within these ceilings, 23–25 strategic submarines carrying 390–420 partially unloaded SLBMs will be maintained.[58]

The present [as at October 1994] Russian submarine potential consists of sixty-two submarines (a 20.8 per cent decrease since 1991) deployed on five naval bases of the Northern and Pacific Fleets. Assets of the Pacific Fleet include: nine nuclear submarines at the Pavlovskoye naval base (62.5 per cent decrease since 1991), all of them the older Yankee-I and Delta-I classes (Navaga and Murena classes in Russian), fifteen at the Rybachiy naval base on the eastern coast of the Kamchatka Peninsula (no decrease since 1991), with 60 per cent of them of the Delta III class (Kalmar class in Russian), as well as modern weapons deployed in the Far East. Assets of the Northern Fleet are: thirty-eight submarines stationed in three bases on the Kola Peninsula (no decrease since 1991), the majority being modern classes and including six Typhoon class and six Delta-IV class.[59] Data presented by Joshua Handler and William Arkin indicate that 66 per cent of all Russian SLBM warheads are deployed within the Northern Fleet, but recent official documents by the Russian Defense Ministry state that the missiles are divided proportionally, at a ratio of 63:37 in favor of the Northern Fleet.[60] Regardless of Soviet efforts to build a sanctuarized SLBM base in the Sea of Okhotsk during the 1970–1980 period and efforts toward free access to open seas through the base on the Kamchatka Peninsula in the 1980s, the Kola Peninsula remains the primary base for Russian naval strategic forces. Submarine modernization in the 1980s affected the Northern Fleet; the potential for a sanctuarized Sea of Okhotsk became outdated with START-II. It is highly notable that reductions of Russian naval strategic forces were performed exclusively at the expense of the Pavlovskoye base in Kamchatka.

Because it is illogical to maintain the assessed number of twenty-three to twenty-five nuclear submarines in two separate fleets, technical parameters are in favor of concentrating Russian SLBMs in the Northern Fleet. Furthermore, three of the four submarine-building shipyards in Russia are scheduled to close. The one remaining, which will cut its production in half, is the *Severniy* shipyard at Severodvinsk (Arkhangelsk Oblast).[61] Elimination of shipyard facilities in the Far East appears incompatible with the importance of Pacific naval nuclear forces.

Political factors may force Russia to abandon the Northern SLBM option and return to a Pacific one. Even if SLBMs are deployed there, the Northern Pacific does not appear to be an area of additional political troubles for Russia. Russia's major political partners in the region are the United States and China who do not insist on naval arms control or reductions. The only opponent would be Japan, but the current uneasy state of Russo–Japanese political relations, shadowed by the territorial dispute, permits Russia to ignore Japanese objections.[62]

An additional factor in the military build-up in the Far East will be created if Russia decides upon the Pacific option. The logic behind this option is of the kind that adds to Japanese concerns about regional military balance. Yasuhide Yamanouchi of the International Institute of Global Peace in Tokyo (now Institute for International Policy Studies) indicates:

> The home bases for the SSBNs, Petropavlovsk at the southern tip of the Kamchatka Peninsula and Magadan on the northern end of the Sea of Okhotsk, are both geographically isolated, making them difficult to supply and guard for long periods. The Soviet Union's sea fortification program cannot be carried out safely over a long time without secure ties between Vladivostok and the other Soviet coastal bases. The sea lane linking Vladivostok and the other Soviet coastal bases in the Okhotsk Sea are the lifelines of the Soviet Union's Sea Bastion strategy.[63]

There are indications that after losing shipyard facilities in the Ukraine, Russian military leadership has tended to rely on the sea bastion strategy. An article by General-Lieutenant I. Skurlatov in *Voyennaya mysl'* is indicative of this. The author writes: 'To increase fleets' capacities of coastline defense, it is more realistic to take the line of further qualitative improvement and development of all components of coastal troops: coastal missile and artillery complexes, divisions of coastal defense and marines.'[64]

CONCLUSIONS

The issues discussed above allow us to conclude that the Russian contribution to international security in the Asia–Pacific region is a much more complex problem than is its role in Europe or in Russian–American relations. The military establishment is the component of the former Soviet elite that has changed the least since 1991. It remains cautious of close cooperation with the West and remains hopeful about the military factor of Russia's great power status. With the collapse of the Warsaw Treaty and the USSR, attention has shifted to political and conflict issues within the CIS territory. Expectations for military build-up are limited by lack of finances, problems of troop withdrawal from abroad and the general chaotic situation in Russia.

The results of Gorbachev's détente and arms reduction policies toward the United States and Western Europe, along with the new geopolitical realities resulting from the collapse of the USSR, limit to a great degree the geographical scope of post-Soviet Russia's military ambitions. The bargain that was made between Gorbachev and the military establishment for arms reductions in the West in exchange for larger military opportunities beyond the Urals dominates the military mentality.

This is not to say that the present Russian military ambitions are comparable with the 'Soviet threat' of the 1970s and 1980s. Given the current transitional period of military reform and the extensive national conflicts within the CIS, the army is too preoccupied by domestic problems to initiate anything of import on an international scale. At the same time, the problem of Asia–Pacific security in the near future may be much more complicated than the question of whether a Yeltsin-type democracy or nationalist–neocommunist alliance will prevail. Given a more stable situation, even under a Yeltsin-type regime, there is a real possibility of Russian military expansion in the region.

NOTES

1 *Nezavisimaya gazeta*, 7 May 1992.
2 *Nezavisimaya gazeta*, 7 May 1992.
3 If compared to the number of weapons in the USSR at the time the CFE was concluded and with the ceilings set by the CFE for the USSR, Russia may keep only 37 per cent of the initial number of tanks (58 per cent of the CFE ceiling), 43 per cent of armored vehicles (64 per cent), 58 per cent of artillery systems (59 per cent), 57 per cent of planes (73 per cent), and 60 per cent of helicopters (59 per cent). *Izvestiya*, 31 August 1994.
4 *Nezavisimaya gazeta*, 29 July 1992.
5 Mikhail Kolesnikov, 'Ugroza pryamoyy agressi protiv Rossii znachitel'no snizilas,' *Nezavisimaya gazeta*, 5 October 1994.
6 *Izvestiya*, 7 May 1992.
7 *Ibid.*
8 *Izvestiya*, 7 May 1992.
9 'Osnovnye polozheniya voyennoy doktriny Rossiyskoy Federatsii,' *Izvestiya*, 18 November 1993.
10 *Segodnya*, 19 January 1994.
11 *Izvestiya*, 7 May 1992.
12 Valentin Larionov, 'Otkuda gosudarstvu zhdat' voyennuyu ugrozu?,' *Nezavisimaya gazeta*, 15 May 1992.
13 *Kraznaya zvezda*, 22 May 1992.
14 *Izvestiya*, 1 June 1992.

15 *Vek*, no. 15, 16–22 April 1993.
16 A.S. Sinaysky, 'Geopolitika i natsional'naya bezopasnost' Rossii,' *Voyennaya mysl'*, no. 10, 1992, p. 10.
17 Viktor Stefashin, 'Varianty razvitiya voyenno-politicheskoy situatsii na Dal'nem Vostoke,' *Problemy Dal'nego Vostoka*, nos. 1–3, 1992, p. 62.
18 *Ibid.*, pp. 66–9.
19 *Nezavisimaya gazeta*, 30 July 1992.
20 *Ibid.*
21 S.B. Lavrov, 'L.N. Gumilyov i yevraziystvo,' L.N. Gumilyov, *Ritmy Yevrazii*, Moscow: Ekopross, 1993, p. 9.
22 N.S. Trubetskoy, *Vavilonskaya bashnya i smesheniye yazykov*, cited in L. N. Gumilyov, *Zametki poslednego yevraziytsa: Predisloviye k sochineniyam kn. N.S. Trubetskogo*, p. 61.
23 *Ibid.*, p. 39.
24 L.N. Gumilyov, *Ritmy Yevrazii*, p. 190.
25 See Vladimir Zhirinovsky, *Posledniy brosok na yug*, Moscow: IK Bukvitsa, 1993.
26 *Krasnaya zvezda*, 10 October 1992.
27 See *Kommersant*, 4–11 May 1992; *Nezavisimaya gazeta*, 6 June 1992.
28 *Nezavisimaya gazeta*, 13 May 1992.
29 *Izvestiya*, 13 May 1992.
30 *Krasnaya zvezda*, 22 May 1992.
31 See *Izvestiya*, 16 May 1992.
32 *Novosti* program, Ostankino TV, 16 April 1993.
33 *Izvestiya*, 30 December 1993.
34 *Izvestiya*, 2 February 1994.
35 *Izvestiya*, 13 May 1992.
36 *Krasnaya zvezda*, 22 May 1992.
37 *Izvestiya*, 13 May 1992.
38 For a more extended discussion of the concept of sufficient defense in Gorbachev's policy, see Alexei V. Zagorsky, 'Political Dimensions of Pacific Security: The Soviet View,' Miles Kahler, (ed.), *Beyond the Cold War in the Pacific*, IGCC Studies in Conflict and Cooperation, vol. 2, San Diego: University of California Press, 1991, p. 111.
39 V.P. Luzyanin, 'Strategicheskaya stabil'nost' i mnogopolyarnaya model' sderzhivaniya,' *Voyennaya mysl'*, nos. 8–9, 1992, pp. 10–11.
40 Yu. A. Nikolaev, 'Oboronnaya dostatochnost': Kriterii i metody otsenki,' *Voyennaya mysl'*, nos. 4–5, 1992, p. 28.
41 V.P. Luzyanin, V. S. Yelizarov, 'Podkhod k opredeleniyu sostava gruppirovki sil i sredstv oboronnoy dostatochnosti,' *Voyennaya mysl'*, no. 11, 1992, p. 26.
42 *Izvestiya*, 16 November 1992.
43 Alexei Arbatov, 'Kakim budet vybor Rossii?,' *Nezavisimaya gazeta*, 31 December 1993.
44 Boeicho, *Boei Hakusho, Heisei 5 nen* [Defense white paper, 1993], Tokyo: Okurasho Insatsukyoku, 1993, p. 46, and Boeicho, *Boei Hakusho, Heisei gannen* [Defense white paper, 1989], Tokyo: Okurasho Insatsukyoku, 1989, p. 41.
45 *Disarmament and Security, 1988–1989: Yearbook*, Moscow: Novosty Press Agency for IMEMO, 1989, p. 496.
46 *International Herald Tribune*, 16 January 1990.
47 *Pravda*, 14 January 1990; *Izvestiya*, 17 April 1991.
48 *Izvestiya*, 30 December 1993.
49 *Nezavisimaya gazeta*, 29 July 1992.
50 This figure may be compared with data from *Military Balance*. According to this source, the Soviet equivalent within the CFE area of what is now the Russian army was ninety-six divisions at the end of 1989. *Military Balance 1989–1990*,

London: Brassey's for the International Institute of Strategic Studies, 1989, pp. 38–42.

51 *Ibid.*, pp. 41–2.
52 Boeicho, *Boei Hakusho, Heisei 3 nen* [Defense white paper, 1991], Tokyo: Okurasho Insatsukyoku, 1990, p. 48.
53 *Pacific Research*, vol. 4, no. 1, (February 1991), pp. 13–14.
54 *Izvestiya*, 2 December 1992.
55 *Segodnya*, 5 July 1994.
56 *Izvestiya*, 20 November 1993.
57 The figure of 2,804 warheads on Russian SLBMs was published by the General Staff of the CIS Navy as data for the beginning of 1992. *Izvestiya*, 12 March 1992.
58 *Nezavisimaya gazeta*, 23 March 1993.
59 *Izvestiya*, 20 November 1993 and 12 March 1992.
60 Joshua Handler and William M. Arkin, *Nuclear Warships and Naval Nuclear Weapons: A Complete Inventory*, Neptune Papers, no. 5, Washington, DC: Greenpeace, 1990, pp. 74–5, and *Izvestiya*, 20 November 1993. Handler and Arkin's data on the number of Russian warheads on SLBMs (3,802) does not coincide with the data published by the General Staff of the CIS Navy in 1992, but the data on the number and type of submarines are identical.
61 *Vek*, 22–9 January 1993.
62 The situation in Northern Europe is quite different. Russian willingness to expand the Northern European cooperation system centered around the Scandinavian nations, as well as the nature of Russo–Finnish relations, make her rather vulnerable to Scandinavian demands for regional denuclearization. In the end, political considerations may outweigh strategic ones.
63 Yasuhide Yamanouchi, *Japan's Security Policy and Arms Control in North East Asia*, IIGP Policy Paper, 60E, Tokyo, October 1991, p. 5.
64 I.S. Skurlatov, 'Problemy oborony morskogo poberezh'ya,' *Voyennaya mysl'*, nos. 4–5, 1992, p. 20.

Part II

Economic development in the Russian Far East

3 Economic challenge in the Russian Far East

Tsuneo Akaha, Pavel A. Minakir and Kunio Okada

INTRODUCTION

After ten years of *perestroika* and thirty months of 'Radical Economic Reform', the economic situation in Russia has not improved. On the contrary, it is worse now than ten years ago. In 1990–91, there was widespread confidence in Russia that the improvement of the economic situation depended on taking decisive steps in the direction of a market economy. Today many Russians look back and feel that they have suffered unnecessary economic losses because of their government's haphazard and often inconsistent policies. Although the jury is still out on the wisdom of radical economic reform to turn Russia into a market economy open to the world, it is clear that those who live in the struggling transition economy cannot wait for the reform policy's painful consequences to disappear.

The introduction of radical economic reform and the accompanying political confusion in post-Soviet Russia have brought about a severe recession throughout the country, including the Russian Far East. The departure in 1993 of the architect of the reform plan, Yegor Gaidar, did not alter the key objectives of the reform program, namely a reduction of federal budget deficits, control of currency and credit circulation, and privatization of large state enterprises. On the eve of the Russian presidential election in June 1996, many outside observers feared the rise of anti-reform forces among nationalists and Communists throughout the country, some even predicting a sweeping roll-back of reform. After defeating Communist Alexandr Zhuganov in the run-off election in July, Yeltsin retained Prime Minister Viktor Chernomyrdin and other pro-reform members of his cabinet and added new reform-oriented advisors. The policy of reform survived the pre-election jitter.

In many respects, however, the reform has been a curse to the Russian Far Eastern economy. Inflation has been rampant, industrial production has plummeted, domestic investment capital has virtually disappeared, and unemployment has climbed higher than ever before. Moscow is no longer in a position to provide the economic subsidies on which the Russian Far East had long depended during the Soviet era. Only in 1995 did the region's economy begin to show some signs of 'bottoming out.'

ECONOMIC CHALLENGES UNDER REFORM

In 1994, only one parameter appeared to become more stable in the Russian economy: inflation. The inflation rate during the May–August 1994 period was about 3–5 per cent a month. The government and the Central Bank used two special instruments to control inflation in the country. First, monetary and fiscal pressures on the economy were used. As a result, the nation's industrial output dropped by 18 per cent in 1992, 14.1 per cent in 1993, and 20.9 per cent in 1994 (see Table 3.1). An associated consequence of the anti-inflation measures was a drastic decline in general domestic demand. Exports also dropped as a result of high customs duties and relatively low exchange rates. The shrinking aggregate demand became the most serious constraint on economic development.

Regulation of the exchange rate on interbanking currency exchanges was instituted in 1994. Consequently, the ruble–US dollar exchange rate was more or less stabilized. Import prices were also more or less stable. This was important because imported foodstuffs and consumer goods represented more than 30 per cent of the domestic market in Russia.

The general economic situation of the nation was very unstable, however. It was impossible to keep exchange rates low for an extended period of time. Imports grew at uncontrollable rates as domestic production declined and personal income went up. It was also impossible to limit the money supply when non-payment reached almost 100 trillion rubles. As a result, by September 1994 the inflation rate was increasing by 8 to 10 per cent a month, and the exchange rate (rubles to US dollars) began to change fast against the ruble.

Table 3.1 Industrial production in the Russian Far East
(change as percentage of previous year)

	1986–90 average	1991	1992	1993	1994	1995
Russia	2.6	−8.0	−18.0	−14.1	−20.9	−6.0
Far East	2.3	−2.7	−14.4	−12.3	−20.8	—
Sakha Republic	3.8	−2.4	−20.2	−3.9	0.4	2.0
Jewish Autonomous Oblast	4.4	−5.0	−25.4	−33.3	−29.0	−32.0
Primorskii	2.8	−3.7	−6.9	−11.8	−29.3	−1.0
Khabarovsk	2.8	−1.2	−13.6	−18.2	−41.5	−23.0
Amur	2.2	−6.4	−17.3	−7.4	−22.9	−18.0
Kamchatka	2.4	−7.9	−26.9	−6.5	−30.8	9.0
Magadan	−0.2	−3.1	−8.1	−10.6	−11.6	−21.0
Sakhalin	0.2	3.1	−21.8	−26.9	−10.0	9.0

Source: Roshia Sangyo Kiso Chosa: Ekonomikku Torendo, 1995 [Basic survey of Russian industry: economic trends, 1995], Tokyo: Roshia To'o Boekikai Roshia To'o Keizai Kenkyujo, 1995, p. 90

In 1995, the average monthly inflation rate stood at 7 per cent. Although there were some signs of improvement in the export sector, particularly fuels and raw materials exports, domestic demand dropped. As a result, the overall industrial output declined by 6 per cent for the year. Other major trends in the Russian economy were an upturn in the financial market, a continuing decline in production-related investment, a drop in personal disposable income, and a seemingly endless increase in income disparities. The continuing economic reform in the Russian economy had far-reaching effects on the nation's regions. Generally, cuts in central fiscal subsidies and varying economic sovereignty of the regions widened the wage gap between the 'haves' and 'have-nots' in the regions.[1]

The initial impact of the radical reform on the Russian Far East was relatively favorable as compared with most other parts of Russia. An important factor was the rapid growth of export earnings through the liberalization of foreign trade. This factor, together with the continuing state support for economic development during 1992, put an end to discussion about establishing an independent Far Eastern Republic. Moscow relaxed its control over the region's cooperation with the countries of Northeast Asia, and the region received new opportunities for international cooperation.

Beginning in the second half of 1992, however, the Far East's economic situation began to deteriorate, a process that has continued to this day.

The financial situation worsened progressively as a result of the consistent deflationary policies of the central government. The aggravation of financial problems in Russia's economy had a considerable effect on the financial performance of enterprises in the Far East. The number of unprofitable enterprises increased steeply. Factors such as higher production costs per unit of production, the end of state compensation for input price differentials, and the rising cost of the 'hard components' of production (heat and electric power, transportation costs, etc.) led to a dramatic decrease in the competitiveness of the region's products in the domestic markets of Russia and the Commonwealth of Independent States (CIS).

Cut off from the domestic market as a result of the reforms, the Far East began to insist on special privileges for foreign economic relations. As early as March 1992, all of the governors of the Far Eastern territories had forced the central government to adopt a special decree providing privileges for exporters. The Gaidar government was very reluctant to grant these privileges, however, and by the middle of 1992 the privileges had lost their meaning as the result of the introduction of a new system of licenses and quotas for the export of raw materials (the principal export commodity of the region). With the introduction of the new quota system, Moscow regained full control over regional exports.

In 1993, the volume of investments continued to decline. Although the reduction of budget allocations from the central government was not compensated for by the stimulation of private investment activities, in 1993 the part of profit that was used for capital investment was free from taxation.

However, enterprises continued to prefer to invest in capital transactions and consumption. As a result, the process of decapitalization ('eating out') of the economy which had begun in 1992 continued in 1993.

The fiscal condition of both the state and the private sector deteriorated. In the Russian Far East, the cumulative debts of the public and private enterprises reached 760 billion rubles in September 1993. This amounted to one-half of the total industrial output during the January–September period. Outstanding bank loans in the region stood at 970 billion rubles. With 30 per cent and 10 per cent of the region's public and private enterprises in debt, respectively, many factories were closed down and the payment of workers' salaries was delayed by as many as four months.[2] Industrial output has continued to decline. By 1993, the region's industrial production had fallen to the 1983–85 levels.

High inflation rates continued. In 1993, the region's inflation rate was a whopping 1,100 per cent, surpassing the national rate of 1,000 per cent. The average wage in the Russian Far East in September 1992 was 40,000 rubles, but it increased to only 114,000 rubles a year later. As a result, consumer purchases were constrained and retail sales, including consumer durables and foodstuffs, dropped by 11 per cent from 1992 to 1993. However, goods on local markets were increasingly diversified, including luxury items such as passenger cars, computers, and electric home appliances. Although market prices of these items went up by 20–30 per cent, their supplies were stable and even growing. The market in better housing was also moving, with demand exceeding supply.[3] These trends indicated a growing gap in purchasing power among the region's population.

Investment activities in the Russian Far East also continued to slow down. In 1987 prices, the total investment in the region in 1993 amounted to only 1.1 billion rubles, compared with the 4 billion rubles that was invested in the region's economy in 1987–88. Far Eastern enterprises had to use most of their profits to pay rising wages in an attempt to counter the effects of the fast-growing inflation. To hedge against inflation, banks would issue only short-term loans, the average term of a loan being only 3–4 weeks, and charge interest as high as 260–280 per cent.[4]

Although privatization proceeded in the region, this did not necessarily improve the region's economic life. By the end of 1993, as many as 1,700 enterprises had been privatized, of which 450 were large enterprises. About 26–27 per cent of large state enterprises had been privatized, but all of them were experiencing financial difficulties. Most enterprises had to lay off workers. The official unemployment rate in the Russian Far East was less than one per cent as of August 1993, but the number of jobless people (28,000) was three times as large as a year earlier. Capital shortages also strained private farms in the region, which numbered about 15,000. Their output accounted for a mere 1.5–5 per cent of the total production of agricultural products in the Russian Far East.[5]

The situation has not improved much. On the contrary, most economic indicators have shown deepening problems. The most significant of these signs has been the continuing decline in industrial output. Particularly notable has been the drop in machinery production in Primorye and Khabarovsk. The defense industry, one of the most important sources of industrial production and employment in these territories, has reduced its output substantially due to shrinking government procurement. Rising costs of transportation and increasing electric power prices have also contributed to the decline in industrial production. Machinery production in Primorye and Khabarovsk dropped by as much as 42 per cent and 62 per cent respectively in 1994.[6] In 1995, industrial production in the Russian Far East continued to decline, albeit at slower rates (4–5 per cent). Industrial machinery output dropped by 27.3 per cent in Primorye and 43 per cent in Khabarovsk. Declining domestic investment in industrial machinery was a major problem, as were skyrocketing prices of energy and transportation. Regional investment from indigenous sources had dropped by more than 60 per cent from 1992.[7] As a result, 42 per cent of all industrial enterprises in the region were operating in the red.[8] Consumer prices continued to rise at alarming rates in the region, 250–310 per cent in 1994 and 200–240 per cent in 1995.

One important consequence of industrial deterioration and inflation has been widening unemployment. Although the official jobless rate appeared tolerable (3 per cent in Primorye, 5.2 per cent in Khabarovsk, and 4.3 per cent in Kamchatka), more realistic unemployment rates based on ILO formulae in these territories were 9 per cent, 11 per cent, and 18 per cent, respectively.[9]

ONE BRIGHT SPOT: FOREIGN TRADE

Amidst these generally negative trends in the Russian Far East, one bright spot has been the expansion of international trade, particularly with Asian countries.

The beginning of economic reform in 1992 had brought expectations for immediate liberalization of the economy and reorientation of economic potential throughout Russia toward international markets. Taking into consideration the rapidly falling competitiveness of Far Eastern products in the domestic market, such reorientation was particularly desirable. Trends at the beginning of 1992 seemed to indicate that this idea was realizable. It seemed that the idea of the 1960s, of exploiting foreign markets for stimulating economic development of the Far East and producing internationally competitive raw materials and other goods which were unprofitable if produced for the internal markets (an idea that was never realized in the thirty years under the planned economy), was being realized. There was a sharp increase in regional exports and imports in 1992, 30.4 per cent for exports and 260 per cent for imports, caused by the euphoria over the liberalization of foreign trade. In 1993, foreign trade turnover increased by a much smaller but still encouraging rate, 11 per cent, to $3 billion. The increase in 1993 was wholly attributable to the 18.4 per cent growth of exports; the figure for imports was only 2 per cent. These figures looked rather favorable as compared with those for Russia as a whole, which experienced only a 1.4 per cent increase in exports, to $43 billion, and an almost 30 per cent drop in imports, to $27 billion. In the Russian Far East, the share of exports in industrial production increased from 4 per cent at the end of the 1980s to 8.5 per cent in 1992.

However, a closer examination of the seemingly healthy growth in international trade in the Russian Far East revealed some disconcerting facts. The growing importance of foreign economic relations had an artificial character and was not evidence of the emergence of a truly open export-oriented economy in the region. First, export growth, as mentioned above, was observed under the conditions of sharp production decline in industries, which undermined the future prospects for industrial development. Second, the commodity structure of exports was very unstable and had little in common with the long-term needs of economic development in the Russian Far East. Additionally, an increasing share of the exports in some important commodity groups (petrochemicals, rolled steel, non-ferrous metal scrap and

Table 3.2 Russia's trade with Asian countries, 1992–94
($US millions)

Trade partner	1992		1993		1994 (forecast)	
	Exports	Imports	Exports	Imports	Exports	Imports
Afghanistan	84.4	214.3	50.0	861.7	60.0	900.0
Vietnam	78.9	112.1	112.0	154.0	150.0	150.0
Bangladesh	10.2	12.5	21.7	23.0	23.5	26.5
Iran	258.3	48.1	686.1	37.0	1,050.0	250.0
India	568.9	822.1	450.0	550.0	800.0	1100.0
Indonesia	16.6	9.6	17.0	60.0	18.0	132.0
N. Korea	400.0	200.0	350.0	80.0	400.0	200.0
S. Korea	203.8	753.1	960.0	560.0	1,400.0	600.0
China	2,737.2	1,669.3	5,080.0	2,600.0	5,000.0	3,000.0
Laos	0.9	4.3	9.3	2.7	14.0	4.0
Malaysia	24.5	5.8	26.0	20.0	30.0	22.0
Mongolia	235.0	176.0	257.0	135.0	225.0	172.0
Pakistan	52.6	64.6	35.9	11.3	31.0	40.0
Singapore	143.8	510.8	161.0	534.0	182.0	553.0
Thailand	271.4	224.9	476.2	205.5	500.0	560.0
Turkey	649.3	384.0	1,362.5	492.5	1,500.0	560.0
Philippines	31.9	3.7	157.2	9.2	160.0	10.0
Japan	1,568.7	1,680.1	1,850.0	1,350.0	1,850.0	1,450.0
Australia	7.9	52.4	8.0	66.0	8.0	66.0
New Zealand	3.6	363.0	2.5	33.0	2.5	33.0
Taiwan	455.2	44.5	480.0	110.0	550.0	100.0

Source: Russian Ministry of Foreign Economic Relations

alloys) was carried out by a few enterprises. This created a progressive narrowing of the export base of the region. Third, the growth of exports did not result in capital good imports for the modernization of export industries. Fourth, a major part of enterprises and industries of the region remained isolated from export activities and were not likely to survive the waves of economic reform. Fifth, the poorly diversified industry and commodity structure of regional exports meant that the Far East was highly vulnerable to changing international markets, a pattern long observed in developing countries as they became integrated with the more advanced economies of the world.

It is none the less true that international trade has grown and become a very important part of the region's economic life. Especially important is the growing trade with the neighboring Asian countries. In 1993, Russia's trade with its Asian partners reached almost $20 billion, up $5 billion from the previous year. This was particularly noteworthy because the nation's world-wide trade had declined during the same period. As Table 3.2 shows, Russia's most important Asian trading partners in 1993 were China (two-way trade reaching $7.68 billion), Japan ($3.2 billion), Turkey ($1.86 billion), South Korea ($1.49 billion), India ($1 billion), Afghanistan ($911 million), and Iran ($723 million).

A large portion of Russia's trade with Asian countries was and continues to be conducted by the Russian Far East. In 1994, Japan was by far the most important trading partner of the Russian Far East, with the two-way trade reaching $1,105.1 million, or 48.9 per cent of the region's total international trade valued at $2,260.3 million (see Table 3.3). The other important trade partners were South Korea ($261.9 million in two-way trade), China ($250.6 million), and the United States ($176.0 million).

The region's trade with Japan, South Korea, and the United States has experienced a fairly steady growth. In contrast, China's trade with the Russian Far East has shown drastic fluctuations. In 1993, China emerged as the region's most important trading partner with the two way trade reaching $1,188.3 million and surpassing the region's $1,100.2 million trade with Japan. The dramatic drop in China's trade in 1994 was largely due to Moscow's decision in February of that year to tighten the control of the influx of Chinese traders and laborers in the region. The action was taken in response to the region's growing concern over the large and visible presence of Chinese, including an estimated 400,000–500,000 illegal workers.[10] There were also concerns about the shoddy quality of Chinese consumer goods that were flooding the market. Whether these concerns were warranted or not, Moscow's action obviously had a dramatic impact on the trade flow between the two countries.

Primorye leads the rest of the Russian Far East territories in international trade. It is followed by Khabarovsk, Kamchatka, Sakha, Amur, Sakhalin, Magadan, and the Jewish Autonomous Oblast (Table 3.4). There is potential for further expansion in the region's foreign trade if its dilapidated

Table 3.3 Russian Far East trade by partner, 1994
($US millions)

Trade partner	Exports (value)	%	Imports (value)	%	Total (value)	%
Total	1,610.5	100.0	649.8	100.0	2,260.3	100.0
Japan	995.0	62.0	110.1	16.9	1,105.1	48.9
S. Korea	163.3	10.2	98.6	15.2	261.9	11.6
China	156.0	9.7	94.6	14.6	250.6	11.1
USA	63.6	4.0	112.4	17.3	176.0	7.8
Singapore	25.7	1.6	14.5	2.2	40.2	1.8
Australia	31.1	1.9	7.7	1.2	38.9	1.7
Canada	19.1	1.2	19.2	3.0	38.3	1.7
Germany	19.3	1.2	17.4	2.7	36.7	1.6
Switzerland	15.5	1.0	19.7	3.0	35.2	1.6
Norway	21.5	1.3	3.4	0.5	24.9	1.1
Italy	8.2	0.5	13.8	2.1	22.0	1.0
Hong Kong	18.9	1.2	2.3	0.4	21.2	0.9
Other	73.3	4.2	136.1	20.9	94.2	9.2

Source: Roshia Kyokuto Data Book [Russian Far East data book], Tokyo: Roshia To'o Boekikai Roshia To'o Keizai Kenkyujo, 1996, p. 9

Table 3.4 Foreign trade in Russian Far East territories, 1994
($US millions)

Territory	Exports (value)	%	Imports (value)	%	Total (value)	%
Far East Total	1,610.5	100.0	649.8	100.0	2,260.3	100.0
Sakha	171.8	10.7	132.3	20.4	304.1	13.5
Primorskii	435.0	27.0	156.0	24.0	591.0	26.1
Khabarovsk	403.1	25.0	130.2	20.0	533.3	23.6
Amur	69.1	4.3	36.6	5.6	105.7	4.7
Sakhalin	219.4	13.6	43.9	6.8	263.3	11.6
Magadan	13.9	0.9	59.6	9.2	73.5	3.3
Jewish AO	10.2	0.6	6.2	0.9	16.4	0.7
Kamchatka	288.0	17.9	85.0	13.1	373.0	16.5

Source: Roshia Kyokuto Data Book [Russian Far East data book], Tokyo: Roshia To'o Boekikai Roshia To'o Keizai Kenkyujo, 1996, p. 8

transportation and communication infrastructure is improved, but this will require enormous investment. Given the serious shortage of capital affecting the entire country, the region will have no choice but to turn to the international community for the necessary funds. However, the Russian Far East must compete against the other capital-short regions of Northeast Asia, particularly China. Competition also exists within the Russian Far East.

There are two other important aspects to the growing international trade

Table 3.5 Composition of Russian Far East exports, 1993–94
($US millions)

Item	1993 (value)	%	1994 (value)	%
Total	2,048.1	100.0	1,610.5	100.0
Machinery, plant, transport equipment	212.8	10.4	32.0	2.0
Fuels, minerals, metals	559.3	27.3	464.0	28.8
Chemicals	51.6	2.5	19.8	1.2
Consumer goods	70.3	3.4	3.1	0.2
Construction material	6.0	0.3	4.3	0.3
Timber, forestry products	430.1	21.0	317.2	19.7
Foodstuffs, food materials	687.8	33.6	704.0	43.7
Freight, port, distribution fees	13.7	0.7	53.2	3.3
Other	16.5	0.8	12.9	0.8

Source: Roshia Kyokuto Data Book [Russian Far East data book], Tokyo: Roshia To'o
Boekikai Roshia To'o Keizai Kenkyujo, 1996, p. 10

activities in the Russian Far East. One is that natural resources constitute the most important export sector. As shown in Table 3.5, this sector, including fuels, minerals, metals, construction materials, timber and forestry products, and fish and other foodstuffs, accounted for over 90 per cent of the region's total exports in 1994. One can expect their importance to continue as the region develops closer economic ties with the many resource importers in the Asia–Pacific. This, of course, will have important implications for resource conservation and management in the Russian Far East, as we will examine later.

FOREIGN INVESTMENT AND JOINT VENTURES

Another important point about the region's growing trade with Asia–Pacific countries is the role of international joint ventures. At the very early stages of economic reform, in 1987, special incentives (tax holidays, preferential taxation, etc.) were introduced to the Far East in order to attract foreign investment. Moscow hoped to shift the burden of economic development in the Far East to foreign investors. In reality, however, the expectations that direct foreign investment, together with the natural and productive resources of the region, could quickly improve productive capacity of the Far East and expand foreign trade turned out to be only partially realistic.

Beginning in 1991, the process of establishing joint ventures started at a very rapid pace. By the end of 1991, there were 206 joint ventures in operation. The main incentives for foreign investors at that time were the ease of access to natural resources, preferential taxation, and favorable conditions for export. In 1992, however, these preferential measures were cancelled due largely to the unfounded fear in the central government that the foreign investors were interested only in destroying socialism. In spite of this, the establishment of foreign capital firms accelerated, but investment began to be directed toward non-productive activities (mainly trade operations). This process was favored by the decentralization of foreign economic activities and the liberalization of foreign economic and exchange transactions, as well as by the announcement of plans for the establishment of free economic zones. The euphoria of 1991–92 was more or less understandable; benefits connected with entry to a newly opened market often outweigh fears of high risks involved in investing in a politically unstable country. Establishment of joint ventures and wholly owned foreign subsidiaries continued well into 1993, in spite of the aggravations of political instability in the country and constant changes in foreign investment legislation. By the beginning of 1994, over 1,500 firms with foreign capital participation were registered in the Russian Far East. This represented a 70 per cent increase over the 1988–92 period.

In 1993, the number of joint ventures in operation increased by 36 per cent (28 per cent in 1992). However, the total number of joint ventures remained insignificant against the background of the economic troubles of the region noted earlier. Foreign investors were very reluctant to invest new funds in the Far East. No large-scale investment programs were realized. In spite of the number of joint ventures established, the foreign investment situation became even more difficult than in 1992. For example, in Khabarovsk Krai, which has one of the highest numbers of foreign capital firms in the Far East, 207 such companies were registered in 1993 as compared with 155 in 1992, but the total value of foreign investment had dropped more than eightfold.

The large increase in the number of registered foreign companies was, almost exclusively, connected with the growing Chinese presence. In 1993, joint ventures with Chinese participation accounted for over 40 per cent of the total number (27.6 per cent in 1992). The second highest foreign capital investor was Japan (15.5 per cent in 1993 and 22.3 per cent in 1992). The main sphere of activities of Chinese-affiliated enterprises was connected with both domestic and foreign trade, within which framework the traditional exchange of raw materials and consumer goods was performed. Very few Chinese joint ventures were engaged in construction or production of consumer goods because the primary goal of Russo–Chinese joint ventures was the extraction of extra profits from existing price differentials for raw materials and consumer goods between the two countries. A conspicuous feature of Chinese-affiliated enterprises was the negligible size of their authorized capital. The average value of Chinese investment was only $50,000; the comparable figure for companies with Japanese capital participation was over $300,000. Many Chinese-affiliated enterprises, particularly 100 per cent-owned subsidiaries, were dummy companies engaged in real estate transactions and other spheres of activity that did not appear in their charter documents.

Between 1988 and 1994, there were a total of 624 enterprises with foreign capital participation in the Russian Far East (Table 3.6). Eight hundred and eighty-eight were with Chinese partners, 280 with Japanese companies, 274 with US investors, and 177 with South Koreans. Business enterprises with international capital accounted for as much as $190.5 million in exports and $122.8 million in imports in 1994. They were most active in the export of fishery and other marine products and timber and other forestry resources and in the import of food, consumer goods, and industrial machinery and equipment. In 1994, over 62 per cent of their exports were in fish and other marine products, 11.7 per cent in timber and forestry products, 17.1 per cent in ferrous and non-ferrous metals. The bulk of their imports were in foodstuffs (40.0 per cent), consumer goods (32.3 per cent), and industrial machinery and equipment (17.3 per cent).

In general, the hopes that foreign investment would compensate for the decrease in national production and contribute to the modernization of production have not materialized. The main spheres of interest to joint ventures are foreign trade, wholesale and retail trade, the restaurant and hotel business, and tourism. They have shown only limited interest in the material production sphere for foreign investors, including the processing of natural resources and import substitution of consumer goods. Moreover, they are becoming hostages to the internal financial and economic turmoil and unpredictable legislation.

Foreign investors have reacted quickly to the deterioration of the investment climate in the Far East, or, to be more precise, to the deterioration of prospects for improvement. The average value of foreign investment began to fall dramatically, particularly after 1992 when the central government cancelled all preferences for foreign entrepreneurship.

The continuing economic instability of the region (and the country as a whole) remains the primary negative factor influencing the scale, industrial

Table 3.6 Enterprises with foreign capital participation, 1988–94

Territory	US	Japan	China	South Korea	Other
Far East Total	274	280	888	177	624
Khabarovsk	77	65	209	45	108
Primorskii	110	90	460	50	254
Sakhalin	48	95	25	65	98
Kamchatka	13	16	5	7	39
Amur	4	3	95	3	11
Magadan	10	7	25	3	31
Jewish Autonomous Oblast	2	1	60	1	12
Sakha	10	3	9	3	71

Source: Roshia Kyokuto Data Book [Russian Far East data book], Tokyo: Roshia To'o Boekikai Roshia To'o Keizai Kenkyujo, 1996, p. 11

structure, and final results of the activities of foreign-affiliated companies. Very few joint ventures are established in the sphere of manufacturing. The main spheres of joint venture activities continue to be foreign trade, services, and intermediary activities. Frequent changes in legislation, not always well-grounded, do not foster the creation of a favorable investment climate. Under the present conditions, the imposition of national business regulations on foreign investors and the cancellation of tax privileges for newly established foreign capital firms in the region exercise negative influence on the scale of foreign investment in the region, as well as on the development of international trade activities of foreign-affiliated firms.

The waning of the Cold War gave birth to a host of proposals for international development projects and renewed interest in cooperative projects that had been on the back-burner during the Cold War years. Many of these projects directly involve the Russian Far East: natural gas development in Yakutia (Sakha Republic), oil and gas development on the Sakhalin continental shelf, development of the Tumen River Basin, development of the greater Vladivostok area, construction of a new bridge over the Amur River connecting the Russian city of Blagoveschensk and the Chinese city of Heilongjiang, expansion and improvement of port and harbor facilities in the Russian Far East, repair of the Khabarovsk-Amur railroad bridge, development of forestry resources in the Russian Far East, and establishment of a free economic zone (FEZ) in Nakhodka.

It is beyond the scope of this analysis to describe each of these projects, except to point out some common features among them. First, they all require extensive international cooperation, as they call for enormous capital investments which are not available locally. For example, the Tumen River Project, as envisaged by the UN Development Program, calls for the investment of tens of billions of dollars. The Greater Vladivostok Concept envisages an investment of $15–20 billion for the development of transportation, communication, and industrial infrastructure. One of the Sakhalin offshore oil and gas development projects and the Russian–US–Japanese project to build pipelines to transport natural gas from Yakutia to Japan is expected to cost 1 trillion yen each. A second common characteristic among the proposed development schemes is that they all have important environmental implications. The Tumen River Project, for example, envisages major infrastructure development, including the construction of railroads, roads, ports and harbors, and other transport/communication facilities. Needless to say, all resource development projects have implications for the region's natural resources. One of the forestry resource development projects envisages the export of 6 million cubic meters of raw timber and 400,000 cubic meters of lumber over a five-year period. Although this is expected to add $1.4 billion to the Russian–Japanese two-way trade, major environmental impact cannot be denied. Although hard currency shortages on the Russian side have long delayed the start of the project, both sides continue to show interest.[11]

NATURAL RESOURCE DEVELOPMENT

The need to balance the exploitation and conservation of natural resources in the Russian Far East is as acute as the need to balance energy development and environmental protection. The fundamental problem is that the region's economic life depends heavily on the development of its natural resources but resource conservation measures are lacking and what limited regulations exist are not effectively enforced. One of the most important natural resources in the region is surface water (mainly river water), which is used as the main source of water supply in the region. In Primorye, for example, water use amounts to 1,800 million cubic meters per annum, of which 37 per cent is for industrial use, 31 per cent for agricultural irrigation, and 19 per cent for public use and drinking. Because of the irregular river run-off, there is a shortage of water in almost one-half of the territory, particularly in Vladivostok and Artyom. There is an acute problem of water quality as well. Causes of the problem include violations of health regulations in water reservoir areas, the overloading of treatment plants during rainfall seasons, and shortage of coagulants.[12]

The rational management of forestry resources remains a very difficult task under the current political and economic condition in the Russian Far East. Although 73 per cent of Primorskii Krai is covered by forests, the resource situation is rather serious. The mixed coniferous-broad-leaved forests, a main economic asset of the territory, are substantially overexploited by large-scale logging. The decision of the Council of Ministers of the USSR on the Improvement of Forestry and Logging Management of 10 March 1988 had an adverse effect on the forestry resources in the territory. The decision transferred most of the valuable forests and governmental forest protection agencies to the administration of the logging industry under the jurisdiction of regional production associations. This resulted in the reduction in the public reporting of illegal logging activities. In response, on 17 January 1991, the Council of Ministers issued a decree on the Improvement of Forestry Management, whereby all management of forest areas and forestry resources was returned to government bodies. Moreover, the Primorskii Krai soviet made a decision to set up an out-of-budget fund for forest resource protection and regeneration, in which 5 per cent of the wholesale price of each cubic meter of timber logged in the territory would be deducted beginning on 1 January 1993. It was hoped that these actions would improve the situation. However, as the Svetlaya controversy demonstrated, this was not the case.

Svetlaya is a Russian–South Korean joint venture in logging capitalized at $32 million (50-50 split between the partners), with a production capacity of 1 million cubic meters a year for thirty years. The company was registered with the Monetary and Economic Department of the Ministry of Finance on 20 August 1992. Its founders are the Primorsklesprom Association, the Terneyles Association, and Hyundai. Each year over a thirty-year period 400,000 cubic meters of over-mature spruce-fir forests in Terney District and

600,000 cubic meters in Pozharski District are scheduled to be logged. A feasibility study was approved by the Ministry of Wood Industry, credits were obtained, and equipment was purchased for logging, road construction, chip production, and greenhouse cultivation of 2.8 million seedlings per annum. The joint venture was expected to operate at a profit with the felling of 650,000–700,000 cubic meters per annum. However, in 1992, the company logged 373,000 cubic meters and had losses at the end of the year.

Unfortunately, the rash manner in which the joint venture was established caused a major problem. When the company was set up, agreement had not been secured from the authorities of Pozharski District for the clear-felling of large volumes of timber. Moreover, the felling areas of the joint venture were in the dwelling area of Udege, a small minority people, whose protection against degradation and extinction is a major focus of national attention. The Land Code of the Russian Federation was violated under which land areas associated with economic activities of native peoples must not be allotted without a special referendum. Also violated was the President's decree on the Urgent Measures Regarding the Protection of Areas of Dwelling and Economic Activities of Minority Peoples of the Russian North. Thirdly, the ecological section of the feasibility report was incomplete with respect to reforestation and capacity estimation.

The Administration of Primorye allotted, without consent of the Territory Soviet, wood-cutting areas for Svetlaya on the ethnic territory of Udege. This provoked a stormy reaction of both residents and experts and a confrontation between the parties concerned. In the end, the controversy was discussed by a working group by order of the Russian government, by the krai court which took the side of the krai administration, and by the Supreme Court, which submitted the case for review. In 1992, the public, Udege, Cossacks, and others, placed pickets in the upper reaches of the Bikin River to prevent logging. This action was supported by Greenpeace, which visited Primorskii Krai on the *Rainbow Warrior* in November 1992. The vessel attempted to call attention to Hyundai–Svetlaya's allegedly destructive practices by blocking a company barge transporting logs cut in the Terney forests.

As of May 1994, it was reported that a group of environmentalists, led by Greenpeace activists, chained themselves to timber cutting machines owned and operated by the Russian–Korean joint venture and temporarily stopped the logging operation. The chairman of the krai administration's Natural Resources Committee is reported to have said that his committee had not received any formal complaints about Hyundai's activities in Primorye forests. Relicensing of the logging operation was expected.[13] Thus, the controversy is not likely to disappear in the foreseeable future.

The Ussuri taiga is also subjected to environmental strains of various kinds. Poaching has increased. The main animals are Ussuri tiger, musk deer, and roe deer. Many valuable medicinal herbs, such as ginseng, are collected in large quantities. According to the new provisional regulations on hunting which were established in 1992, the krai administration manages the hunting resources, hunters are all considered tenants of the hunting forests, and nature preservation committees are to ensure compliance. However, there are many loopholes in the legislation and huntsman services are poorly supported. Therefore, the situation is not expected to improve very soon.

Other biological resources in the region are also facing increasing problems. Many rivers, reservoirs, and lakes are important because they serve as spawning grounds for a variety of fish. However, water pollution and illegal poaching in these areas have become a serious threat. For example, because of logging-caused pollution, the Partizanskaya (or Suchan) River, which is an important source of drinking water for Nakhodka, is no longer a major fishing area. The Razdolnaya River, flowing through Ussuriysk, is also losing its significance in fish production.

Recent trends in the development of marine fishery resources in the Russian Far East add to the region's difficult task of developing its natural resources on a sustainable basis. In the 1960s to 1980s, the former Soviet Union developed fairly stable and predictable bilateral regimes with Japan and South Korea for the management of foreign fishing activities in the Soviet exclusive economic zone (EEZ) in the northwest Pacific.[14] However, the dissolution of the Soviet Union and the subsequent political turmoil and economic crisis in Russia have had serious consequences. A combination of the decentralization of resource management authority, the termination of Moscow's subsidies for the region's economy, the absence of regional financial resources, and the rather disorderly process of privatization of industrial enterprises has resulted in a serious weakening of the Far Eastern fishing industry. Fishing boats and equipment are in disrepair, investments in repair facilities are woefully inadequate, and underpaid or unpaid crews are leaving the industry for other opportunities. Moreover, both regional fishing concerns and their foreign partners in joint ventures and other cooperative arrangements have rushed to catch their allotted or purchased fish quotas for more immediate financial gains, ignoring the long-term resource consequences.[15]

Visible declines in the regional authorities' ability to enforce fishery laws and regulations have led to increases in poaching by both Russian and foreign fishermen. Smuggling by Russian fishermen has increased, depriving the Russian and regional governments of important tax revenues. Illegal poaching by foreign, particularly Japanese, fishermen has also increased.[16] These developments have increased international tensions. In the spring of 1994, Russia began a major campaign to crack down on Russian smuggling and foreign poaching. In the process, the Russian Border Guard have resorted to shooting at foreign fishing boats suspected of illegal fishing. As of August 1994, seventy-seven Japanese fishermen had been captured.[17] In September, one Chinese fishing boat and one South Korean boat were captured by the Border Guard and in the process two fishermen died.[18]

Amidst these unfortunate developments a new area of Russian–Japanese cooperation was proposed in 1994. The mayor of the southern Kuril district of Sakhalin, Nikolai Pokidin, proposed that the Japanese pay fees for fishing in the waters surrounding the disputed Northern Territories. If implemented, the proposed scheme would bring some badly needed hard currency to the depressed economy of the islands. The defective transportation system of Russia does not guarantee a regular supply of fuel to the islands and the fishing and marine product processing industries there have deteriorated to dangerous levels. Pokidin hopes that his proposal will expand transactions between the people of Hokkaido and the residents of the Russian-controlled islands and arrest the latter's economic deterioration.

Hokkaido's fishing industry and the prefectural government have welcomed the proposal. However, the Japanese Foreign Ministry is concerned that Japan's agreement to pay fishing fees in the Russian-controlled waters would imply *de facto* recognition of Russian jurisdiction over the disputed territories. It is reported that the Japanese government would prefer a private arrangement between Japanese fishing industry groups and their Russian counterparts. Such an arrangement might include joint research of the state of marine resources in the area, such as crabs which are reportedly being depleted. The resources caught under the name of joint research could be sold on the Japanese market, and a portion of the sale should be paid to Russia as Japan's contribution to the joint research. Following preliminary discussions, Tokyo and Moscow began formal negotiations on this issue in March 1995, but the talks have not produced a mutually acceptable arrangement.

INTERNATIONAL COOPERATION

Effective international cooperation for the sustainable development of the Russian Far East requires, first and foremost, the recognition on the part of the region's leaders of the need to cooperate with the neighboring countries. Second, the recognition must be translated into institutional support and resource commitment for carrying out cooperative efforts. As one of the participants in international cooperation, the Russian Far East must possess the necessary legal authority, administrative capacity, and financial, technical, and other resources. Since the region is critically handicapped in these capabilities, it must be given access to the resources of its neighboring countries. Thirdly, the cooperating parties must have the political will to overcome obstacles to cooperation. For example, territorial disputes and domestic jurisdictional conflicts must not be allowed to disrupt cooperative arrangements between the Russian Far East and its neighbors. Fourth, there must be a reasonable expectation and fairly short-term demonstration of tangible benefits to the parties. Finally, each cooperating party must have sufficient confidence in the others' ability to carry out their respective responsibilities and obligations.

Under the present circumstances of political uncertainty and economic crisis in Russia in general and in its Far Eastern region in particular, it is unrealistic to expect that all these conditions will be satisfied in the near future. One must be realistic about the prospects of cooperation, particularly in terms of the readiness of the Russian Far East region. There are some indications of regional support for international cooperation. However, there is also ample evidence that suggests that caution, care, and sensitivity are necessary in developing international cooperation involving the Russian Far East.

A 1992 opinion survey by the Institute of History, Archeology, and Ethnography in Vladivostok revealed important facts about Primorye residents' attitudes toward international cooperation.[19] A survey which was conducted in nineteen southern Primorye cities and towns in the period August–September 1992 elicited 1202 responses. Interviews were also conducted with 120 high-ranking officials in regional and Vladivostok administrations, the biggest state enterprises, new economic organizations, scientific institutions, universities, and others. The respondents were asked to state their opinions on such issues as the Nakhodka Free Economic Zone (FEZ), the Vladivostok Project, the Tumen River Project, and the integration of the Russian Far East into the Asia–Pacific economy. The survey revealed general support for expanding the region's international economic ties, but there were some significant differences of opinion among various groups. There was great reluctance among directors of state enterprises and those who were older and less educated. It was also evident that only administrative officials and economic leaders were relatively well informed of the various proposals and prospects for international cooperation.

In the immediate areas where international projects and the FEZ were planned, three-fourths of the respondents to the 1992 survey favored such projects. Those most enthusiastic were the managers of new private economic organizations, followed by their employees, industrial and transportation workers, agricultural workers, students, out-of-industry intellectuals, military personnel, pensioners, company officers and engineers, and housewives, in that order. Respondents from the Nakhodka area, where major international ports are located, were the most supportive regional group, reflecting their positive experiences with foreigners. The support among the region's high-ranking administrative officials was based on expectations of improved living standards, higher production and consumption levels, enhanced private initiatives, resolution of regional problems, chances of economic reform, and improved local economic and social conditions. These were also the most informed group of individuals about the various development projects. They also favored private property and the provision of real estate and other forms of long-term credits to finance such projects, and also urged compliance with international law and other standards in foreign affairs. However, between one-tenth and one-fifth of non-industrial experts, directors of state enterprises, and managers of scientific institutions and new economic organizations feared that the proposed international projects might place Primorye in the status of a dependent supplier of raw materials.[20]

Many groups in Primorye were more supportive of the Nakhodka Free Economic Zone and the Vladivostok Project than the Tumen River Project.[21] Moreover, in the Russian Far East, the possible ecological consequences of the Tumen River Project have received very limited attention. There are virtually no Russian environmental experts involved in the study of the project.[22]

Successful international cooperation will also depend on the Russian Far East people's attitude toward the neighboring countries. The 1992 survey in southern Primorye cited above revealed a high level of confidence in Japan as the most reliable business partner, with almost one-half of the respondents giving preference to their neighbor to the southeast. The United States was favored by 40 per cent of the respondents, South Korea and Germany by 20 per cent, and China by 10 per cent. Administration officials, directors of state enterprises, and business organizations in southern Primorye favored economic integration first with Japan, South Korea, and the United States, and then with China, Taiwan, Australia, Germany, and North Korea. The largest proportion of southern Primorye residents (40 per cent of the respondents) believed that Japan should be the most interested in the Vladivostok Project, followed by the United States, China, South Korea, North Korea, and Mongolia. For the Tumen River Project, the residents ranked as their preferred partners China, Japan, South Korea, North Korea, and Mongolia, in that order.[23] Japanese and German firms were the most preferred business partners among the southern Primorye population, followed by South Korean, US, Chinese, Taiwanese, and Australian firms. Administrative officials wanted to work with US, Japanese, German, South Korean, Taiwanese, and Chinese firms, in that order.[24]

A vast majority of the southern Primorye people acknowledge the need to receive foreign economic assistance, with younger and more urban segments accepting this necessity more readily than agricultural workers and older generations. Preferred forms of aid, particularly among the people in their thirties, out-of-industry intellectuals, people with advanced technical education, and leaders of new economic organizations, are high technology, technical training, and managerial training. Additionally, regional administrators and economic experts recognize that foreign investments and other foreign business involvement in the region will require the granting of privileges to foreign business concerns, including (in the order of preference) reduced import-export fees, favorable terms for repatriation of capital and profits, low income taxes, freedom to invest capital in any economic sector, and guarantees for long-term credits including real estate.[25] However, a substantial number of individuals whose organizations receive state budget allocations, e.g., university administrators and directors of scientific institutions and state enterprises, see little need to invite foreign investments. The granting of credits involving real estate and natural resources is not a popular choice among most leaders in southern Primorye. All in all, the strongest support for granting special privileges to foreign businesses is found among city mayors and their deputies, experts and consultants of public bodies, and chairmen and vice-chairmen of the soviets. Limited support comes from the leaders of new economic organizations and directors of scientific institutions. Resistance can be expected from army officers, directors of state enterprises, and presidents and vice-presidents of universities.[26]

How are joint ventures seen by the residents of Primorye? There is substantial interest (50 per cent) among regional and local administrative officials in working in joint ventures with US, Japanese, and German firms, in that order. Among the general public, there is much less interest, although one-third would be ready to work for Japanese and German companies, 10–20 per cent for South Korean firms, and a very small proportion for Chinese and North Korean businesses.[27] When it comes to the local impact of joint ventures and other cooperative business schemes, however, serious questions are raised about the distribution of benefits both within the communities and between Russian and foreign participants in such arrangements.

Generally favorable attitudes toward international economic and environmental cooperation exist among the better educated and the more internationally experienced segments of the population, with the greatest support coming from regional and local administrators. One should remember, however, that there is significant reluctance among those who are supported by state institutions. It should be remembered that cooperative arrangements may not necessarily generate tangible benefits that can be readily and equitably shared between parties with disparate resources and capabilities.

CONCLUSIONS

The results of radical economic reform are more severe for the Far East than for European Russia or even Western Siberia. The high prices of energy, transport tariffs, and labor have made Far Eastern products, even raw materials, uncompetitive in the domestic market. This has considerably strengthened the eagerness of the Far East for cooperation with the countries of the Pacific Rim. However, the realization of the reorientation strategy of the regional economy to foreign markets will be possible only with real state support. This support must be provided by the central government of Russia in the form of the establishment of more flexible and liberal economic regimes in the Russian Far East in the fields of taxation, customs regulations, and economic legislation.

How can the Russian Far East develop indigenous foundations of economic development? The region is blessed in three areas: the enormous reserves of natural resources, the geographical location as a major transit point for east–west trade, and the proximity to the capital-rich Asia–Pacific countries. Clearly, until manufacturing and service industries are sufficiently developed to compete in the already competitive markets of Asia–Pacific, the region must depend on an export-led development strategy focused on natural resources. This near-term strategy must be balanced with the longer-term economic and environmental needs of the region.

It is clear that Moscow and the Russian Far East must develop a mutually acceptable arrangement for a degree of autonomy for the economic development of the latter. Striking a new balance between centralization and localization of economic authority is fundamentally a political decision and must await the establishment of a stable federal system with clearly demarcated division of power between the levels of government. An important part of the question has to do with the level of dependence on or vulnerability to international economic forces that will be politically acceptable in the Russian Far East. Center-region consensus is unlikely to emerge, however, until national politics stabilize. In the meantime, the economy of the Russian Far East will continue to be at the mercy of the politics of reform in Moscow and exposed to the vagaries of foreign capital and markets.

NOTES

1 *Roshia Sangyo Kiso Chosa: Ekonomikku Torendo, 1995* [Basic survey of Russian industry: economic trends, 1995], Tokyo: Roshia To'o Boekikai Roshia To'o Keizai Kenkyujo, 1995, pp. 6–7.
2 Pavel Minakir, 'The Present Condition and Future Prospects of the Russian Far East Economy,' *Rotobo Chosa Geppo* (Rotobo monthly survey), no. 2, February 1994, Tokyo: Rotobo, 1994.
3 *Ibid.*, pp. 46–7.
4 *Ibid.*, p. 48.
5 *Ibid.*
6 Kunio Okada, 'Enkaichiho ni okeru Minkan Sekuta no Keisei' [Private sector formation in Primorye), *Hokuto Ajia Chiiki Keizai Koryu no Genjo to Tenbo* [The current situation and prospects of economic exchange in northeast Asia], Tokyo: Roshia To'o Boekikai Roshia To'o Keizai Kenkyujo, 1996, pp. 40–1.
7 Pavel A. Minakir, 'Kainsenkyogo no Roshia Kyokuto no Seiji-keizai Josei' [The political–economic situation in the Russian Far East after the Duma election], *Roshia Kyokuto Boeki Chosa Geppo, February 1996*, Tokyo: Roshia To'o Boekikai, 1996, p. 54.
8 *Roshia Sangyo Kiso Chosa: Ekonomikku Torendo, 1995* [Basic survey of Russian industry: economic trends, 1995], Tokyo: Roshia To'o Boekikai Roshia To'o Keizai Kenkyujo, 1995, pp. 90–1.
9 *Ibid.*
10 James Clay Moltz, 'From Military Adversaries to Economic Partners: Russia and China in the New Asia,' *Journal of East Asian Affairs*, vol. 9, no. 1, Winter/Spring, 1995, p. 177.
11 *Asahi Shimbun*, 23 April 1993, p. 12.
12 Evgeny E. Jarikov, 'The Current Situation of Environmental Protection in Primorsky Territory,' in *Primorsky Territory: Its Political, Social, and Economic Situation and Environmental Protection*, Vladivostok: Center for Pacific Economic Development and Cooperation; and Monterey, California: Center for East Asian Studies, Monterey Institute of International Studies, 1993, p. 19.
13 *Vladivostok News*, 27 May 1994, p. 2.
14 Tsuneo Akaha, 'From Conflict to Cooperation: Fishery Relations in the Sea of Japan,' *Pacific Rim Law & Policy Journal*, vol. 1, no. 2, Summer 1992, pp. 225–80,

and Akaha, 'The Postwar Japan-Soviet Fisheries Regime and Future Prospects,' *Ocean Yearbook*, Chicago: University of Chicago Press, 1992, pp. 28–56

15 Akaha, 'Japanese-Russian Fishery Joint Ventures and Operations: Opportunities and Problems,' *Marine Policy*, May 1993, pp. 199–212.

16 *Hokkaido Shimbun*, 4 June 1994, p. 1.

17 *Asahi Shimbun*, 17 May 1994, p. 3, and 16 August 1994, p. 3.

18 *Hokkaido Shimbun*, 14 September 1994, p. 31.

19 The survey was named 'The Public Opinion in the Southern Primorye in connection with the Greater Vladivostok Project, Tumangan Project, and Incorporation of the Russian Far East into the Economic Structures of the Asia–Pacific Region.' Results of the survey are summarized in Nikolai G. Shcherbina, 'The Reaction to the Foreign Presence in the Primorsky Region,' a report prepared for the Center for East Asian Studies, Monterey Institute of International Studies, March 1993.

20 Shcherbina, pp. 4–6.

21 *Ibid.*, pp. 2–3.

22 *Utro Rossii*, 21 July 1994, pp. 1 and 3.

23 Shcherbina, pp. 8–9.

24 *Ibid.*, p. 9.

25 *Ibid.*, p. 11.

26 *Ibid.*, p. 14.

27 *Ibid.*, p. 14.

4 Problems of resource development in the Russian Far East

Evgenii B. Kovrigin

INTRODUCTION

Until recently the term 'Russian Far East' in the Asia–Pacific region and elsewhere was, as a rule, associated with the Soviet naval and military threat to its neighbors. Within the Soviet Union, the region was viewed differently – mainly as an almost inexhaustible reservoir of natural resources such as timber, fish, fur, conventional and precious metals, and diamonds. These traditional images have recently changed, however, as the Soviet threat has vanished and, domestically, *glasnost* has made it clear that the region's natural riches are not without limits and, moreover, are badly damaged.

Many of the resources in the Far East are enormous in quantity. In fact, the region is one of the world's last frontiers of natural wealth. However, the times when natural resources were extracted in easily accessible places are gone; a switch to deposits and sites which are more difficult to reach and which require heavier production costs is inevitable.[1]

In this chapter, the author's intention is to briefly consider some important aspects of resource development in the region. Among these aspects are:

1. the availability of natural resources;
2. the sector's role in the economy of the Far East;
3. legal issues of resource development;
4. problems of financing primary industries;
5. social problems linked to resource utilization; and
6. international implications including export problems and foreign investments in the region.

THE FAR EAST'S NATURAL RESOURCE POTENTIAL

Since the Russian Far East's early colonization, its development has been based on the maximum use of the region as a source of raw materials for the needs of the whole empire (Tsarist or Soviet). At present, resource-extracting industries constitute the largest segment of the Far East's economy, their share in overall industrial output reaching nearly one-third of the total.

At the start of the current economic reforms, extraction of non-ferrous ores and precious metals, forestry, and fisheries were the three main pillars of the region's economic order. The system of resource exploitation was extremely centralized, monopolized by central ministries, and separated between them. Although all mineral and biological resources were officially state property, they were often referred to as 'nobody's property.' Profits originating from their exploitation were channeled to the national budget and then partially re-allocated to the region. The system was characterized by non-complex resource utilization, low levels of processing, and primitive technology. Neglect of such major needs as environmental protection and social infrastructure development was also characteristic of this system.

Nevertheless, for a period of time this type of investment policy secured high growth rates. Average growth rates in the 1970s for the Russian Far East's 'locomotive' industries, such as fisheries and non-ferrous metals, were as much as 14 per cent.[2] However, friction resulting from this strategy began as the distribution of state subsidies between resource industries and other sectors was increasingly distorted. By the second half of the 1980s almost all opportunities for regional economic development had vanished.

The economic reforms which followed the period of *perestroika* raised questions about radical change in the resource sector and its adjustment to market relations. Reform in the resource sphere turned out to be as complicated and controversial as that in other sectors of economic life. All attempts to introduce market principles into resource development have been countered by opponents of the reforms and by the inertia of the old economic establishment. The region boasts large quantities of some seventy different kinds of minerals and fuels. However, residents joke that the number of major problems involving raw materials utilization surpasses the amount of fossils and minerals.

The Far East is Russia's largest economic region in area. Its territory occupies 6.2 million square kilometers. Two hundred and eighty-one million hectares of the territory, exactly 100 times the size of the total arable land in the region, is covered with forests. The forests contain about 21 billion cubic meters of wood, more than 80 per cent of which is valuable conifers and the remainder deciduous species such as oak, ash, lime, and various kinds of birch. The Russian Far East's forest yield reached its peak in 1986 at 36 million cubic meters of harvest. It decreased to 26 million cubic meters by 1992. Non-timber resources of the Far Eastern taiga include herbs, wild vegetables, mushrooms, berries, fur-bearing animals, and other zoological species.

Marine biological resources in the Russian exclusive economic zone of the Pacific Ocean and adjacent seas amount to 26 million tons. It is believed that up to 6 million tons of fish and 2 million tons of other marine animals could be caught annually without damage to the regenerative cycle. However, annual catches have been dwindling. In 1990, for example, 5.2 million tons were taken, but by 1992 the amount had dropped to only 3.1 million tons, with diminishing stocks of herring, iwashi (sardine), mintai (pollack), and crab being the main culprit. The annual catch of salmon, locally considered the most valuable fish, has reportedly dropped from 100,000 tons under the old Soviet regime to 5,000 tons today.[3] On the other hand, some stocks such as cod, halibut, squid, and shellfish remain under-exploited.

The Russian Far East's share of the national mineral resources is high at an estimated 34.4 per cent. The region accounts for 95 per cent of total national production of tin ore, 37 per cent of tungsten, 49 per cent of lead, 91 per cent of fluorspar, and 14 per cent of coal and zinc. The region's contribution of boron, antimony, and mercury is also substantial. The Sakha Republic (Yakutia) is the monopolistic supplier of Russia's diamonds, with an estimated annual output of 20,000 to 30,000 carats, or one-fifth to one-quarter of the world's total production.[4] Some 100 tons of gold and 300 tons of silver are believed to be excavated annually. Ferrous metal ores, whose explored reserves constitute 4.4 billion tons, are not being extracted. There are many proven and explored deposits of other minerals that remain idle.

Reserves of crude oil and gas are almost entirely located in Sakhalin and Yakutia's Lena–Viluisk geological provinces. According to recent Japanese estimates, predicted reserves of oil and gas in the region are 18 billion tons and 56 trillion cubic meters respectively.[5] Confirmed petroleum and natural gas reserves amount to 308 million tons and 1.5 trillion cubic meters, respectively. Explored coal reserves amount to 18 billion tons, while predicted reserves are estimated at 255 million tons. In 1992, the Russian Far East extracted 40.6 million tons of coal, 1.7 million tons of crude oil, and 3.4 billion cubic meters of natural gas. Lately, however, annual yields of both coal and petroleum have drastically dwindled. In spite of the great resource potential, energy shortage is currently the most critical problem in the Pacific areas of Russia.

There is general agreement that practically all of the raw materials in the Russian Far East have a good base, and prospects for further development are high. In the long run, in terms of natural resources, the region is said to be able to sustain itself and satisfy the demands of the rest of Russia and beyond. These forecasts contrast sharply with the current shortages of fuel and minerals in the region.

Regretfully, exploitation of mineral and biological resources in the Russian Far East has not always been rational. The irrationality has resulted from the rudimentary character of initial exploration, abnormal losses during transportation and storage, and the low level of processing. Simple (not complex) utilization means that only the most accessible and highest-quality deposits have been developed. The production and marketing of this 'cream of the crop' requires minimal effort on the part of the parties involved and in the short run guarantees the highest profits.

Meanwhile, lack of the necessary technology prevents upgrading the degree of processing. For example, practically all excavated metallic ores are locally processed only to the phase of concentrates. Only 25–80 per cent of the possible amount of round wood is harvested in each wood-cutting area.[6] The incomplete utilization of the region's raw materials leads to many undesirable results, the primary one being the untimely exhaustion of reserves which can no longer be exploited by traditional methods.

Increasingly intensive and utterly irrational human pressures during the last decades have brought about either a sharp distortion of the raw material base or, not infrequently, its complete exhaustion in terms of available technology. As a result, considerable amounts of valuable raw materials are left in sites (as tailings) undeveloped. Development is usually resumed later when new technology becomes available, but each subsequent return to the site requires new capital investment.

For example, the Solnechny ore-processing complex (Khabarovsk Krai) operates a tin deposit which is presumably the largest in the world and which, in addition, contains eight other metal ores.[7] However, due to the obsolete technology used at the site (dating back to the 1950s), only 50–60 per cent of available tin, 60 per cent of copper, 40 per cent of tungsten, and 25–30 per cent of available zinc and lead are extracted, with the remaining percentage left as tailings. In a similar manner, the low technological level of wood-cutting in the Russian Far East results in numerous returns, up to seven or eight times, to the same timber-harvesting sites.

Examples of the complete exhaustion of natural resources leading to the closure of enterprises and the evacuation of workmen's settlements are numerous. Abandoned fish-processing factories on the Kamchatka coast, wood-cutting areas south of Primorskii Krai and Sakhalin Oblast, and abandoned deposits of brown coal in Amur Oblast are clear examples of such degradation. The increasing exhaustion of natural resources had become evident by the middle of the 1980s and intensified the crisis in such industries as forestry and coal. Nowadays, raw materials-related enterprises are constantly driven northward or farther away into the mountains. Ever worsening conditions of extraction reduce the quality of resources involved, aggravate environmental problems, and drastically increase production costs.

It is obvious that the existing simple-extensive use of natural resources should be replaced by resource-saving utilization based on advanced, mostly foreign, technologies. Unfortunately, previous foreign involvement in the resource sector of the Far East did little in this respect. Major general agreements on forest development with Japan, in spite of the large-scale import of Japanese machines and equipment, yielded economic 'enclaves' and made practically no contribution to the dissemination of advanced technology in the region.

LEGAL ISSUES

Exportation of fish and timber has long been an important specialization in the Russian Far East and in this sense the region has been closely, though indirectly, linked to the overseas market. Under the command-administrative economy, the competitiveness of exported products was maintained by the free use of first-class sites and deposits. However, the largest portions of fish and timber, as well as nearly all non-ferrous metals, were sold in the guaranteed domestic market, which, though not highly profitable, did support the stability of the resource-related industries. While the central ministries were always winners, the system guaranteed the survival and stability of the industries in question. In sum, the system could be called 'perverted paternalism.'

The post-*perestroika* market reforms, in beginning to change the entire system of the resource utilization, have meant, first of all, an end to planned financing and domestically guaranteed sales. The problem of property rights in real estate and natural resources has come to the foreground and has not yet been solved.

The fate of land legislation has turned out to be one of the most intricate issues of the economic reforms in post-Soviet Russia. Twice in late 1993 (in October and in December), President Boris Yeltsin issued decrees on land, the first being far more democratic than the second. The draft land code was forwarded by the government to the State Duma in May 1994. It was bitterly criticized in Russia for its less than concise and insufficient market character. The draft code has not yet been approved. The liberal daily *Izvestiya* has written in this connection that the legal vacuum gives local authorities complete control over land transactions and makes all such transactions criminal in modern Russia.[8] The long-lasting confusion reflects the struggle within the new Russian establishment for property in real estate, the most lucrative in the country. At present, this confusion makes the position of industrialists, especially foreign ones, utterly unstable and prevents them from increasing investment throughout Russia, including the Far East.

So far, only agricultural land and industrial sites can be privatized. This means that about 61 per cent of the Russian Federation's territory is still state-owned.[9] In the Far East this share is bigger because the terrain is largely covered with wooded mountains. In addition, land cannot be sold to foreign citizens, including those engaged in joint ventures; it may only be leased or used as the Russian partners' contribution to the fixed capital of joint ventures. Meanwhile, although it remains politically controversial, the officially guaranteed right to purchase and sell land remains the ultimate condition for a breakthrough in foreign investment in Russia.

It is clear that genuine market economic systems assume the existence of various forms of land property and a developed land market. But it is equally clear that the *de jure* recognition of private ownership for all land will sooner or later lead to the private ownership of other natural resources (timber, minerals, fuels etc.) all of which are still proclaimed state property. At present, even timber industry enterprises are not allowed to privatize the woods they exploit and must lease them instead. Raw materials are the very basis of resource-related enterprise activity. Pressure from such enterprises, which are no longer state-owned and which are eager to obtain resources, will only increase. There is no doubt that eventually a large portion of natural resources will belong to private owners in either explicit or implicit form.

The problem of natural resource management is closely connected with the problem of property rights. It is true that the formerly super-centralized system of control has shifted considerably to the provincial and municipal authority level. However, many control levers are still vested in central agencies in Moscow. Under these circumstances, contradictions between provincial and central authorities occur frequently. For example, proposed oil and gas development off Sakhalin became hostage to a power struggle between the oblast's government, the leadership of the domestic Sakhalin Ocean Oil and Gas Production Corporation, and the Russian Energy Ministry.

These contradictions result mainly from the controversial and incomplete demarcation of legal rights among the levels of official hierarchy. New state acts, e.g., laws on payments for land, on mineral wealth, on forests, and on environmental protection are, in some cases, inconsistent and contradictory. However, these laws and local rules and regulations are laying down new foundations of natural resource government. Meanwhile, the idea that the resources, or at least a part of them, could be governed through the system of local tenders and auctions, as well as through the sale of licenses and the leases of resource-rich sites to the users, is gaining popularity throughout the Far East. However, this work is still in an embryonic state.

THE CHANGING FINANCIAL SITUATION

The resource sector suffers from the current financial hardships more than other sectors of the regional economy because most extractive industries depend on the continuous influx of investment, e.g., for the construction of mines, roads and loggers' settlements, as well as for prospecting and oil-well drilling. However, centralized investments have been either abolished completely or reduced to the degree where they have practically no influence on the development of production. Significant investments have become so rare that they require special governmental decrees, e.g., the December 1993 decree issued for the financing of a new coal mine in Urgal District.[10] Those engaged in the primary sector confront the necessity to fund themselves, a task which is, at present, unachievable by most people.

The reduction of state investment has sharply complicated production and export of raw materials from the region. There is practically a unanimous opinion in the Far East that if the central government wants to avoid social unrest and wishes the Russian Far East to be the nation's link with the Asia–Pacific economy, it should resume providing funds for the raw material sector of the region. Some scholars have even indicated the desirable share of the republican budget to be devoted to this cause. One of them, for example, suggests the following distribution as adequate until the year 2015: the republican budget 45 per cent of the total, local provincial budgets 30 per cent, and funding from corporations involved, including foreign firms, 20 per cent.[11]

The state's exact share in the overall financing of the Russian Far East's primary sector is subject to discussion, but the highest priorities in this respect seem to be energy facilities, industrial infrastructure, and geological prospecting. To avoid an inefficient geographical scattering of centralized investment and credit, the territorial distribution of firms receiving state subsidies should be clearly determined and concentrated in several 'economic growth zones'. Perhaps the establishment of joint-stock companies involving private and state funds could finance some vital industries, e.g., a joint-stock company for the energy complex in Khabarovsk Krai.[12]

Direct financing and subsidization are not the only roles the central authorities could play in support of the Far East's primary sector. The central authorities should also negotiate with foreign governments for loans aimed at the development of resource-related industries and other associated industries which could boost exports and reinforce the regional economy. Of special importance to the Russian Far East would be international assistance in the adoption of efficient mining technologies and in the processing of tailings in ore-dressing enterprises.

In the academic circles of the Russian Far East, participation of foreign private capital in the development of natural resources is considered an absolutely necessary, or even 'the only reliable' source of funding available.[13] The primary objectives of foreign investment will not only be the infusion of capital funds but the introduction of foreign advanced technologies in the form of transfer of machinery and equipment, as well as know-how. However, with the exception of fisheries and forest projects, Japanese and other international businesses are not in a hurry to invest in primary industries.

For example, in regard to large-scale resource projects, no progress has been seen in the Russia–Korea–Yakutia consortium for the development and transportation of Yakutia oil and gas to South Korea. Progress in the development of two major oil/gas projects on Sakhalin (the projects known in Russia as SODECO and MMMS) which involve major Japanese, American, and West European businesses could also be speeded up. In addition, some industries that are vital to the Far East's energy supply, such as coal mining, have not even aroused interest abroad. Assertions that neither Japanese nor Americans are truly interested in the development of hydrocarbon deposits in Sakhalin have become increasingly frequent in the Russian mass media. Prime Minister Chernomyrdin's decision to give the Russian quasi-governmental Gasprom concern the exclusive rights to develop the Sakhalin shelf might be a reflection of such views.[14]

An important element of the new system of financing resource development should be the active participation of local administrations. Additional local funding could be generated through revenues from domestic and joint venture taxation, the sale of local government's natural resource quotas to exporters, and charges on the use of natural resources.[15] The recent proposal of the administration of Yuzhno-Kurilsk District in Sakhalin Oblast that Japanese fishermen pay for the right to fish in Russian territorial waters is a vivid example of this approach.[16] It seems appropriate that the major part of local revenues be allocated to the improvement of the region's infrastructure.

In the Russian Far East, the problem of financing the extraction and processing of raw materials is closely linked to the problem of the region's outrageously underdeveloped industrial and social infrastructure. In the past, infrastructure was built and maintained with financial allocations from the central ministries. The funds were minimal in quantity and, as a rule, were barely adequate to maintain temporary facilities. As a result, although the subsidies helped to reduce construction costs in the end, they led to economic loss.

Nowadays, as centralized financing has sunk into oblivion, the idea that a substantial part of infrastructure costs should be covered by local budgets is becoming increasingly popular. Payment for the use of natural resources, akin to royalties in the west, and new local taxes, originating from the growing number of enterprises and jobs, would be the basic source for financing of infrastructure projects.

For the time being, the local authorities unfortunately keep insisting that natural resource developers should develop the necessary infrastructure themselves. This approach is not constructive as it scares away potential investors. Those enterprises which do venture to open new production facilities tend to minimize infrastructure expenses which results in heavy damage to the resource base and environment. Given this, the December 1993 resolution by the Russian government to permit up to 20 per cent of customs revenues in Khabarovsk Krai to be used for the improvement of local infrastructure seems to be a sound decision.[17]

In the near future, however, local budgets will hardly be sufficient to finance industrial and social infrastructure development. The provincial administrations are not in a position to undertake large-scale borrowing from private foreign sources either. International assistance, therefore, is both desirable and necessary. Indeed, at the start of *perestroika*, Soviet planners had begun to entertain glowing prospects of foreign, primarily Japanese, corporations eagerly improving the region's obsolete infrastructure to meet the requirements of the twenty-first century in exchange for the Far East's natural resources. When their expectations regarding Japanese involvement failed, Soviet/Russian hopes switched to South Korea. There was much talk, for example, about the intention of Hyundai to build a cutting edge industrial complex on the shores of the Bay of Svetlaya in the Pozharski District of Primorskii Krai as part of a major Russo–Korean wood-cutting joint venture. The Russian mass media envisaged that, thanks to Hyundai's efforts, the remote village's infrastructure would become 'a mini-South Korea.' This expectation never materialized.

The Soviets/Russians failed to understand that, when it comes to international cooperation, construction of industrial infrastructure in developing countries (considering the Russian Far East a developing region) is not the responsibility of private corporations but a goal of official development assistance (ODA). In the Far East, future ODA flows should be directed to the revitalization of the region's obsolete infrastructure as well as to the modernization of export-oriented extracting industries.

Low-interest 'soft' loans from Japan's Overseas Economic Cooperation Fund (OECF) seem to be the most logical option in this regard. The terms and conditions of these loans should be similar to those of the numerous infrastructure loans provided by Japan to the People's Republic of China and the loan recently negotiated with Kyrgyzstan, i.e., repayment over thirty years, with a ten-year period of grace and annual interest of 3 per cent.[18] Unfortunately, however, bilateral and domestic political problems are impeding the inflow of the badly needed international official aid.

Since the start of the current economic reforms in Russia, the necessity of payments for the use of natural resources has been taken for granted. However, the implementation of this idea has turned somewhat chaotic and inconsistent. Of course, although the above mentioned state acts and specific local rules constitute a certain framework for the regulation of resource development, they cannot embrace all kinds of resources and all methods of utilization. Some of the state mandates and local rules remain mere declarations because no effective mechanism for their implementation has been created.

The new laws and regulations have introduced many kinds of payments, local taxes, and fines that natural resource users are subject to, some of which contradict each other. Among them, the current principle that the user should pay for the amount of extracted resources rather than for the right to use the developed site or reserve is arguably the most controversial one. For example, the law on mineral wealth adopted in 1993 implies payment for the use of resources, but the rate of payment is dependent on the market value of the products, not on the rate of raw material use. Therefore, resource-saving is not encouraged, and ores other than the primary one will continue to be left as tailings.[19]

The current approach to economic control in the raw materials sector cannot be called systematic. Instead, many state acts and local regulations seem to be aimed at confiscation of part of the users' revenue for the benefit of national and municipal authorities. In other words, they constitute a system of legalized extortion.[20] Some payments whose parameters should be significant for users are not. Hardly a single measure, except for fines, serves as a stimulus for the rational utilization of resources in the Far East. For example, the differentiation of land taxes on the basis of the type of soil, geographic zones, and method of use is illogical and often inexplicable. Some auxiliary payments, such as those for the reproduction and protection of forests through the end of 1993, were much higher and more devastating than the payments (royalties) for the right to harvest timber. While the payments for the rights to exploit fishing grounds, oil and gas fields, and gold mines seem to be sound (they fluctuate around 10 per cent), those related to other kinds of natural resources are so insignificant, between 1 and 5 per cent, that they cannot serve as real regulators of resource utilization.

SOCIAL ISSUES

Many of the current difficulties in the primary sector of the Far Eastern economy stem from social drawbacks, for example, labor force problems. Nowadays, the primary sector absorbs a significant portion of the region's population, the forestry industry alone supplying jobs to 12 per cent of available manpower.[21] However, employment in this sphere has been losing its prestige in regional society. The low level of the sector's social infrastructure in the already inferior Far East is, perhaps, the most discouraging factor. As a result, the influx of young men and women into resource industries has dwindled, and the median age of the personnel has persistently increased. The previous system of organized worker recruitment from other regions of Russia has collapsed because former non-Russian Soviet republics, previously a reliable source of manpower, have become foreign states.

Many analysts, both Russian and foreign, speculate that local Russian manpower will be insufficient and import of workers from densely populated China (and construction of housing facilities for them) will be inevitable. Unlike other major Russian economic regions, the Russian Far East has a long record of attracting foreign workers. By the end of 1992, North Korean, Chinese, and Vietnamese workers engaged in agriculture, construction, light industries, and forestry, numbered over 35,000.[22] It is feared that intercultural and ethnic problems might arise if the number of 'guest workers,' especially those from China, grows without control in the future. So far, Chinese workers have not been used in extractive industries.

Another social problem accompanying resource development is environmental. Mining, wood-cutting, and other resource industries have always been associated with environmental problems. The period of *glasnost* and loosening of censorship prior to the dissolution of the USSR and during the first years of Russian statehood have generated an avalanche of frightening ecological information which had been kept secret. The psychologically unprepared society apprehended the situation as a real environmental disaster; the rise of the region's 'green movement' was its quick response. The environmentalists have joined with two other local movements, the first of which demands more economic rights for the indigenous populations of the Far East, and the second of which speaks out against the employment of foreigners in the primary sectors of the region.

The force resulting from these movements is in total opposition to resource development. 'Green' extremists oppose any foreign investment and the influx of alien manpower. The movement is counter-productive and capable only of aggravating the current economic crisis. Unfortunately, a sizable part of the Russian Far East's population supports the green approach. An American magazine referred to the Far Eastern commoners' concern that 'the Hyundais of the world will sweep up raw materials without leaving any milling or processing industries behind.'[23] The view that it would be better to leave the Russian Far East undeveloped than to allow the influx of foreigners who 'are eager to grab the region's natural wealth' is not uncommon.

In general, administrations and local 'new' businessmen are inclined to cooperate with the foreign industrialists. At the same time, the 'old' entrepreneurs who, because of their previous Communist connections possess valuable business information, oppose the influx of powerful foreign investors in order to preserve their monopolistic positions. In the Far East, their animosity is especially sharp in the forestry sector, as has been demonstrated by the failed negotiations with the American timber giant Weyerhouser and the curtailment of production by the Russo–South Korean wood-cutting enterprise Svetlaya, the largest joint venture in Primorskii Krai and the whole Russian Far East. Svetlaya became the victim of resistance from the local small Udege minority and the adjacent Cossac community. In 1992, those groups put forward demands to company headquarters to stop the destruction of the environment and also organized armed pickets, damaged some of the joint venture's equipment, and prevented the Koreans from launching their next production facility.[24]

THE RFE'S NATURAL RESOURCES AND THE ASIA–PACIFIC REGION

In the past, Moscow authorities earmarked most Far Eastern natural resources (for example, non-ferrous metals) for domestic use. Nevertheless, the region's contribution to the national foreign trade balance was conspicuous because its economic specialization was based on the export of unprocessed wood, fish, and coal. For example, locally produced primary commodities have accounted for some 25 per cent of overall value of Russian exports to Japan. In the second half of the 1980s, the region's shipments accounted for 40 per cent of national timber exports and about one-quarter of total fishery exports. Unfortunately, the region obtained practically no revenues from these exports because timber and fish were always controlled by the central Moscow ministries.

Nowadays, the fact that in the immediate future only resource exports are capable of obtaining either foreign funds or new technologies is increasingly realized in society, among both policy-makers and economic planners. During the last few years the Russian Far East showed a trend of growing reorientation from domestic to external markets. The majority of the region's provinces have increased the volume of foreign trade. The Far East's remoteness from and the weakness of its technological (intra-industry) connections with the core of Russia seem to be favorable factors for improved relations with the advanced countries of the Asian–Pacific region.[25]

In 1980 the share of raw materials in the Russian Far East's total exports was 85 per cent. In 1992, as a result of the sharp fall in the volume of foreign timber shipments, it decreased to 79 per cent. Round wood export reached its peak at 8,204,000 cubic meters in 1988, fell to 4,835,000 cubic meters in 1990, and fell drastically again to a mere 1,804,000 cubic meters in 1992. This can be explained mainly by the sharp reduction of timber shipments to their principal consumer Japan, where Russian round wood is being progressively supplanted with supplies from North America, New Zealand, and others. Moreover, even timber deliveries to former Soviet republics and to Russia itself have dwindled in reaction to increasing transportation tariffs.

Despite the radical curtailment of timber exports, their structure has remained unchanged and is characterized with very low, or in many cases, absent added value. Round wood exports occupy the central position while the export of articles such as saw-timber, wood chips, and pulp remains marginal.

Unlike timber, the shares of fish, fuels, and minerals in the region's exports have been growing since the late 1980s. The rates of growth have been different for each separate commodity. The share of ferrous and non-ferrous metals (without gold and silver) grew to 6.2 per cent by 1992. The export of coal reached its peak in 1990 when it amounted to 7 million tons but then dwindled to 2.9 million tons two years later. Overseas shipments of crude oil and petroleum products, however, grew swiftly from 490,000 tons in 1990 to 726,000 tons in 1992 despite decreases in production and acute domestic shortages.

The countries of Northeast Asia are the main consumers of the Russian Far East's exports, representing 84 per cent of the region's export value in 1992. Since the 1960s, Japan has always been the number one importer of the region's seafood, lumber, fuel, and energy resources. However, as a result of the re-emergence of China as a major trade partner and Russia's deteriorating ability to produce natural resources, both the value and volumes of exports to Japan have decreased since the late 1980s. Japan's share fell from 62 per cent to 47 per cent between 1985 and 1992. After an enormous decrease in 1992, an unexpectedly sharp increase was registered in 1993. Japan continues to dominate Sakhalin, Kamchatka, and Magadan Oblasts' exports and maintains a rather high standing in exports of Khabarovsk and Primorskii Krais. The country was the monopolistic consumer of 95 per cent of Yakutia raw material exports in 1992.[26] Thanks to the halt in imports from Japan, because of accumulation of arrears in Russian payments, nearly all the Far Eastern provinces currently enjoy a positive trade balance with Japan.

The trade bias toward Japan has been considered by many Far Easterners a drawback of the region's trade pattern and a serious deterrent in the diversification of foreign ties. So, the emergence of new counterbalancing partners such as China and South Korea is welcomed in the region. In 1992, China surpassed Japan as the leading trading partner with the Far East; Korea's share amounted to about 9 per cent. The shares of other countries so far have been irregular and inconsistent. The US percentage of the Russian Far East's production is surprisingly small and contrasts with the American role as a conspicuous investor in the region; in Khabarovsk Krai, the US market accounts only for 0.12 per cent of all exports and Yakutia's shipments to the United States in 1993 were valued at an insignificant US$220,000.

Clearly, during the years of economic reform the raw materials orientation of the region's exports has not changed. Meanwhile, appeals for deeper processing of natural resources headed for export can be heard more loudly than before. This push for higher value-added exports is not groundless because the region's manpower is both cheap and skilled enough to accomplish the task. The Russian Far Eastern provinces are eager to convert themselves from a raw materials-oriented region to fully fledged participants in the Pacific's international division of labor. They want the resource policy to be reshaped to help them achieve economic prosperity in the long term. Finding a solution to the capital investment problem is the crucial factor for the implementation of this task. However, direct foreign trade is not the only form of foreign economic exchange available to the Russian Far East. Other forms, such as bilateral general ('compensation') agreements involving Japanese capital, production cooperation in forestry with North Korea and, most recently, the emergence of joint ventures and free economic zones have also been important.

Most former Soviet exports to Japan, the main consumer of the country's raw materials, were carried out through the mechanism of 'compensation' agreements. The three successive agreements in forestry (1969–74, 1975–79, and 1981–86) were supplied almost completely by the Far East's forests. Under these agreements, Japan extended credits through the ExIm Bank for the purchase of Japanese machines, equipment, and consumer goods to the Soviet Union. The USSR carried out its return payments through shipments of lumber from the Far East to Japan, approximately 32 million cubic meters in total.

At present, cooperation with Japan also includes a general agreement for the development of coking coal in South Yakutia (Neriungri) involving annual shipments of 5.5 million tons of coal to Japan and an agreement on hydrocarbon prospecting on the shelf of Sakhalin, which resulted in the discovery of two major natural gas and petroleum deposits.

Compensation agreements have contributed considerably to the development of primary industries in the Far East. But, there is a widespread opinion that they also play a negative role. They have consolidated the raw materials orientation of the region's exports and inhibited the development of import-substitution production facilities. According to Primorskii Krai's politician, Ms Yevdokia Gayer, her native territory has virtually become 'Japan's raw material appendage.'[27] For example, it is generally believed that the realization of forest agreements has not improved the structure of the forest complex. The negative results of earlier Soviet–Japanese forest agreements were taken into account when the Fourth Agreement (1992–97) was negotiated. In the future, Japanese credits will be repaid with more value-added goods, such as half-finished products for the furniture industry.

For the last thirty years, the Russian Far East's provinces have been the arena for Soviet/Russian–North Korean production cooperation in wood-cutting. The Koreans supplied the facilities with mainly unskilled workers, more than 20,000 people in the early 1990s, while the host-country's contribution consisted of dispatching engineers and technicians and the supply of materials, machines, and equipment. As a result of this cooperation, Soviet share of production totalled nearly 70 million cubic meters of round wood and more than 3 million cubic meters of chips successfully marketed abroad. Unfortunately, the low technological level of the facilities and systematic violations of host country's regulations by the Korean lumbermen have prevented rational utilization of forest resources. Therefore, the public attitude to further cooperation with North Korea has deteriorated lately. Additionally, the recent wave of defections of Pyongyang's lumbermen to South Korea threatens to create international frictions.

The number of foreign-affiliated companies, which started to emerge in the Far East prior to the dissolution of the USSR, surpassed 1,000 at the end of 1992. The overwhelming majority of them are joint ventures. These enterprises also concentrate mainly on the utilization of natural resources with little or no added value. The share of fish products in the total value of exports of local joint ventures in 1992, for example, amounted to nearly 77 per cent, while that of forestry products totalled only 7.4 per cent. These figures almost exactly duplicate the share of the natural resources in the region's conventional exports. The raw materials orientation of the joint ventures gives rise to unfavorable criticism on the part of the local population, mass-media, and general public, but for the time being this pattern is surely better than the absence of foreign activity.

At first, investment-based cooperation in the Far East was less active than in the western USSR. The trend has changed noticeably since 1991; nowadays, the percentage of joint ventures in the Far East as compared to their overall number in the Russian Federation is proportionally higher than the region's share in either the nation's population or GDP. The activity of joint ventures during the last few years has certainly drawn Asia–Pacific countries both economically and culturally closer to the Russian Far East. By the end of 1992, locally registered foreign-affiliated enterprises accounted for as much as 22 per cent of the region's trade turnover and, presumably, a higher share of the region's raw material exports.[28] Headquarters of small and medium-size joint ventures have become an integral part of the urban environment in Khabarovsk, Vladivostok, and other cities in the Far East.

Japanese companies were the pioneers in the foreign capital penetration of the Far East. However, lately they have been surpassed by Chinese investors in the number of joint ventures and by Americans in terms of accumulated assets.[29] For example, in Khabarovsk Krai in 1992, as many as twenty Japanese-affiliated joint ventures were established; in 1993 the number of the cases dropped to twelve. Nevertheless, the Japanese contribution to raw materials exports from Far Eastern joint ventures is much greater than that of all other investors combined. In Khabarovsk Krai in 1993, the share of the

Japanese–Russian joint enterprises, which capitalized at only US$18 million, amounted to 74 per cent of the total exports for all foreign-affiliated enterprises.[30] In general, more than half of the 'international' production in the Far East is headed for Japan.

The investment regime in the Russian Far East is still inferior to that in most capital-receiving countries of the Pacific Basin, and the investment 'climate' (to use a broader definition) is blatantly uneven and intricate. In many foreign officials' opinion, their work in the Far East is anything but a pleasure. Moreover, according to Japanese mass media, most Russian–Japanese ventures engaged in raw materials extraction, for example, are still unprofitable. Nevertheless, cases of repatriation of invested capital are rare, due, perhaps, to the relative smallness of sums involved. Quite regrettable has been the liquidation of Okhotsk Suisan Co., a joint venture with 49 per cent stock participation by major Japanese companies whose products were visible in the region's retail outlets.[31]

CONCLUSIONS

During the *perestroika* period, the view that the region must give up its raw materials orientation and switch to the production and export of high value-added goods was widespread in the Far East. Fortunately, the time of such unrealistic euphoria has passed. The economic development and well-being of the Far East must be based on available natural resources. Nowadays, this sector is entering the market system with great difficulty but not hopelessly. The many kinds of local resources, both explored and untapped, are of great and possibly increasing value for the region and for Russia, as well as for the economies of major Asia–Pacific countries.

The Far East is the only Russian region with direct Pacific contact. Of all the basic factors favorable for economic development, apart from its natural beauty and convenient geographical location, the region possesses only raw materials. The manpower in the region is educated but insufficient in number. The present process of economic reorganization and geographical reorientation is inseparably linked to the necessity for a radical change in the methods of resource exploration which, currently, impoverish the very base of the Far East's existence. These extensive and wasteful methods should be changed for intensive methodology favorable for the optimal utilization of the different kinds and qualities of resources. The future system of control must bring into harmony social, economic, and environmental interests and must aim at increasing productivity, conservation and environmental protection. At the present moment, such a cardinal reorganization requires, in addition to self-support, public and private support from outside the Russian Far East, from the central government, and from the international community.

NOTES

1 A series of international academic meetings dealing with the problems of the region's resources have taken place recently, including the Monterey workshops organized by Professor Tsuneo Akaha. In the Russian Far East, relevant studies are concentrated in a few academic organizations, primarily the Institute of Economic Research in Khabarovsk. For example, the *Economic Review of Russia's Far East* (two volumes, 1993) edited by the institute's director, Professor Pavel A. Minakir, is a very valuable source for those interested in the raw materials of the region. The author thanks the institute's deputy director Professor Alexander S. Sheingauz for the use of his materials.

2 P.A. Minakir, 'Prospects for Reform in the Soviet Far East: Options and Agenda,' Peter Drysdale (ed.), *The Soviets and the Pacific Challenge*, North Sydney: Allen & Unwin, 1991, p. 110.

3 *Newsweek*, 26 July 1993, p. 12.

4 *Asahi Evening News*, 8 December 1993, p. 6.

5 *The Japan Times*, 11 November 1993, p. 8.

6 A.S. Sheingauz, 'Prirodopol'zovanie Rossiiskogo Dal'nego Vostoka,' unpublished paper, 1994, pp. 4–5.

7 V.T. Shishmakov, 'Mineral Resources of the Russian Far East: Prospects for Export,' *The Kyungwon Economics and Management Review* (Seoul), vol. 2, 1993, p. 210.

8 *Finansovye izvestiia*, 19–25 May 1994.

9 Sheingauz, *op. cit.*, p. 7.

10 *Tikhookeanskaia zvezda*, 10 December 1993.

11 Shishmakov, *op. cit.*, p. 212.

12 This idea was suggested by the Institute of Economic Research, Khabarovsk. *Priamurskie vedomosti*, 11 March 1993.

13 Tsuneo Akaha (ed.), 'US–Japan Cooperation in the Development of Siberia and the Russian Far East: A Summary of Conference Presentations, 22–4 July 1993,' Center for East Asian Studies, Monterey Institute of International Studies, October 1993.

14 *Izvestiya*, 3 October 1993.

15 Kiichi Mochizuki, 'The Financial Policy for Economic Development Project,' in Akaha, *op. cit.*, p. 5.

16 *Asahi Evening News*, 6 April 1994, p. 2.

17 *Tikhookeanskaya zvezda*, 10 December 1993.

18 E.B. Kovrigin, 'Some Problems of Russo-Japanese Official Economic Cooperation in the Russian Far East,' *Kyushu Daigaku Keizaigaku Kenkyu* (Fukuoka, Japan), vol. 60, nos. 3–4, 1994, p. 31.

19 *Priamurskie vedomosti*, 14 January 1993.

20 Sheingauz, *op. cit.*, p. 11.

21 P.A. Minakir (ed.), *Dal'nii Vostok Rossii: ekonomicheskoe obozrenie*, vol. 1, Moscow: Progress-complex, 1993, p. 47.

22 Judith Thornton and Alexander Temkin, 'The Consequences of Crisis for the Russian Far East and for the Russo–Japanese Economic Relationship,' Tsuyoshi Hasegawa *et al.* (eds), *Russia and Japan: An Unresolved Dilemma between Distant Neighbors*, Berkeley: International and Area Studies, University of California at Berkeley, 1993, p. 327.

23 *Newsweek*, 26 July 1993, p. 14.

24 *Kommersant Daily*, 28 November 1992.

25 Lyudmila Amosova, 'Far East of Russia: Objects of Long-term Cooperation between Russia and South Korea,' *Sino–Soviet Affairs* (Seoul), no. 55, 1992, p. 189.

26 P.A. Minakir (ed.), *Dal'nii Vostok Rossii: ekonomicheskoe obozrenie*, p. 108.
27 *Moscow News*, 25 June 1989, p. 16.
28 P.A. Minakir (ed.), *Dal'nii Vostok Rossii: ekonomicheskoe obozrenie*, p. 117.
29 *Priamurskie vedomosti*, 23 July 1994.
30 *Tikhookeanskaia zvezda*, 28 December 1993.
31 *Asahi Shimbun*, 13 October 1993, p. 2

5 Minerals and mining in the Russian Far East

James P. Dorian

INTRODUCTION

Of particular importance to the mining future of Russia is the Far East region, which was the Soviet Union's leading producer of gold and diamonds, as well as tin, antimony, fluorite and boron. The Far East region, considered by many to be a new frontier for investment, is richly endowed with natural resources and is advantageously positioned geographically along the northwest Pacific rim. It borders on China, Korea, and Japan (already its biggest trading partner), and is also accessible to the North American market. It is an enormous area, covering 6,215,900 square kilometers, or more than 35 per cent of Russia's territory. It is attractive to foreign businesses because of its unique combination of natural resources and advantageous geographical location. The Far East is multinational, with more ethnic groups in the region than anywhere else in Russia. Like Siberia, the Far East has a history of autonomy.

In contrast to past Soviet policy, the Russian government is anxious to open the Far East to foreign investors and increase economic ties with nations in the Asia–Pacific region. In Gorbachev's 1986 speech in Vladivostok, a new era was initiated for the Far East when the then President affirmed that economic cooperation with Asia was needed to realize economic development in the area. As trade among Asia's rapidly growing nations increases, the Far East's economy is likely to become more and more active. Today, interest is growing among both existing and potential trading partners in the region in trade deals, joint-venture projects, and large-scale economic linkages. Enthusiasm is also on the rise among Russian industries and enterprises to penetrate the vast markets of China, South Korea, the ASEAN nations, Australia, Canada, Japan, the United States, and other countries. Decentralization of management within Russian industries has offered them opportunities to solicit profitable and promising clients in East Asia and the Pacific region. Indeed, the Far East's geographical location ensures a window to the populated and rapidly developing Pacific area.

Before the dissolution of the Soviet Union, its Far East region produced about 3 to 4 billion rubles worth of raw materials, goods, and services annually.[1] Extractive industries have traditionally played a major role in the economy of the Far East. In total, the extraction of mineral resources makes up more than 25 per cent of the total volume of industrial output. The leading branches of industry are:[2] non-ferrous metals extraction, timber exploitation and processing, and fishing. Timber areas total 257 million hectares, with reserves of 22 billion cubic meters or 28 per cent of all Commonwealth timber reserves. A major portion is composed of valuable species. The Far East accounted for 40 per cent of Soviet lumber exports to such markets as Japan, Australia, and South Korea.

In an effort to improve economic conditions in the Far East and increase access to international markets, a development program known as 'The Long-Term State Programme for the Economic and Social Development of the Far East Region to the Year 2000' was initiated by the Soviet government in August 1987.[3] The program outlined five principal target areas:

1   increasing the domestic supplies of industrial and consumer goods and services to the regional market;
2   increasing the growth of the raw materials and machine building sectors;
3   developing an export base for raw materials;
4   creating special conditions for enhancing international cooperation through joint ventures, such as defining special economic zones within the Far East region; and
5   providing greater autonomy to Far East officials in selecting economic policies and methods to ensure their implementation.

Most of the raw materials produced in the Far East are exported unprocessed, so an effort was initiated to develop a processing sector. Raw materials, including timber, fish, coal, furs, oil products, and non-ferrous metallic ores, comprise 93 per cent of the Far East's exports.[4]

While the long-range program envisaged high rates of economic growth for the Far East to the year 2000, during the first three years of its implementation the program had little success in stimulating the regional economy. Through 1990, the economy of the Far East region grew at an average annual rate of an estimated 2.5 per cent, which compared to a 7 per cent growth rate envisaged by the long-term program. Over the period 1986–90, the growth of industrial production in the Far Eastern region reached 14.9 per cent compared to the 21 per cent envisioned in the long range plan.[5] The decline of the Russian Far East economy began in earnest in 1991. By the beginning of the year, prices of commodities and services in the Far East had risen 190–210 per cent, paralleling the growth in the population's monetary income.[6] The level of credit granted in the region was even higher, 270–300 per cent, triggering a process of hyperinflation.

According to the Far East's Institute of Economic Research, all Far Eastern industries (except electric power and canned fish) have suffered declines in per unit output since 1990.[7] In general, industry achieved its highest output levels in 1988. During the following three years, however, coal production fell by nearly 20 per cent, steel by 25 per cent, lumber by 32 per cent, cement by 10 per cent and fish by 11 per cent. Non-ferrous metallurgy is apparently the only major industrial sector of the Far East not to suffer during the 1988–91 period; instead, output rose and foreign co-operation increased.

MINERALS AND MINING

Geologically complex and diversified, the Far East contains more than seventy types of minerals, including gold, diamonds, tin, zinc, iron ore, oil, natural gas, and coal. Though vast in area and sparsely populated, the region is relatively well-mapped geographically, with 1:50,000 scale or better maps available for many mineral-producing districts.[8] During the past three five-year development periods, the value of geological surveying activities in the Far East more than doubled.[9] Maps are of high quality and commonly integrate prospecting and mineral resource assessment data.

With its major reserves of non-ferrous, rare and noble metals, diamonds, mercury, graphite, and other non-metallic minerals, the Russian Far East had long been a key provider of mineral resources for the former Soviet Union. More than 90 per cent of Russian diamonds are extracted in the Far East, or Yakutia, while Russia is the world's largest diamond producer and a major exporter. Non-ferrous and precious metals are found in metallogenic zones along the Far East's Pacific coastline (see Figure 5.1 on page 94). Only a limited number of deposits have been sufficiently identified, evaluated, and developed, though some notable exceptions include large deposits of tin, antimony, fluorite, and boron (see Table 5.1). The Far East is the country's leading producer of these minerals, as well as gold and diamonds.[10] The region possesses 95 per cent of Russia's tin reserves, and contributes nearly the same percentage of tin production. The Far East is also a significant supplier of tungsten (24 per cent reserves; 37 per cent production), lead (8 per cent reserves; 49 per cent production), zinc (4 per cent reserves; 14 per cent production), fluorspar (41 per cent reserves; 91 per cent production), and coal (9 per cent reserves; 14 per cent production).

Some of Russia's richest zinc deposits have been discovered in the Far East, particularly within the Sikhote–Alin Mountains of the Maritime Territory, the southern reaches of the Khabarovsk Territory, in Yakutia, and in the Chukchi Peninsula.[11] Tin-ore, or cassiterite, found in the Far East is also of special interest, as is copper ore at Udokan in southern Yakutia and the bauxite deposits of the Khabarovsk Territory. Far East tin discoveries during the 1940s indicated that the region would be a suitable target for commercial tin mining. Dozens of tin deposits have since been successfully exploited in the area.

The Far East region also plays a major role in the production of coal, tungsten, lead and zinc, and cement. Discoveries have been made of major coal and lignite fields, many of which lend themselves to strip mining. Proved coal and lignite reserves approach 13 billion tons, while speculative reserves stand at fifteen times that.[12]

Table 5.1 Characteristics of mineral resources in the Russian Far East

Mineral[a]	Principal characteristics
METALS	
Antimony	The discoveries of the Sarylakhski and Sentachanski antimony deposits in Yakutia indicate some promise for antimony production in the Far East. Mining at the Sarylakhski mine began in 1970, followed by exploitation of the Sentachanski deposit. Remaining reserves at both deposits are small. Significant reserves are possible within the Verkhne-Kolymskaya antimony province in Yakutia or the Republic of Sakha.
Copper	Large copper reserves are possible in Yakutia, where stockwork deposits of copper–molybdenum and copper–tungsten ores (Northern Stankovaya metallogenic zone and Tompo-Bryungadinski ore district), copper–sandstone (Western Aldanskaya metallogenic zone) and other deposits can be found. Similarly large deposits are predicted in the Magadan and Kamchatka Regions, though of a different type – copper–porphyry.
Iron ore	Prospecting activities have been concentrated in the Amur Region and Khabarovsk Territory, where ferruginous quartzites and magnetites have been discovered, and in Southern Yakutia, where the old Southern Aldanski District of magnetite ores is found. The most probable sites for development are the Svobodny town in Amur Region and Chulman township in Southern Yakutia. The prospected reserves at Southern Aldanski are estimated at 1,500,000 million tons. West of this region and near the BAM railway, a major iron-ore district Charo-Tokkinski is found with forecasted reserves estimated at 3,700 million tons. However, the Charo-Tokkinski reserves are almost inaccessible and the mining conditions extremely difficult.
Lead and zinc	The Far East produces a small amount of these metals, and will not be able effectively to increase production in the next decade or so. Dalnegorski is expected to remain the only lead–zinc producer in the region until at least 2000. Several small deposits have been explored and are being developed in Dalnegorski by the Dalpolimetall Production Association. Predicted reserves of lead and zinc rank high in Yakutia. New deposits can be found in the Mamsko-Kyllakhskaya zone and the Southern Verkhoyanski, Western Verkhoyanksi and Tastayakhtasski districts, all of which are nearly inaccessible and underdeveloped. Polymetallic deposits have been discovered in Magadan Region, where the Taskano-Omulskaya zone (strati-bound deposit) shows the greatest promise.
Mercury	Mineralization of mercury is abundant in the Far East, notably in Yakutia and the Magadan and Kamchatka Regions. Several deposits have been discovered in these regions, though none are being developed for economic reasons. Nearly half of Russia's estimated mercury reserves occur in the Far East. In recent

Table 5.1 continued

Mineral[a]	Principal characteristics
	years, surveying and evaluation of the largest discovered deposits – Zvezdochka (Yakutia) and Tamvatpeiski (Magadan Region) – were carried out in the upper and middle Kolyma regions and the Koryakskoye highlands.
Tin	The Far East is the principal supplier of tin in Russia and contains the bulk of the country's reserves. Many deposits are being developed in Magadan Region, Yakutia, and Khabarovsk and Maritime Territories. Placer deposits account for more than 40% of the national output of tin; however, remaining placer reserves are insignificant. Production of tin in the Far East continues to decline as older deposits are depleted, and new regions are being developed slowly. The national demand for tin is only half met, and imports are becoming more costly. The future of the tin-producing industry in the Far East depends on the opening up of new regions. Yakutia (Republic of Sakha) has ample reserves of tin, as do the Central and Southern Yanski districts. Physical environmental conditions in Yanski are very difficult, however. The Magadan Region also holds promise for tin development, second only to Yakutia in estimated reserves, while leading in tin mining and production from concentrates.
Tungsten	Tungsten minerals of wolframite and sheelite are commonly found in association with tin ores. As a consequence, the production history of tungsten in the Far East coincides with tin mining operations. Forty deposits have been identified in Magadan Region, the Khabarovsk and the Maritime Territories, and the Republic of Sakha, accounting for less than 10% of the nation's reserve base of tungsten trioxide. A majority of the deposits are small and insignificant placers. The major Iultinski and Primorski processing facilities are currently operational; tungsten is extracted during tin-ore enrichment at the Solnechny and Deputatski facilities. Prospects for continued tungsten production in the Far East are largely linked with the huge Primorski ore-enrichment plant.
NON-METALS	
Apatites and phosphorites	The Far East agricultural industry is insufficient in mineral fertilizers, particularly phosphorus. Much prospecting is therefore under way in the Udsko-Selemdjinski District in Khabarovsk Territory and the Seligdarskoye apatite deposit in Southern Yakutia. Reserves at Udsko-Selemdjinski are estimated at 1,300 million tons of ore, or 100 million tons of P_2O_5. Prospecting is generally concentrated in the basin's western portion closer to the BAM zone. Exploration work for apatites has been done in the Aldanski district in Yakutia, where the Seligdarskoye deposit holds the greatest promise. Other apatite reserves have been identified in the Khaninski district near BAM in Yakutia and in Khabarovsk Territory. In

Table 5.1 continued

Mineral[a]	Principal characteristics
NON-METALS cont'd	
	recent years, several districts have been selected for phosphate raw materials production, including Yudomo-Maiski, Ayanski, Meginski, Malo-Khinganski, Zeya-Selemdjinski, Oldoe-Urushinski and Badjalski, some of them lying in the BAM zone.
Cement	There are five cement-making plants in the Far East: Teploozerski in the Jewish Autonomous Region, Spasski and Novospasski in Maritime Territory, Poronaiski in Sakhalin and Yakutski. With Novospasski beginning operations and Spasski expanding, demand for cement in the Far East can be met by locally produced raw materials, though supplies are limited to the Northern Far Eastern Region. A new Sakhalinski plant will replace Poronaiski, and will convert to the production of construction lime and ground limestone for agriculture.
Fluorspar	Fluorspar reserves have been discovered in the Khinganski and Jewish Autonomous Region in Khabarovsk Territory, and in the Voznesenski and Pogranichny deposits in Maritime Territory. Minor amounts of fluorspar concentrate are produced in combination with tin concentrate at the Khinganolovo plant and transported to the Ural area. The Voznesenski deposit is the principal supplier for the major Yaroslavski ore-dressing facility.
FUEL RESOURCES	
Coal	The development of coal fields in the Far East began long before the first gold mining operations. The Bering Sea coast experienced coal mining as early as the turn of this century. Proved coal and lignite reserves top 13 billion tons in the Far East, while speculative reserves stand at fifteen times that. The majority of coal reserves (75%) are concentrated in the Republic of Sakha, Amur Region, and Maritime Territory. Four major coal-bearing areas identified include the Okhotsk, Anadyr, Omsukchan, and Arkagala districts. The coals range in rank from brown to anthracite. Most of the coal deposits have a complex geological structure, limiting surveying and development activities. During the 1975–85 period, coal output expanded from 35.2 million to 51.3 million tons, or 1.5 times. Government policies resolve to bring Far Eastern coal production to 82–85 million tons by the year 2000 through the retooling and expansion of existing facilities and the building of new mines.
Oil and gas	The Far East is a major consumer of oil and gas, which are supplied principally from the country's central regions. In recent years, more than 10 million tons of petroleum products and 6.5 million tons of crude oil annually have been transported there by sea and railway, at an annual cost of greater than 300 million rubles. The plan for comprehensive development of the Far

Table 5.1 continued

Mineral[a]	Principal characteristics
	Eastern region to the year 2000 highlighted the need to sharply increase oil and gas prospecting; in the next two five-year development periods the volume of surveying activity is to increase 2.5 to 3 times.

[a] Selected minerals only.
Source: Dorian, James P., August 1993, *Mining in the CIS: Commercial Opportunities Abound*, Financial Times Business Information Ltd, London, p. 152

On an equivalent area basis, the minerals industry of the Far East is more developed than that in Alaska of the United States, even though remote areas in the Far East were not developed until the 1930s or later.[13] The Far East can be conveniently divided into four mining zones:

1 the South Zone incorporating parts of Khabarovsk Territory and the Amur region (tin, gold and coal);
2 the Pacific Zone including the Maritime Territory and the Sakhalin and Kamchatka regions (polymetallic ores and tungsten);
3 the Northern Central Zone including Yakutia, Magadan District and part of Khabarovsk (precious and non-ferrous metals, diamonds, coal, iron ore and natural gas); and
4 the Far North Zone which includes the Chukchi National Area (non-ferrous metals, gold and diamonds).

Exploration in the Far East during the next several years will focus on gold, oil and gas, coal, tin, tungsten, antimony, and phosphate. The Russian government has actively promoted the region as having the greatest potential in the country for joint minerals exploration and development. Clark and Sekisov[14] recently assessed the development potential of the numerous mineral deposit types found in the Far East (Table 5.2). Their evaluation was based largely on geologic favorability, deposit size and grade, infrastructural availability, external markets, and economic development plans. The evaluation is subjective, and subject to revision as political, economic, and market conditions change. None the less, it reveals that despite tremendous resource potential in the Far East, the near-term prognosis for minerals development is optimistic for only a limited number of deposits. Commodities developed to the year 2000 and immediately beyond will generally be restricted to those in short supply and of high quality. Poor transport facilities will continue to constrain minerals development.

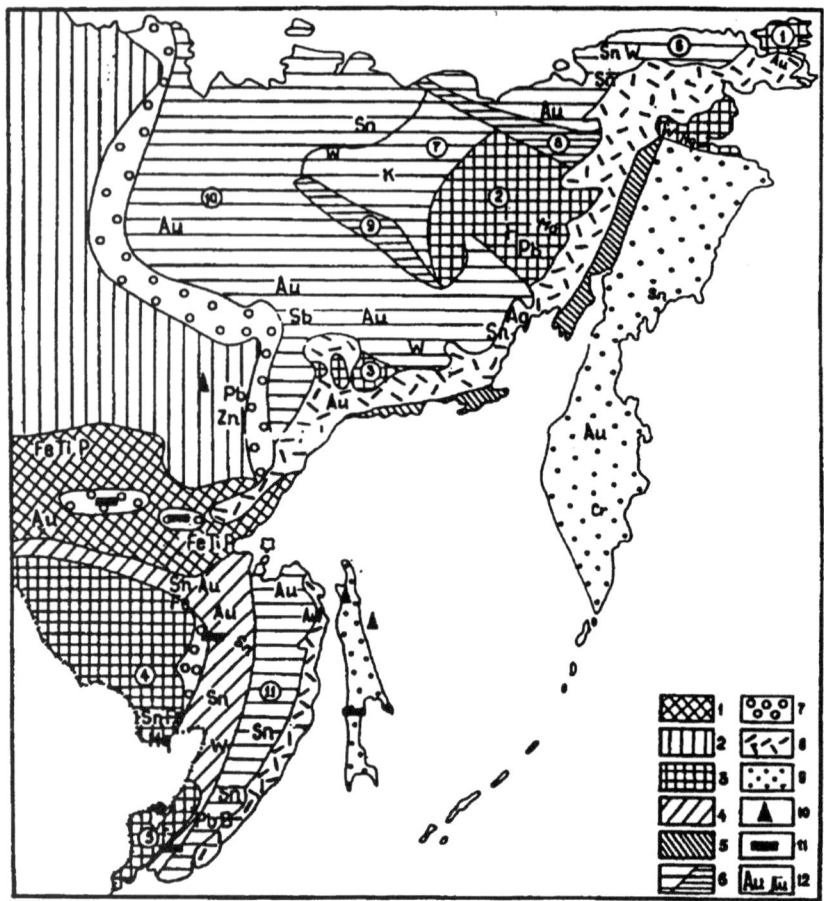

1. Aldano-Stanovoi Shield
2. Siberian platform
3. Medium massifs: (1) Eskimosski, (2) Omonlonski, (3) Okhotski, (4) Burejinski, (5) Khankaiski
4. Amur-Okhotsk Paleozoic geosynclinal-folded system
5. Early-Mesozoic geosynclinal-folded system
6. Late-Mesozoic geosynclinal-folded system: (6) Chukotskaya, (7) Alazeiskaya, (8) Anyuiskaya, (9) Ilin-Tasskaya, (10) Verkhoyano-Kolymskaya
7. Marginal and overlying troughs
8. Marginal-mainland volcanic belt
9. Cainozoic geosynclinal-folded belt

Major deposits of natural resources
10. Oil and gas
11. Bituminous coal
12. Symbols of major useful components in ore-bearing fields (ore-bearing regions are designated with large type symbols; other deposits are designated with small type symbols).

Figure 5.1 Mineral distribution map of the Russian Far East
Source: Yuri I. Bakulin and Vitaly T. Shishmakov, June 1992, 'Mineral Resources of the Russian Far East: Prospects for Export,' paper presented at the Conference on Commonwealth Mining Development: Prospects, Problems and Opportunities for International Cooperation, Institute of Economic Research, 2–5 June, Khabarovsk, Russia

Table 5.2 Subjective evaluation of Far East mineral development potential by deposit type

	Present development potential			Future development potential		
	High	*Med*	*Low*	*High*	*Med*	*Low*
Noril'sk Cu-Ni-PGE	X			X		
Alaskan PGE	X			X		
Placer PGE-Au	X			X		
Diamond pipes	X			X		
Low-sulphide-Au-Quartz Veins	X			X		
Porphyry Cu		X		X		
Cu skarn deposits			X		X	
Porphyry Cu-Mo		X		X		
Sediment-hosted Cu	X			X		
Volcanic-hosted Cu-As-Sb		X				X
Algoma Fe		X			X	
Superior Fe		X				X
Fe skarn deposits		X			X	
Sn veins		X			X	
Sn skarn deposits		X				
Tungsten skarn deposits		X				
Polymetallic veins		X			X	
Sedimentary exhalative Zn-Pb		X		X		
Southeast Missouri Pb-Zn		X		X		
Sandstone-hosted Pb-Zn		X				X
Polymetallic replacement deposits		X				X
Zn-Pb skarn deposits		X				X
Simple Sb deposits		X				
Sepertine-hosted asbestos		X				X
Volcanogenic Mn		X			X	
Sedimentary Mn		X			X	
Upwelling type phosphate deposits		X				X
Laterite type bauxite deposits		X			X	
Lateritic Ni		X				X
Carbonatite deposits		X			X	
Shoreline Placer Ti		X		X		

Source: Clark and Sekisov, 1992

ABUNDANT GOLD

The Far East region is Russia's largest producer of gold. During the period 1970–89, the balance of gold reserves in the Russian Far East increased by 200 per cent.[15] Gold (and diamonds) are mined principally in the basins of the Kolyma and Indigirka Rivers in Magadan and Yakutia and, in the south, in the upper Amur River Basin. In 1992, an estimated 146,000 kg of gold was produced in Russia, with up to 132,548 kg, or 90.1 per cent, coming from the Far East (Table 5.3). Gold production in Khabarovsk Krai increased by 4.8

per cent from the previous year, and the opening up of the industry to commercial activities will likely promote even further development.

Extraction and production of gold in the Far East is dominated by four enterprises: 'Severovosokzoloto'; 'Yakutzoloto'; 'Primorzoloto'; and 'Amurzoloto.'[16] In the 1970s, over 70 per cent of Far Eastern production was in Magadan Oblast (Severovostokzoloto), nearly 20 per cent in Yakutia (Yakutzoloto), slightly more than 4 per cent in Khabarovsk, Primorye, and Sakhalin (Primorzoloto – 4.2 per cent), and 4.4 per cent in Amur Oblast (Amurzoloto). In recent years, output by Yakutzoloto has increased dramatically, as the firm now accounts for around 49.7 per cent of Far East gold production. Sverovostokzoloto's contribution has decreased to 42.7 per cent, while shares by Amurzoloto and Primorzoloto have also fallen to 3.9 per cent and 3.7 per cent, respectively.

At present, most Far East gold production is from placer deposits, particularly from the tributaries and main streams of the Kolyma, Indigirka and Amur rivers. To a great extent, the region's gold potential is unknown and untested, especially in reference to lode gold deposits. However, the close association of gold mineralization with older massif structures and with acidic intrusives within the Pacific fold belt point to a very large potential.[17]

Large gold placers have been discovered in several areas within the Khabarovsk Territory, in Chukotka and on the shelves of the Japan and the Okhotsk seas. In particular, more than eighty prospective areas have been discovered in the southern portion of the Primorye Territory, in the Shantar Islands, along the Okhotsk coast of the Lower Amur, on the western coast of Kamchatka, along the shore of eastern Chukotka, in the Chaun Inlet and the Vanka Inlet. The gold content in the placers is 250–600 mg per cubic meter, with some areas having up to 22 g per cubic meter. Placers are traced at depths to 400 meters and far out into the sea. The thickness of mixed river and marine sands is up to six meters.

Table 5.3 Gold output in the Russian Far East, 1992[a]

Republics and regions	Production (kg)
Magadanskaia Oblast	43,238
Yakutia (Sakha)	30,515
Krasnoyarsk region	10,596
Buryatia	2,725
Primorskii Krai	244
Tuva	131
Other regions including Amur	58,551
Total	146,000 [b]

Source: Russian Committee for Precious Metals and Stones, Moscow
[a] Table includes all producing areas in the Russian Federation, not just its Far East region.
[b] Please note that the total figure from the English weekly Commersant (16 June 1993 issue) was 129,500 kg, or 16,500 kg less than that announced by the Russian Committee.

As an example of the scale of gold mining operations in the Far East, at Susuman in the Kolyma mining district, approximately 150 kilometers north of the town of Magadan, about thirteen dredges and up to 200 open-cut placer mines are operating. Lode mining also takes place, based mainly on stockworks in diorites and sheeted shear zones, and the mineralization is very similar to that which occurs in the Juneau gold belt and Valdez Creek mining district of Alaska. Total production from the Susuman area is some 350,000 troy ounces per year (tr. oz/y) or about 35 per cent of the total annual output from the whole of the Kolyma region. Reportedly, less than 10 per cent of the gold resources in the Magadan region are currently being worked.

In assessing the gold potential of the Far East, it must be emphasized that many gold placers also produce substantial quantities of platinum group metals, cassiterite, scheelite, ilmenite, magnetite, zircon, monazite, rutile, and xenotime. From the latter grouping, a rare earth extraction industry could perhaps be developed in the future.[18]

LICENSING RUSSIAN FAR EAST MINERAL RESOURCES

A precedent was set by Russia in February 1992 when the Federation passed a comprehensive draft law on minerals exploration and development. The legislation appeared in two separate documents:

1 the Law on Subsurface Resources, sometimes referred to as the Law of Mineral Resources (adopted 21 February 1992); and
2 Regulations on Procedures for Licensing the Use of Mineral Resources (adopted 15 July 1992).

Under the law, subjects of entrepreneurial activity, including legal persons and citizens of any country, may become mineral users in Russia, provided they have obtained a license, regardless of the form of ownership. Bodies of the state geological inspection system are to monitor the rational use and protection of Russia's mineral wealth. Royalty payments on mineral projects will be divided as follows: 50 per cent for city authorities (municipal/rural county budget), 25 per cent for regional authorities (republic, oblast, or territorial budget), and 25 per cent for the Russian Federation (federal budget). Payments on oil and gas projects will be: 40 per cent to the federal budget, 25 per cent to the republic, oblast, or territorial budget, and 30 per cent to the municipal/rural county budget. The Russian Parliament approved the minerals legislation by October 1992.

The offer to foreign investors and enterprises in Russia with foreign investments of rights to use land, including its lease, and other natural resources is regulated by the Russian Land Code and other legislation in force in the territory of the Russian Federation. Foreign investors obtain the rights to work and exploit renewable and nonrenewable natural resources through concession contracts concluded with the Russian Council of Ministers. Russia's minerals legislation sets out how exploration and operating licenses will be obtained through tender or auction, and are to be issued jointly by the relevant local authority and the geology committee of the Russian Ministry of Natural Resources and Ecology. Exploration licenses will last for a maximum of five years, while exploration rights are for a maximum of twenty years. The legislation also delineates which authorities will receive which royalties, although for strategically important facilities such levels may be negotiated by federal and local authorities.

The Law on Mineral Resources describes three principal concepts: the State Mineral Fund, licensing of mining activity, and a system of payments or fees for the use of mineral resources.[19] The State Mineral Fund encompasses all of the mineral resources of the Russian Federation. Before the dissolution of the Soviet Union, all explored and identified reserves were transferred to the appropriate ministries for industrial exploitation. Today, all of the mineral wealth will reportedly be permanently housed in the State Mineral Fund, while parts of it are handed over to various juridical and physical entities to use but not to own. The transfer is to be carried out through a system of licensing.

The central government body that supervises the State Mineral Fund is the State Geological Committee of Russia, or more accurately, the State Committee for Geology and Rational Use of Resources. The State Geological Committee was created in March 1992, with its chairman, Victor Petrovich Orlov, formerly of the USSR Ministry of Geology. The committee is well-represented at the regional level, including, for example, the Amur Geological Committee of the Russian Far East. The primary function of the State Geological Committee is to coordinate the licensing of mineral resources utilization in conjunction with other state agencies and local authorities. As a representative of the central government, the State Geological Committee must seek agreement from a number of state agencies before making any recommendations.

According to the minerals legislation, any use of the state's minerals wealth must be agreed upon by the State (or regional) Geological Committee as well as local government representatives where the mineral resources are located. Local authorities must approve any recommendations of the State Geological Committee.

Licensing of mining operations in Russia is complicated and the procedure may be revised as activity increases. Licenses are issued jointly by the State Geological Committee or its regional representatives and by the legislature at the local level (autonomous republic, territorial, municipal or rural county). The means of obtaining a license is through a public auction, a tender process, or competition. An auction is a simpler process, and generally without conditions. Auctions are used for relatively small mineral deposits or resource packages. Foreigners are not expected to compete at most auctions. An international tender, on the other hand, is an application to receive a license based on a development plan.[20] The purpose of the tender is to engage foreign capital with Russian companies and coordinate its usage.

In October 1992 it was announced that licenses will generally be awarded to the highest bidder, although feasibility studies must be submitted. The process will apparently favor Russian enterprises and individuals, but foreign participation in many competitions will be allowed. Competitive bids must be advertised in Russian press reports. There will be no fixed price for the licenses.

Holders of licenses will receive exclusive rights to underground resources within the licensed territory. The corresponding land parcel is transferred to the license holder to manage and utilize, but not to own. The license will contain a number of requirements on how the land and underground resources should be managed. The license will be accompanied by regulations and agreements which include fees and payments for the mineral rights. An agreement can take one of many forms including concession, product sharing, or service contract. The terms of a license can be for a specific time period or indefinite; all licenses can be subject to renewal.

Prices and fee schedules, part of the license arrangement, are organized in two parts: a fixed part (down payment), plus monthly installments or royalty payments based on the identified reserves and other characteristics of the deposit. New investors will be eligible for other additional payments and fees in addition to the license fee itself, including application fees, excise taxes (imposed when the profitability surpasses a certain level), special fees for the use of water, land taxes, payments for geological surveying data, and environmental usage fees.[21]

In Amur Oblast, the third largest gold producing region in Russia, licenses are being prepared for several gold deposits with huge potential. Two organizations in Amur have been competing for control over the licensing of mining rights: the Amur Geological Committee (representing Moscow), and the Amur legislature (or Soviet). In Magadan, any enterprise can undertake precious-metals mining if it has a license to do so. In 1992 the Northeastern Geological Committee announced the first auction of mineral-rights licenses: thirteen gold reserves (of an estimated 5.5 tons), a tin deposit and some reserves of semi-precious stones. In Khabarovsk, the legislature issued a decree on 24 July 1992 regarding the procedures for licensing mineral rights in the Krai. The ruling affirmed the authority of the Far Eastern Geological Committee to provide permission for mineral use; licenses will be issued on the basis of tenders.

JOINT VENTURE ACTIVITIES

Foreign mining companies pursuing investment opportunities in the Far East will tend to concentrate their surveying efforts on precious metals or other high unit-value commodities that require smaller infrastructural commitments than do bulk commodities. Many of Russia's deposits being offered to foreign investors occur in the Far East region, notably:

1   Udokan – a stratiform copper–sandstone body;
2   Bugdainskoe – a tungsten–molybdenum stockwork;

3   Agylkinskoe – a copper–tungsten skarn;
4   Katuginskoe – a tantalum-niobium body; and
5   Bolshoi-Seyiim – a titanium body.[22]

While gold was long considered a strategic commodity in the Soviet Union, Far East authorities today recognize that the metal is economically attractive to most mining companies. Diamond mining will also become an attractive area for joint ventures in the Far East. Soviet authorities had calculated that if $2 billion were invested in modernizing mining techniques in the area, diamond production could increase by about 20–25 per cent.[23] In general, future exploration activities for all minerals will focus on the already developed regions of the Far East, as well as new territories which are comparatively accessible.

In an effort to provide extra incentive to foreign companies considering investing in the Russian Far East, in December 1988 the USSR Council of Ministers issued the resolution 'On Further Measures to Develop the External Economic Activities of State-Run Establishments, Cooperatives and Other Non-Governmental Entities,' giving the Far East special status in developing external economic relations. Specifically, joint ventures in the region were exempted from profit tax for the first three years of operation, compared with two years for other parts of the former Soviet Union. After three years of operations, regardless of the directions of the activities of the joint venture, a 10 per cent profit tax rate is established for them, as compared to 30 per cent for the remainder of the country.

Measures are also being considered which would make local industries and administrative bodies of the Far East self-sufficient in hard currency. The source of funding to cooperative projects remains a central concern to potential foreign investors. Though Far East industries provide raw materials and related services worth a reported 3–4 billion rubles annually, most raw materials are exported unprocessed. With its insufficient manufacturing base, a major area of business for foreign companies in the Far East – one that would provide Russia with hard currency – is the processing at primary and finishing levels of raw materials that would then go into finished and semi-finished products. Primary industries could then provide a sound financial basis from which to expand joint ventures and restructure the regional economy. However, modernization of primary industries will take a long time, indicating that raw materials will continue to lead economic expansion and foreign trade links. In this context, Russian Far East industries will likely be oriented towards the manufacture of specialized equipment for construction, mining, quarrying, and fish processing.

Table 5.4 lists many of the economic and financial incentives which exist or are being considered in the Russian Far East to stimulate foreign investment. The region's economic development is being oriented towards establishing and expanding ties with nations of Asia, notably Japan and South Korea. An essential element of this policy is offering incentives for investments and

Table 5.4 Investment incentives possible/previously offered on
Far East joint-venture projects[a,b]

Tax reductions
A three-year deferment in payment of profit tax granted to all enterprises; a five-year deferment granted to projects involving foreign partners.

Within first five years the revenues of joint-venture projects as well as the incomes of employed foreign staff are tax free.

Foreign companies and joint ventures operating in the region should be tax free on the part of their declared profit used to fund social projects and industrial infrastructure projects.

Accelerated amortization of fixed capital should be permitted to all enterprises in the region.

The general rate of profit tax should average about 20%; enterprises using advanced technology and manufacturers exporting much of their output may have their profit tax reduced as much as 50%.

Financial and tariff incentives
All foreign companies and joint ventures should have the opportunity to convert their ruble funds into foreign currency at the commercial exchange rate.

Foreign companies, joint ventures, and Russian enterprises in the first five years of operation should be offered favorable rents and charges.

Organizational incentives
The region should have a simplified registration procedure for foreign companies and joint ventures.

All enterprises should have the right to conduct commodity-exchange and intermediate-trade operations involving commodities and services produced in the region.

Uniform business and financial accounts based on foreign standards and methods should be adopted for all enterprises.

Joint ventures and foreign companies operating in the region do not have to get a license to engage in external trade.

Favourable customs rules
Commodities and services produced in the region that are exported and commodities and services imported for industrial or consumer utilization within the region should be exempted from customs duties.

Payment of customs duties on commodities and services produced in the region and brought to the Russian domestic market should be deferred and the duties should be lowered according to the value of imports in the total value of those commodities and services.

The value added to exported goods and services delivered from Russia's inland regions through the Far East and Trans-Baikal region to customers outside Russia (when finishing production, packing, or other operations are performed in the region) should be exempted from export duty.

Table 5.4 continued

Reorganization of financial system

It is necessary to establish a Far Eastern Bank for Economic Development and a network of commercial banks and local branches of foreign banks.

One major function of the Bank will be to convert into hard currency that part of ruble deposits corresponding to the volume of economic activities within the region on the basis of export operations and fair exchange rates.

To enable the Bank to convert rubles and guarantee foreign investments and loans it will be necessary to create a security fund.

Source: Dorian, James P., August 1993, *Mining in the CIS: Commercial Opportunities Abound*, Financial Times Business Information Ltd, London, p. 152
[a] Incentives intended to stimulate foreign investment and entrepreneurial business activity.
[b] Actual incentives will vary by project and timing.

entrepreneurial activity. Note that the specific conditions of any investment agreement involving foreign capital will vary by goods being produced/marketed, countries included in the project, export/import plans, and a host of other variables. Projects are negotiated on an individual basis whereby laws and regulations serve as guidelines to establishing specific conditions.

While the Far East accounts for just a small share of Russia's overall national product, nearly one-fifth of the country's joint ventures to date are based in the region. At the beginning of 1993, approximately 1,000 joint ventures and other companies with foreign capital were registered in the Far East, with a majority of the companies engaged in the export of natural resources.[24] Export shipments by joint ventures have risen significantly in recent years, and their share in the combined exports of the Far East increased from 2 per cent in 1989 to 24 per cent in 1992.

In the minerals field, while many foreign companies have expressed interest in the Far East region, problems have discouraged significant investments. None the less, the abundance of natural resources in the area continues to attract many of the world's largest mining companies including US-based Cyprus Minerals Company, Canada's Placer Dome, Inc. and Teck Corporation, and Australia's Broken Hill Proprietary Co. Ltd and CRA Ltd. Joint venture agreements have already been established, including one with a Norwegian company – Norsk Hydro – to develop a brucite deposit in Khabarovsk Territory. Joint venture negotiations are also under way to explore and develop coal and other resources by South Korean and Chinese firms, and mine building materials by a Swiss company.

In 1992, the Japanese diamond importer A. Alder of Tokyo and the Republic of Sakha (Yakutia) diamond producer, Toimada Diamond, created a joint venture diamond polishing company.[25] Sakha's diamond output has been estimated at 18 million carats annually; the region is one of the world's biggest diamond producers. The joint venture company was to set up in Sakha and commence operations in August 1993, with all of the polished diamonds destined for export to Japan, which has become the largest single market in the world. The joint project reportedly was established on a 50:50 equity share basis.

In 1991, Japan's polished diamond imports soared to 279.2 billion yen from 135.2 billion in 1985.[26] Russian diamonds are considered extremely popular due to their high quality. The Sakha–Japan operation expects to export 50,000 to 100,000 carats of polished stones per year. Traders view the new operation as a challenge to DeBeers group, which controls nearly 80 per cent of the international rough-diamond trade. DeBeers already markets Russian rough diamonds under a five-year deal signed in 1990 with the former Soviet central government.

A. Alder of Tokyo reportedly decided to establish this joint venture after the Republic of Sakha secured the right in December 1991 to sell 10 per cent of its rough diamonds independently. That share was increased to 20 per cent in March 1992. Historically, Sakha had to sell its output to the state-controlled national diamond ministry in Moscow. A second Japanese jewelry company, FR Corporation, will be responsible for distributing the diamonds that Sakha produces.

One of the more active companies exploring mineral investment opportunities in the Russian Far East is Australian-based CRA Ltd, which recently established a joint venture with the Far Eastern Institute of Raw Materials (FEIMS) and Dalgeologia (a branch of the Russian Ministry of Geology and Metallurgy). This joint enterprise is to pursue development of precious metals and other commodities in Khabarovsk Territory.

CRA signed its preliminary joint venture agreement with FEIMS and Dalgeologia in March 1992, to conduct exploration activities in the Khabarovsk Territory and northern parts of the Far East. Negotiations took place over a two-year period. CRA received two separate licenses for undertaking exploration activities for a variety of mineral commodities (including gold) over an extended period of time. Importantly, these were the first exploration licenses given to a major international company in the Far East.

While the licenses allow CRA to undertake their own exploration activities, the firm intends to subcontract exploration activities to its DAL Pacific minerals subsidiary joint venture company, also based in the Far East. If a viable mineral deposit is discovered, CRA will probably seek to establish a Contract of Work (COW) agreement with the various joint venture partners. Conditions for a COW may be set gradually while exploration is in progress. Even if the Russian minerals law were fully operational, and taxation, import/export, and foreign investment codes were stable and in place, a COW would probably be sought by CRA or other interested foreign firms as it allows for some flexibility in the conditions and terms of the contract according to the specific characteristics of the deposit.

The nearest and potentially large investor in the Russian Far East is Japan, though for reasons rooted in conflicting territorial claims as well as in economic realities, the Japanese have adopted a slow and deliberate strategy.[27] In

1992, however, the Japan External Trade Organization (JETRO) had reported that Japanese firms were becoming increasingly interested in business in the Russian Far East and that their commitment to that region would likely increase.[28] By mid-1993, Japanese-affiliated enterprises accounted for a significant share of the Russian Far East's total foreign trade. The majority of Japanese ventures in the Far East are small-scale and limited to barter deals in which natural resources, not finished products, are traded for consumer goods.

South Korea, also interested in investing in the Russian Far East, is expected to emerge as the primary foreign investor, if the Seoul government dispenses the remaining $1.5 billion of the $3 billion credits it had promised.[29] Hyundai has nearly completed building a lumber processing facility capable of handling 1 million cubic meters of timber. It has also begun construction on a world class hotel and business center in Vladivostok.

Industrial organizations play a major role in the joint development of Russian Far East mineral deposits. Mining companies interested in pursuing joint ventures in the Russian Far East can cooperate with any one of a number of state or territorial organizations. State agencies include the regional branches of the Russian Ministry of Geology and Metallurgy. Local partners may include the Far Eastern Research Institute of Raw Materials, Khabarovsk, the Institute of Mining, Khabarovsk, Dalgeologia, Khabarovsk, Primorgeologia (Primorskii Geological Production Amalgamation), Vladivostok, Sakhalingeologia, Yuzhno-Sakhalinsk, Taezhgeologia, Blagovecsensk, Yakutskgeologia, Yakutsk, Sevvostgeologia, Magadan, Kamchatgeologia, Petropavlcvsk-Kamchatski, Yakutalmaz (Yakutia Diamond), Yakutsk, and Primorzoloto (Primorskii Gold), Vladivostok.

Though major deposits of gold, diamonds, and tin exist in the Russian Far East, specific information about their location, size, and quality is sometimes difficult or costly to obtain or is considered strategic data. At present, special permission can be acquired to obtain information about the potential for development of a deposit. The question of ownership and control of the deposit, whether it be federal or local government, is critical. With destatization, authorities on all levels are attempting to gain control over natural resources. Conflicts are not uncommon.

Economic, political, and social instability are also cause for concern, as are labor strikes which plagued some Far East mines in 1991 and again in 1992. At the Darasunskii gold mines (Chita) and the Severovostokzoloto mines in Kolyma miners struck in 1991 for increased wages, improved housing, and more equipment, food, and other consumer goods. Safety issues are also important in respect to Far East mining operations, as outdated technology and machinery can sometimes lead to disasters, such as that of the Primorskii Gold Association (Primorzoloto) in its gold facility near Nikolaevsk-na-Amure.

BAM MINERAL EXPORTS TO ASIA

With a large yet still untapped minerals base in the Russian Far East and parts of Siberia, nearly two decades ago Soviet authorities initiated the construction of the 3,100-kilometer Baikal–Amur Mainline (BAM). Now operational, the railway is intended to relieve congestion on the Trans-Siberian Railway while providing transport access to the Pacific Basin. The BAM railway was built to serve as a catalyst for domestic economic development while promoting Soviet international relations. Successful operation of the BAM mainline is crucial if Far East (and Siberian) mineral deposits, such as the Udokan copper project which has an estimated 700 million tons of reserves averaging 1.5 per cent copper, are to be exploited. Long-term opportunities for minerals extraction, processing and transport essentially predetermined the selection of the BAM route.

Though the BAM railway was completed in November 1989, it has been plagued with numerous problems. The Soviet Ministry of Railways none the less promoted the project as one that would have tremendous economic impact on the country. Soviet economists had estimated that BAM, constructed at a cost of several billion US dollars, would pay for itself within a few years of operation. A part of the BAM railway that stretches north into the mineral-rich region of Yakutia already is earning revenues, based on Russian ministry reports. This little offshoot is reportedly carrying 10 million tons of coking coal annually from the large open-pit fields of Neryungri, in Yakutia, to the central BAM railway. The reports admit, however, that BAM cannot be profitable until industrial projects, whose products will be transported by the railway, are built.

The resource base surrounding the BAM service region is large, varied, and relatively underdeveloped (see Figure 5.2). Though mineral exploration activities have, until recently, been limited in many parts of the service zone, geologists are confident that the Far East and eastern Siberia are geologically promising. Exploration efforts near the BAM mainline have intensified in recent years, suggesting that previously discovered deposits will probably be better delineated and defined, while new deposits will be found.

In view of the growing economic relations between the Russian Federation and Asian nations, the BAM railway is expected ultimately to serve as an export outlet of commodity goods to the Pacific Basin as a means of earning hard currency. The Russian Far East currently accounts for more than half of all Russian trade with Pacific Basin nations. The export potential of the BAM railway will be dependent on a number of factors, including minerals supply capacity in Russia, Russian/Commonwealth demand requirements, the Russian need for hard currency, commodity prices, the import needs of the Pacific Basin, and external competition. The potential impacts of BAM mineral exports to Asia are listed in Table 5.5. The table is restricted to listing geologic resources in the Far East region.

Commodities with the largest geologic potential in the Far East include

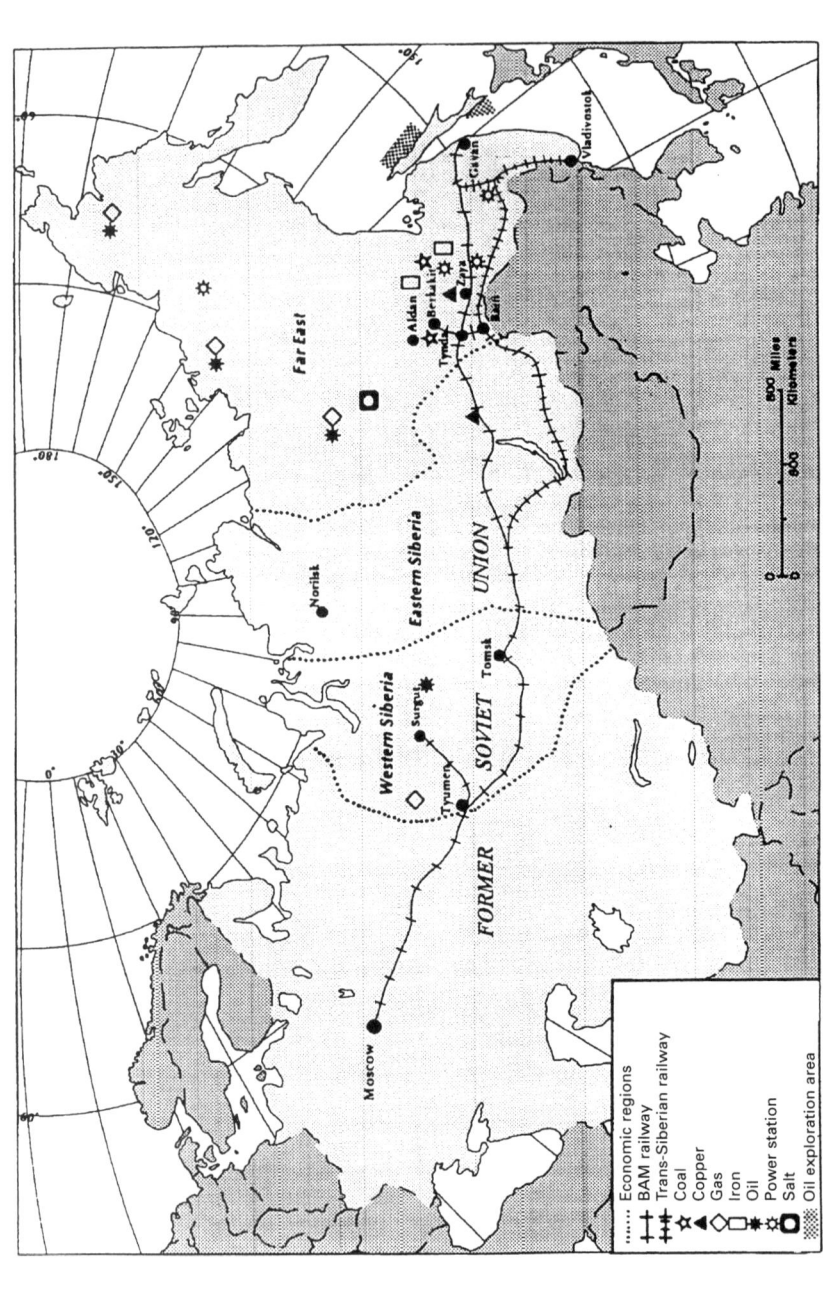

Figure 5.2 The Baikal–Amur Mainland (BAM) railway and nearby mineral deposits

Table 5.5 Potential impact of BAM mineral exports to Asia

Mineral commodity	Geologic resources in Far East[a]			Principal markets[b]	Principal competition[c]
	Major	Some	Potential		
Antimony	X			Japan	China, Canada, Thailand
Boron	X			Japan, New Zealand	China, US
Cement		X		US, Hong Kong, Singapore	Japan, Canada, S. Korea
Coal (bituminous)		X		Japan, S. Korea, Taiwan	Australia, S. Africa, Canada
Copper ore			X	Japan, S. Korea, Canada	Canada, US, Philippines
Diamonds[d]	X			Japan, India, Thailand	Australia, India, Singapore
Fluorite	X				
Gold[e]	X			Japan, US, Canada	Canada, US, Australia
Graphite			X	US, Taiwan, India	China, S. Korea, N. Korea
Iron ore			X	Japan, US, S. Korea	Australia, Canada, India
Lead ore		X		Japan, US, Australia	Canada, US, Australia
Mercury			X	Hong Kong	China
Natural gas			X	Japan, Taiwan, S. Korea	Indonesia, Malaysia, Australia
Petroleum			X	US, Japan, Singapore	Indonesia, China, Singapore
Phlogopite (mica)			X	Japan	US, S. Korea, India
Phosphate			X	Japan, India, Canada	US, Nauru, Christmas Island
Tin ore	X			Malaysia, Singapore, S. Korea	Singapore, Australia, China
Tungsten ore		X		US, Japan, Hong Kong	China, Hong Kong, Mongolia
Zinc ores and concentrates		X		Japan, US, S. Korea	Canada, Australia, US

Source: Dorian, James P., *Mining in the USSR: Investment, Trade and Cooperation in a Changing Environment*, Special Report No. 2133,
Economist Intelligence Unit, London, p. 98

a Based on published Russian resource assessment data and personal visits to major mineral deposit areas. Status of individual resources likely to change given
new releases of Russian geological data and additional exploration activities.
b Major importing nations in Asia–Pacific region in terms of quantity.
c Major exporting nations in or to Asia–Pacific region in terms of quantity.
d Rough, unsorted.
e Non-monetary.
Raw materials and mineral/energy products imported by Hong Kong and Singapore are largely for re-export.

antimony, boron, diamonds, fluorite, gold and tin ore. These or other commodities of high unit-value may be subject to export to selected Asian countries if conditions become economically favorable. Only unprocessed materials will be exported initially, however, until funds are available to construct processing facilities and related infrastructure.

CONCLUSIONS

With increased geological surveying activities scheduled for the remainder of this decade, additional large mineral deposits may be discovered in the Russian Far East. Regardless, minerals mining and processing will continue to influence economic development in the region, particularly in Yakutia (Republic of Sakha) and Magadan where mining plays such a dominant role. During the 1990s, the Far East will remain a primary base for boron, diamonds, fluorspar, gold and tin production. In the longer term, increased output of copper, phosphorus fertilizer, mercury and natural gas is likely, and the development of a steel-making facility is possible. The mining of minerals and fuels clearly represents the Far East's greatest potential for long-term economic growth.

NOTES

1 USSR Chamber of Commerce and Industry, 'The Soviet Union and Asian-Pacific Countries: Outlook for Business Cooperation,' *Bulletin of Commercial Information* (Moscow), no. 3, 1989, pp. 1–3.
2 Pavel A. Minakir, 'Economy of the Soviet Far East: Prospects for Development and Cooperation in the Asian-Pacific Region,' paper presented to the Third PECC Minerals and Energy Forum, Manila, 27–28 July 1989, p. 6.
3 'A Concept of Resolving the Crisis and Stimulating the Social and Economic Development of the Far Eastern Economic Region and Trans-Baikal Region Until 2000,' Khabarovsk, 1991; and Pyotr Baklanov, 'A Concept of the Development of the Far East,' *Far Eastern Affairs*, no. 4, 1991, pp. 3–8.
4 Pavel A. Minakir, 'Prospects for Reform in the Soviet Far East: Agenda and Options,' paper prepared for the Workshop 'Soviet Reforms and Relations with the Pacific,' Australia National University, 5–6 February 1990.
5 Baklanov, *op. cit.*
6 Pavel A. Minakir, 'The Russian Far East: Economic Conditions and Prospects for Cooperation in Northeast Asia,' conference on 'Commonwealth Mining Development: Prospects, Problems, and Opportunities for International Cooperation,' Institute of Economic Research, Khabarovsk, Russia, 2–5 June 1992.
7 *Ibid.*
8 Tom Bundtzen, 'Far East trip report notes to Division of Geological and Geophysical Surveys,' Anchorage, Alaska, 1 November 1989.
9 Novosti Press Agency, *Soviet Far East: Minerals and Resources*, issued by the Soviet National Committee for Asian-Pacific Cooperation and Novosti Press Agency, Moscow and Vladivostok, 1989, p. 81.
10 *Ibid.*
11 Evgenii B. Kovrigin, 'The Soviet Far East,' in John J. Stephan and V.P.

Chichkanov (eds), *Soviet-American Horizons on the Pacific*, Honolulu: University of Hawaii Press, 1986, pp. 1–16.

12 USSR Chamber of Commerce and Industry.

13 Bundtzen, *op. cit.*

14 Allen L. Clark and Genady V. Sekisov, 'Geology, Mineral Resources and the Mineral Development Potential of the Russian Far East,' paper presented at the 'Conference on Commonwealth Mining Development: Prospects, Problems, and Opportunities for International Cooperation,' Institute of Economic Research, 2–5 June 1992, Khabarovsk, Russia.

15 Vladimir T. Shishmakov, 'Estimation of Mineral Resources in the Russian Far East,' unpublished manuscript, Far Eastern School of Interbusiness, Khabarovsk, Russia (in Russian), June 1992.

16 *Ibid.*

17 Clark and Sekisov, *op. cit.*

18 *Ibid.*

19 James P. Dorian, August 1993, *Mining in the CIS: Commercial Opportunities Abound,* London: Financial Times Business Information, 1993.

20 *Russian Far East Update*, April 1993, Seattle: Russian Market Information Services, p. 4.

21 *Russian Far East Update*, September 1992, Seattle: Russian Market Information Services, pp. 6–8.

22 James P. Dorian and Pavel V. Karaulov, 'Joint Mining Ventures in the Former Soviet Union: A Focus on the Russian Federation,' in James P. Dorian, Pavel A. Minakir, and Vitaly T. Borisovich (eds), *CIS Energy and Minerals Development: Prospects, Problems and Opportunities*, Kluwer Academic Publishers, the Netherlands, 1993.

23 Vladimir Kvint, 'Go East, Young Man,' *Forbes*, 26 November 1990, pp. 234–8.

24 'Foreign Investment and the Russian Far East,' *Russian Far East Update*, August 1993, Seattle: Russian Market Information Services, p. 5.

25 *Asahi Shimbun*, 22 March 1992, p. 6.

26 *Los Angeles Times*, 20 July 1992.

27 Bradley Martin, 'Moscow's Last Frontier,' *Newsweek*, Pacific Edition, 18 September 1989, pp. 34–5.

28 *Nikkei Weekly*, 1 February 1992, p. 8.

29 *Japan Times*, 30 June 1992, p. 3.

6 The present situation and future problems of energy production in the Russian Far East

Takashi Murakami

ENERGY PRODUCTION IN THE RUSSIAN FAR EAST

The conditions affecting energy production in the Russian Far East have deteriorated to the worst ever. The general failure of the Russian economy and steep industrial output decline have resulted in shrinking energy production. The Far East region, remote from major Russian economic areas, is greatly affected by the skyrocketing transportation costs due to price liberalization.

Oil extraction has always been an insignificant part of Far Eastern energy production, covering no more than 10 per cent of total petroleum consumption in the area. Oil production in the Far East from the beginning of the 1970s to the middle of the 1980s fluctuated around 2.45–2.5 million tons a year. By 1993, production had plunged to 1.69 million tons. It has since recovered somewhat, to 1.78 million tons in 1994 and an estimated 1.97 million tons in 1995.

Currently, the only significant oil production in the Russian Far East is taking place in Sakhalin (Table 6.1). Development of Sakhalin's oil has a really long history. It started about a century ago. As a result of such long-term low-technology exploration, about 60 per cent of deposits were extracted and production actually is coming to its final stages. Geological conditions are worsening and oil deposits are becoming smaller and smaller. Due to the economic crises and critical capital-equipment shortages gripping the region, those oil wells which were in need of repairs just stopped production.

Similar to oil, natural gas is produced in the area of Sakhalin Island (1.5 billion cubic meters in 1994 and 1.6 billion cubic meters in 1995) and in the Sakha Republic (1.63 billion cubic meters in 1994 and 1.65 billion cubic meters in 1995) (see Table 6.2). Production of coal, which is the most important energy resource for the Far East, peaked at 5.7 million tons in 1988. Production dropped to 3.9 million tons in 1993 and 3.2 million tons in 1994. 1995 saw a small recovery, to 3.5 million tons. Production increases in 1995 were seen in Sakhalin (an increase of 30.5 per cent over the previous year), in

Table 6.1 Forecast of oil production in the Russian Far East
(in millions of metric tons)

	1993	*1994*	*1995*[1]	*1996*[2]	*1997*[2]	*2000*[2]	*2005*[2]
Far East	1.69	1.78	1.97	2.12	2.55	3.51	20.80
Sakhalin Oblast	1.56	1.58	1.90	2.82	4.50	12.05	18.20
Sakha Republic	0.13	1.63	1.78	1.84	2.10	2.30	18.98[3]

Source: *The Situation, Problems, and Perspectives of Russian Oil Production*, Tokyo: Institute
for Economic Research of Russia & Eastern Europe, March 1994, p. 105, and *Long-term
Development Plan for the Far East through 2005*, Moscow 1996, p. 212
[1]   Estimate.
[2]   Forecast.
[3]   Assumes Sakhalin continental shelf production.

Table 6.2 Forecast of natural gas production in the Russian Far East
(in millions of cubic meters)

	1994	*1995*	*1996*[1]	*1997*[2]	*2000*[2]	*2005*[2]
Far East	3,115	3,293	3,573	3,689	3,523	21,978
Sakha Republic	1,634	1,650	1,680	1,750	2,000	2,480
Kamchatka Oblast	—	—	—	20	600	550
Sakhalin Oblast	1,481	1,643	1,893	1,919	2,023	18,948[3]

Source: *Long-term Development Plan for the Far East through 2005*, Moscow 1996, p. 213
[1]   Estimate.
[2]   Forecast.
[3]   Assumes Sakhalin continental shelf production.

Table 6.3 Forecast of coal production in the Russian Far East
(in millions of metric tons)

	1994	*1995*[1]	*1996*[2]	*1997*[2]	*2000*[2]	*2005*[2]
Far East	32.33	35.19	37.69	42.39	49.97	59.49
Sakha Republic	11.39	11.96	12.10	12.20	12.20	12.20
Jewish Autonomous Oblast	—	—	0.25	0.30	0.80	1.50
Primorskii Krai	9.90	10.76	10.95	14.47	16.52	20.04
Khabarovsk Krai	1.48	1.60	1.80	2.00	4.80	5.80
Amur Oblast	4.30	4.50	6.00	6.00	6.10	9.10
Kamchatka Oblast	0.04	0.04	0.05	0.08	0.20	0.20
Magadan Oblast	1.30	1.50	1.50	1.70	1.80	2.10
Sakhalin Oblast	2.93	3.82	4.14	4.69	6.45	7.45

Source: *Long-term Development Plan for the Far East through 2005*, Moscow 1996, p. 213
[1]   Estimate.
[2]   Forecast.

Magadan (15.4 per cent), and in Primorskii Krai (8.6 per cent), with production dropping in all other territories of the Russian Far East (Table 6.3).

Although energy production in the region improved in 1995, serious shortages continue. Even at the peak of oil production in the Russian Far East, the region had to import 90 per cent of its petroleum needs from other regions of the country. Most of the oil produced in the Russian Far East is consumed in the immediate surrounding areas. Even coal production in 1995 amounted to only 61 per cent of the peak year of 1988, necessitating imports from outside the region.

There are several major problems in the energy situation in the region. The first is a shortage of electric power and heating energy. Electric power shortages have the most serious impact on the ordinary citizens in their daily life. Enterprises that fail to pay their electric bills are threatened by power cutoff, although so far there are no cases of power being cut off from individual households unable to meet their payments. At the same time, owing to skyrocketing transportation costs and non-payment of shipping costs, many electric power plants are not receiving coal and are suffering serious fuel shortages. Electric/thermal power plants cannot supply enough electricity and heating steam. In Khabarovsk Krai, Primorskii Krai, and Sakhalin Oblast, temporary shut-offs of electric power have become a more or less routine and chronic phenomenon. Foreigners visiting the Russian Far East also experience life in hotels with no hot water. Shortages of electricity and heating power have become normal for ordinary citizens. One might even say they are used to such experiences. Primorye suffered the most serious energy shortage in the summer of 1996. Although coal production in the territory increased, power companies had to reduce purchases of coal because many consumers were unable to pay for their power. The situation was made worse when coal miners went on strike in protest against pay delay of over six months.[1] The problem highlighted the urgent need to expand energy production in the Russian Far East.

The second problem is a declining refining capacity in the region. In 1992, about 60 per cent of the petroleum products used in the Russian Far East were refined in the region itself. Currently, there are two oil refineries in Khabarovsk and Komsomolsk-na-Amure with a total annual capacity of 10 million tons. Ninety per cent of oil for these two refineries comes from western Siberia more than 5,000 kilometers away. Liberalization of oil prices and skyrocketing transportation costs gave a strong shock to the Far Eastern refinery plants whose supplies were carried by rail. Due to the rising transportation costs, petroleum products of the Far Eastern refineries became one and a half to two times as expensive as those of the Siberian refineries, whose crude oil is supplied by pipeline. Transportation of crude by rail now costs about ten times more than by pipeline. With 90–94 per cent of the costs of production being raw material (crude) costs, both Khabarovsk and Komsomolsk refineries have an extremely limited ability to reduce their production costs.

Third, price liberalization and transportation cost increases are producing a completely new situation for Russian consumers. Purchasing foreign-made petroleum products is gradually becoming cheaper than buying from domestic sources. This trend is especially apparent in such remote areas as Magadan and Kamchatka Oblasts. Russian domestic prices of petroleum products have come close to international prices and, in some cases, have already overtaken them. In such circumstances, the situation of the ruble exchange market and the existence of import tax will be the key factors determining consumers' behavior.

POLICY FOR SOLVING THE ENERGY CRISIS

Sakhalin continental shelf oil and gas development

The most effective way to expand the energy supply in the Far East would be to develop the abundant oil and natural gas reserves on the Sakhalin continental shelf. Confirmed reserves of oil (A+B+C1) in the shelf area amount to 44 million tons, gas condensate, 46 million tons, and natural gas, 600 billion cubic meters. In addition, it is believed that there are vast reserves that have not yet been confirmed.[2]

April of 1972 was the starting date for development of the Sakhalin offshore oil and gas deposits. At that time, during the fifth meeting of the Japanese–Soviet Economic Cooperation Committee in Tokyo, the Soviet side suggested joint prospecting and development of oil and gas in the offshore areas of Sakhalin. It was just after the 1973–74 oil shock when prices escalated, and Japan, with virtually no domestic oil, gas, or coal reserves that are commercially exploitable, felt the need to diversify its energy supplies. A public corporation, SODECO, was established with participation of various financial institutions in the country. The undertaking had the appearance of being a major national project. The Soviet side had almost 'zero' experience in prospecting and developing offshore oil and gas, but under the project it received the necessary capital, technology, and equipment from Japan.

The prospecting and development project, later called 'Sakhalin-1,' led to the discovery of Odoptu and Chaivo oil fields. In 1982, the participating countries prepared a plan for starting oil exploration, but due to the decline of international oil prices the project became economically less urgent. At present, eighteen years after the signing of the general framework agreement for the project, 'Sakhalin-1' has come to a standstill. During this period, the Soviet side, using technology and equipment obtained under the 'Sakhalin-1' project, discovered several other deposits independently from Japanese partners. Subsequently the Russian government opened the project to competitive international bidding to select a group of developers for several of the oil and gas fields.

In May 1991, Russia announced the bids for a feasibility study (F/S) for Lunskoe and Piltun-Astokhskoe, large deposits in the northeastern part of

Sakhalin. After a fiery competition between six different groups of companies, the 3M group, including Mitsui & Co., McDermott International Inc., and Marathon Oil Co. were selected as partners in the F/S execution. Later, Royal Dutch Shell and Mitsubishi Corp. joined the so-called 'Sakhalin-2' project in addition to the three original partners, forming the expanded consortium called the '4MS.' A holding company, Sakhalin Energy Development Co. Ltd, was established and registered in Bermuda with capital participation of the 4MS partners. On 23 June 1994, Russian Prime Minister Victor Chernomyrdin and American Vice-President Al Gore watched the signing of a product-sharing contract between the Russian Ministry of Fuels and Energy and the 4MS. Pending necessary national legislation for product sharing, the agreement required declaration of a commencement date within two years of its signing. On 30 December 1995, President Yeltsin signed the legislation after it was revised to eliminate many provisions favoring foreign investors. Foreign investors expressed concern over the new law.

The new law was an expression of resource nationalism in the country. Earlier drafts of the legislation exempted foreign investors from customs duties but this privilege was eliminated against the background of heavy tax burdens on domestic producers. The final legislation also eliminated protection against unilateral changes in response to the international market condition. A third concern to foreign investors is that under the new law international contracts that are considered strategically important require parliamentary approval, a condition that would expose foreign investors to the vagaries of domestic politics. Fourth, the law on product sharing gives priority to domestic entities as subcontractors, suppliers, and transporters. There is also a requirement for domestic contents in gas development technology and equipment. Yet another point that troubles foreign investors is the very distinct possibility that in case of a dispute or conflict affecting their investments in Russia they may be at the mercy of unilateral Russian decisions.

In spite of these concerns, the official commencement of 'Sakhalin-2' was declared on 21 May 1996. Commencement of 'Sakhalin-1' was also declared on 10 June 1996, as the 30 June 1995 product-sharing agreement between Russian and foreign investors in that project was found valid. The agreements governing these projects were not subjected to parliamentary review because they had been concluded prior to the new national legislation. As nationalism continues to influence the domestic political situation, however, they may very well come under closer 'political' scrutiny at the national level. It cannot be said that stability is secured for these Sakhalin gas development projects. Already a comprehensive bill has been introduced to the Russian Parliament to revise the Law on the Continental Shelf, the Law on Underground Resources, and various tax laws.[3]

The decisive difference between 'Sakhalin-1' and 'Sakhalin-2' has to do with the composition of business consortia. Russian investors separately participate in 'Sakhalin-1,' but Russian investors have joined together to form a

Sakhalin Energy Investment Company as the operator of 'Sakhalin-2'. 'Sakhalin-1' stockholders include the Japanese consortium SODECO (30 per cent), Exxon (30 per cent), Sakhalinmorneftegaz (23 per cent), and Rosnefte (17 per cent), with Exxon serving as the gas field operator. The 'Sakhalin-2' stock is shared by Mitsui (20 per cent), Mitsubishi (10 per cent), McDermott (20 per cent), Marathon (30 per cent), and Royal Dutch Shell (20 per cent).[4] Another difference between the two projects is that the ultimate decision-making authority for 'Sakhalin-1' rests with a Russian government entity to be established, while 'Sakhalin-2' has a Supervisory Council as the highest decision-making body with six representatives of the Russian government, the Sakhalin Oblast government, and foreign investors.[5] The exploitable reserves of Arktun-Daginskoe in 'Sakhalin-1' are estimated at 245 million tons of oil, 287 billion cubic meters of gas, and 26 million tons of gas condensate. Chaivo holds an estimated 17 million tons of oil and 97 billion cubic meters of natural gas reserves, and Odoptu 28 million tons of oil and 41 billion cubic meters of natural gas reserves.

In July 1993, a new international bid on 'Sakhalin-3,' involving a large part of the Northeast Sakhalin coastal shelf, took place in Denver, Colorado. In December 1993, it was announced that the rights to prospecting for six years and subsequent development for nineteen years on the basis of feasibility studies were given to Exxon (Blocks 1 and 2) and to a Mobil–Texaco consortium (Block 4). No company entered the bid for another block (Block 3). Russia also plans to open the next, fourth project, or 'Sakhalin-4,' involving coastal shelf areas of the Sakhalin Gulf and Block 3 of 'Sakhalin-3.' The biggest obstacle to this project is that parliamentary approval, as noted above, may be susceptible to highly nationalistic sentiments. Exxon has already negotiated a product-sharing contract with the Russian partners and, pending parliamentary approval, plans to start the project in the summer of 1997.[6]

The idea of merging 'Sakhalin-1' and 'Sakhalin-2' is also being considered in order to increase the profitability of the two projects. Cooperation in pipeline and export terminal construction, which can be used jointly, can substantially improve the economic efficiency of the two projects.

In these oil and gas development projects, the most contentious issue involves conditions for foreign investments. If the projects are successfully carried out, they will be a major boost to the entire Russian Far East economy and will help ease the depressed energy situation in the region. They will also provide environment-friendly energy resources for Northeast Asian countries. They will become a symbol of a new era of cooperation in Northeast Asia.

Many problems must be solved before the Sakhalin projects can be realized. For the most part, solutions to the problems depend on the Russian side. Approval of proper legislation concerning oil and gas development is the most pressing issue. More precisely, it is necessary for the Russian government to approve the Oil and Gas Law and the Law on Production-Sharing, and to revise the Underground Resources Utilization Law. These are currently being discussed in the State Duma, the lower house of Russian Parliament. If legislative action proceeds, it may be possible to start project works in the spring of 1995 [see p. xxiii], when the development sites are freed from the long freezing winter.

Russia is quite eager to begin oil and gas exploration as soon as possible. According to the 'Sakhalin-2' development plan, initial production is slated for 2001 and guaranteed production for sometime after 2005. 'Sakhalin-1' is scheduled to come on stream two years later, with initial production expected in 2003. Payments of royalties and premiums to the Sakhalin Region Infrastructure Development Fund were expected to begin in 1994. Therefore, progress in 'Sakhalin-2' will bring substantial economic benefits to the Sakhalin Region.

Natural gas development in the Sakha Republic (Yakutia)

A real possibility exists to ease the future energy situation in the Russian Far East if the huge reserves of natural gas in the Sakha Republic can be successfully developed. The first step in the development was taken as early as the mid-1970s, when Japan, the United States, and the Soviet Union signed a trilateral general agreement on Yakutia natural gas prospecting. About 1 trillion cubic meters of natural gas reserves were found. However, following the Soviet invasion of Afghanistan in December 1979, the international project came to a halt. In the spring of 1990, the Soviet Union sought Japan's cooperation in the so-called 'Vostok Plan' to build a pipeline from Yakutia through North Korea and South Korea, supplying natural gas to Japan. The plan was also shelved after the breakdown of the GOSPLAN (State Committee for Planning) and central planning system with the Soviet Union's collapse.

In the autumn of 1992, President Yeltsin suddenly cancelled his scheduled visit to Japan but visited Korea instead, to the consternation of many Japanese. Russia and South Korea agreed that the Yakutia natural gas development, which would supply 25 billion cubic meters of natural gas annually, would be the centerpiece of economic cooperation between the two countries.[7] The Korean side established an eight-company consortium, but since then very little has happened. It was reported that President Yeltsin had proposed the Yakutia development idea without consultations with the Sakha Republic and that this upset the Sakha President Mikhail Nikolaev. In June 1994, the two countries agreed that the development should proceed. It appears, however, that the public display of interest in the development of Yakutia natural gas was a routine political gesture on the part of the Russian president. In December 1992, Russia and South Korea agreed to conduct a preliminary feasibility study. Korea Petroleum Development Corporation and thirteen other companies participated in the study, which was completed in November 1995. The study shows that the projected development will take three times as much capital as initially estimated.

In the meantime, the Sakha Republic is seeking cooperation with Japan. In June 1992, at the invitation of the Republic president, a delegation of Japanese specialists visited the Republic. Both sides agreed to reopen the discussion on the development project. In March 1994, President Nikolaev visited Japan and requested Japan's cooperation in natural gas development. Three months later, a fact-finding delegation of Japanese government officials and industry representatives visited Yakutia.

The Sakha Republic is eager to move the project forward, but so far neither South Korea nor Japan has taken any steps in that direction. A complicating factor is the growing interest in Moscow and in the Sakha Republic to combine the development of natural gas in Yakutia with that of gas exploitation in the adjacent Irkutsk. The Sakha Republic's earlier plan was to ship its natural gas by pipeline southward to the trans-Siberian railroad and eastward to Khabarovsk and Vladivostok, on to North Korea, South Korea, and Japan. When President Yeltsin visited Beijing in April 1996, however, Moscow and Beijing agreed to cooperate in building a pipeline to ship natural gas from Irkutsk to Beijing and Tienjin through Mongolia. Both Japan and South Korea have shown initial interest, although they are cautious before they commit themselves.

The general approach of the Sakha side to the natural gas development project is that an increase and export of natural gas supply to the Far East would require an expansion of discovered gas reserves from the original 1 trillion cubic meters to 2 trillion cubic meters. For this purpose, the Republic would like to invite foreign investments and conduct the necessary pre-feasibility studies and prospecting. Korea's potential role will be limited in terms of the size of investment required for the project, and Japan's participation will be necessary. Because of the bad geological conditions in Sakha and the need to construct a 3,000 kilometer pipeline connecting the production sites to the markets in East Asia, the investment requirement for the Yakutia project would far exceed the level of investment envisaged for the Sakhalin Coastal Shelf project. Korea by itself would not be able to come up with the necessary capital.

As for Japan, private companies would be willing, in principle, to take part in pre-feasibility studies, but at the prospecting stage participation of the Japanese government and commitment of public funds would be necessary. In view of the recent international bidding for the Sakhalin projects which has resulted in increases in the price of geological information and benefits favorable mostly to the Russian side, private companies in Japan are not likely to jump in quickly or act independently. Prospective Japanese participants, including some of the largest electric power companies and gas companies in the country, along with large trading houses, engineering firms, and steel pipe producers are forming a group that would work under the umbrella of the Japanese–Russian Economic Cooperation Committee and develop 'in-house' information. It is unlikely that a large number of Japanese companies will participate if the Sakha side should open the project to competitive international bidding. In contrast to the Sakha Republic's eagerness to start the project as soon as possible, Japanese companies are moving very deliberately and slowly, with one eye on the developments surrounding the Sakha project and one eye on the Sakhalin projects.

In the long term, the development of oil and gas on the Sakhalin continental shelf and gas in the Sakha Republic will help ease the energy situation in the Russian Far East. However, major developments will have to wait until the twenty-first century. In the meantime, in order to overcome the energy shortages, the Russian Far East must find other means of obtaining the necessary supplies. The construction of nuclear power plants is receiving serious consideration in the region, but it too must wait until the next century for implementation if at all.

CONCLUSIONS

In April 1996, the Russian government approved the 'National Plan for the Long-term Development of the Far East through 2005,' which envisions gradual expansion of oil production in the region until it reaches 3.5 million tons in the year 2000. A more dramatic increase in petroleum production will have to wait until the Sakhalin offshore development begins in 1999. Even at that point, however, about one-half of the oil produced in Sakhalin is destined for exports and the Russian Far East will continue to depend on imports from other parts of the country. Natural gas production in the Russian Far East is not expected to grow significantly until production on the Sakhalin continental shelf starts, after the year 2000. Oil and natural gas production in the Sakha Republic cannot change this situation until after 2005. Coal production in the Russian Far East will be a non-factor because it is estimated to recover to the 1988 level in 2005. Primorskii looks to coal development as a way of improving its energy self-sufficiency. It has an ambitious plan to double its coal production between 1995 and 2005. Khabarovsk is even more ambitious, trying to expand its coal production by 360 per cent during the same period. These estimates are highly unrealistic in view of the aging and deteriorating mining operations and inadequate investment capital.

In conclusion, we expect that the Russian Far East will be forced to continue to transport oil from Siberia and, at the same time, supplement it with imports as well as with the coal produced within the region. Capital shortage and economic instability will probably continue in the foreseeable future, limiting the region's ability to expand its energy supply. There do not seem to be any bright prospects for quite some time.

NOTES

1 *Delovoi mir*, 1 August 1996. Thirteen of the fourteen coal mines in the territory were shut down during the strike in which 12,000 miners participated.

2 Interfax, *Oil & Gas Report,* no. 28, 15 July 1994.
3 Presentation by N. Pavlova, Deputy Director, Continental-Shelf Mineral Resources Development Bureau, Sakhalin Administration, in Sapporo, 7 August 1996.
4 *Interfax Siberian Business Report*, 30 May 1996, p. 8. The total investment is $12 billion.
5 The total investment is $15 billion.
6 *Interfax Siberian Business Report*, 30 May 1996, p. 9.
7 Interfax, 16 June 1994.

7 Environmental challenge in the Russian Far East

Tsuneo Akaha

INTRODUCTION[1]

The Russian Far East's economic development depends critically on the exploitation of its rich natural resources, the most important, and arguably the only asset the region has to offer for its own exploitation and for export. However, the combination of limited political support, an underdeveloped legal regime, fragile social institutions, and constrained financial and technological resources for environmental protection in the region mitigates against ecologically sustainable development of these natural resources. Given the geographical contiguity and trans-border environmental impact of industrial and resource development activities in the economies of Northeast Asia, including that of the Russian Far East, cooperation among them in both industrial and resource development and environmental protection will be particularly important. International cooperation is not only morally desirable but also economically and politically essential.

The purpose of this brief analysis is to ascertain the prospects for international cooperation in the sustainable development of the Russian Far East. I will discuss the challenges to its environmental protection and resource conservation and management. I will then assess the region's readiness for international cooperation. I will conclude with a set of norms and principles that will be essential for the development of international cooperation in this area.

ENVIRONMENTAL CHALLENGE

The environmental situation in the Russian Far East is serious. There is a systemic problem of ineffective environmental protection and resource management throughout the region.

There are many instances of accidental and intentional pollution. In 1993, for example, there were thirty-four discharges of harmful substances in Khabarovsk Krai, with damages totalling an estimated 130 million rubles. For violating ecological regulations in the Krai, 560 people were called to administrative responsibility and three to criminal responsibility. The total sum of fines reached 58 million rubles. Production at eight plants was halted after they violated environmental regulations. In Primorye, the situation was no better. There were 144 accidental discharges of pollutants with an esti-mated 248.5 million rubles in damages and 492 people were called to administrative responsibility for violating environmental laws and fined a total of 16.1 million rubles. Enterprises were fined 708.5 million rubles. Another 734 individuals were called to administrative responsibility for vio-lating hunting, fishing, or plant regulations, and were fined 14.4 million rubles.[2]

Ironically, however, the economic recession in the last several years has been something of a 'blessing' to the region's environment in that the decline in industrial production has led to a reduction in industrial discharges. In 1992, for example, the output of industrial waste in Primorye dropped by an average of 12.5 per cent. A survey of 220 enterprises in the region for the first six months of 1994 revealed that the total amount of industrial waste had dropped by 18.2 per cent from a year earlier. On the other hand, sixty-three enterprises, mostly in construction, public utilities, and transportation, increased the amount of waste by 20,200 tons. The use of poor quality fuels and old treatment facilities was blamed for this problem.[3] Power plants in Primorye increased their atmospheric emissions. During the first half of 1994, electric power enterprises accounted for 53.7 per cent of pollution in the territory. Also increasing pollution in recent years are private vehicles, many of which are imported from Japan. Atmospheric emissions in Primorye include gaseous and liquid pollutants, including sulfuric anhydride (60 per cent of the total), carbon oxides (26 per cent), and nitrogen oxides (11 per cent). In Primorye, the most polluted air is found in Vladivostok, Artyom, Partizansk, Luchegorsk (where thermal power plants are located), Spassk (cement production), and Dalnegorsk (fertilizer and boron chemicals pro-duction). The amount of dust in the air in Vladivostok exceeds the maximum permissible level by 50 per cent; nitrogen dioxide levels in the atmosphere in Vladivostok, Partizansk, and Ussuriysk are two-and-a-half times the per-mitted levels; and benzopyrene (a carcinogen) is found at levels two to three times higher than allowed in Vladivostok, one-and-a-half times in Partizansk and Dalnegorsk, and five times in Ussuriysk.[4]

One of the most important natural resources in the Russian Far East is sur-face water (mainly river water), which is used as the main source of water supply in the region. In Primorye, for example, water use amounts to 1,800 million cubic meters per annum, of which 37 per cent is for industrial use, 31 per cent for agricultural irrigation, and 19 per cent for public use and drink-ing and the rest for other purposes. Because of the irregular river run-off, there is a shortage of water supply in almost one-half of the whole territory, particularly in Vladivostok and Artyom. Water quality is an acute problem as well. Causes of the problem include violations of health regulations in water reservoir areas, the overloading of treatment plants during rainfall seasons, and shortage of coagulants.[5]

The level of pollution in reservoirs, rivers, and coastal sea areas in

Primorye is also high. The main causes of this problem are the shortage of treatment facilities, out-of-date treatment technology, suboptimal locations of treatment plants, and waste dumping. In 1992, eighteen enterprises were cited for violating water disposal regulations, fined, and ordered to halt their operations. These penalties have had no apparent effect, however, and illegal waste water discharges continue. Sewage discharge is about 800 million cubic meters a year, of which 42 per cent is raw sewage and 57 per cent untreated service water. As a result, high levels of ammonium nitrogen are found in many small rivers of Primorye, in some areas as high as five to ten times the maximum permissible levels.[6] There are no purification systems for sewage in Vladivostok, and 96 per cent of raw sewage flows into Amurskii Bay. Lack of funding is the major problem and has delayed plans to construct special treatment facilities and the introduction of new methods of treatment, including the use of micro-organisms. Only 100 million rubles were set aside for these purposes in 1994.[7]

The major polluters of water reservoirs in Primorye are utility establishments, accounting for over 50 per cent of the total sewage discharge, farms (10 per cent), mines (9 per cent), and metallurgical works (5 per cent). Many coastal sea areas are seriously contaminated by organic and biogenic substances, particularly pesticides. Seventy per cent of Golden Horn Bay is covered by patches of oil. The most contaminated body of water in Primorye is the Peter the Great Bay, with river run-off in the area carrying transit waste water and a large volume of sewage from Vladivostok and Nakhodka.[8]

Efforts to protect the environment are focused on water pollution control, which is receiving as much as 90 per cent of Primorye's budget for environmental protection. Air quality protection receives a scant 7 per cent of the krai's anti-pollution budget.

The bad environmental situation is continuing throughout the Russian Far East. During the first half of 1994, twenty cases of accidental release of pollutants into water resources were reported in Primorye, with damages totalling 67.1 million rubles. There were eight reported cases of illegal industrial discharges at land sites in Primorskii Krai, with an estimated 17.4 million rubles in damages. There were 121 enterprises which exceeded maximum permissible levels for waste discharged into water reservoirs and sixty enterprises similarly polluted land areas. The total penalties for these violations were 188.2 million rubles. There were 188 persons who were called to administrative responsibilities and fined 13.5 million rubles and five individuals were called to criminal responsibilities.[9]

In combination with the poor food situation, vitamin deficiencies, and the high rate of female labor, the deteriorating natural environment of the Russian Far East is taking a heavy toll on people's health. For example, 16 out of every 1,000 residents in Primorye suffer from endocrine illnesses and nutritional and metabolic disorders, and 370 and 60 persons experience respiratory and digestive diseases, respectively. The death rate in Primorye increased by 8.4 per cent from 1991 to 1992.[10] According to specialists from the Mechnikov Medical Society based in the Institute of Epidemiology and Microbiology of the Siberian branch of the Russian Academy of Sciences, over the last twenty years there has been a 40 per cent increase in the mortality rate from cancer in Primorye. The specialists' surveys indicate a direct link between the increased incidence of cancer and the state of the environment in the region. The alarm has been sounded about the state of health of the residents in the areas where open-cast enriched ore mining is conducted and in the city of Bolshoi Kamen where a nuclear-powered submarine repair dock is located.[11] According to D. Fefelof of Yakovlevskii *raion* of Primorye, the poor quality of drinking water in his region is the result of a money shortage for repair work on water systems and activities of military plants. In 1993, over 3,000 cases of infectious diseases were reported in the area.[12]

A 1992 study of the environmental condition of Magadan indicates alarming levels of pollution and serious health consequences.[13] The level of atmospheric pollution in the oblast is quite high, the largest polluter being thermal power stations (35 per cent of the total air pollution), followed by motor transport (33.5 per cent), city industrial plants (20.5 per cent), heating stations (10 per cent), and other sources (1 per cent). In 1990, 661 sources of air pollution were counted, including 21,000 units of transport vehicles, many unpaved roads, machine building plants, construction plants, construction materials and cement producers, and ore plants. Only ninety-eight of these sources, or 14.8 per cent, were equipped with dust traps, of which only half were working properly. High levels of dust, sulfur dioxide, carbon oxides, nitrogen dioxide, and benzopyrene are found in the atmosphere. Air pollution has resulted in high incidents of deaths from respiratory and blood diseases and allergies.[14] Garbage collection and recycling are poorly done. The Kamenuschka River, an important reservoir in Magadan, is contaminated by chromium, organic substances, and bacteria. Many cases of infection and gastric diseases have been reported.[15] The quality of water in the Gertner Bay and the Nagaeva Bay is bad, with high concentrations of oil products, phenol, and ammonium nitrogen found in these bodies of water, which are used for recreational and fishing purposes.[16]

An outbreak of trichinosis and salmonella has also been reported in Primorye and in Amursk, respectively. The growing human consumption of wild animal meat, especially in taiga areas, has been blamed for the trichinosis outbreak and contaminated food is the suspected cause of the outbreak of salmonella.[17]

NUCLEAR ENVIRONMENTAL HAZARDS

As if these environmental problems are not enough, the Russian Far East is facing another potential environmental disaster, the dumping of nuclear waste in the Sea of Japan (known in Korea as the East Sea). In 1993, it was revealed that between 1959 and 1991, the Soviet Union dumped nuclear waste from old battleships into the Arctic, more precisely at five points in the

Barents Sea and at eight points in the Kara Sea. The dumping included seven nuclear reactors containing radioactive material. The Russian government also admitted that the former Soviet Union had dumped nuclear waste, including two nuclear reactors, into the Sea of Japan. The announcement came as a shock to the Japanese and Koreans, especially to those involved in fishing. It was also acknowledged that the Russian navy resumed dumping of nuclear waste in the Sea of Japan in 1992.

The Russian government asserted that the nuclear dumping of low-level radioactive waste did not violate the 1973 London Convention banning the dumping of high-level radioactive material in the sea.[18] Moscow repeatedly stated that the dumping did not pose any threat to people's health, and the report prepared by a special commission appointed by the Russian president to investigate the ecological effects agreed.[19] Japan's Science and Technology Agency also stated there were no apparent effects on Japanese territories. However, the general public in Japan and elsewhere protested against the continuing dumping of nuclear waste by the Russian government. Greenpeace obtained and made public in April 1993 a Russian government report which indicated the former Soviet Union had designated ten dumping sites at sea and that after the collapse of the Soviet Union, the Russian navy continued to dump small amounts of radioactive waste into the ocean. The report concluded that the Russian navy would continue this potentially hazardous practice until ground disposal facilities were built in 1997.

In April 1993, the Japanese government decided to conduct a study on the environmental effects of the nuclear dumping in the Sea of Japan and asked for Russian cooperation. This preliminary study determined in August that the current level of nuclear waste dumping by the Russian navy did not affect human health. International concerns did not go away, however. At the 5 June 1993 'sherpas' meeting' in preparation for the G7 Summit later that year, it was agreed that the G7 members would cooperate in the study of environmental effects of Russia's nuclear waste dumping into the ocean and to prepare a new plan to assist Russia in developing alternative ways of disposing of nuclear waste.

On 17 October 1993, four days after President Boris Yeltsin had paid an official visit to Tokyo to promote bilateral cooperation, Greenpeace reported that the Russian navy resumed nuclear waste dumping in the Sea of Japan. Many Japanese were stunned by the announcement and the Japanese government protested. The US government demanded that Russia stop nuclear waste dumping into the ocean and questioned whether the Russian navy was keeping the standards required under the London Convention. On 21 October, Prime Minister Chernomyrdin stated that Russia would not conduct nuclear waste dumping in the near future. The statement was reiterated by the Minister of Atomic Energy. Ten days later, however, the Commander of the Pacific Fleet of the Russian navy said that dumping in the Sea of Japan would take place again soon because the ground storage facilities were filled to capacity. Local opposition to the nuclear waste dumping was also registered, with Primorye Governor Nazdratenko openly criticizing the navy's action.[20] Conflicting statements continued into 1994, with the Russian government announcing in May that it would dump into the sea in three months' time radioactive waste that had been stored on tankers in the Vladivostok port.[21]

One of the byproducts of the controversy was that at the November 1993 meeting of the London Convention members a resolution was adopted banning the dumping of low-level radioactive waste for twenty-five years. Of the forty-two countries participating in the vote, the United States, Japan, Canada, and thirty-four other countries voted in favor of the resolution, but Russia, Britain, France, China, and Belgium abstained.[22]

Another consequence of the controversy over the dumping of nuclear waste in the ocean was the agreement between Russia, Japan, South Korea, the United States, and the International Atomic Energy Agency (IAEA) to cooperate in the study of the environmental impact on the Sea of Japan. After several postponements, the study was conducted in March–April 1994. It found no particular abnormalities in seawater and seabed samples collected at seven spots southeast of Vladivostok.[23] Japan and Russia also agreed in June 1994 to cooperate in the building of a disposal plant for liquid nuclear waste near Vladivostok. Japan's contribution to the project will come out of the $70 million Japanese grant for the dismantling of Russian nuclear weapons and nuclear waste disposal. The facility, to be built through international bidding, would filter radioactive substances from the liquid waste. In the coming years Russia will dismantle some sixty nuclear submarines. Several storage ships, including a 2,000-ton tanker fully loaded with nuclear waste, are currently moored off Vladivostok, but the vessels are worn out and could pose a serious environmental threat.[24]

Another nuclear development in the Russian Far East that is raising international concern is the proposed construction of nuclear plants in the region. The economic crisis in Russia has led to the breakdown of old energy supply networks and has therefore increased the need for reliable energy sources. Under these circumstances, in January 1993, the Russian government announced it would begin construction of three nuclear power plants, ending the moratorium imposed after the Chernobyl disaster in 1986. The new reactors were scheduled to be constructed by 1995 at the cost of $58 million. Feasibility studies were also planned to study the possibility of building up to twenty-three additional reactors. The Russian Far East is seen as a prime location for some of these nuclear reactors.[25] The heads of administration of seven *raions* of Khabarovsk and Primorye have asked the government to begin work on a feasibility study for building small atomic power stations in remote villages in their areas.[26] Serious consideration is also being given to the possibility of using nuclear reactors from submarines to supply electricity to Primorye.[27] Some are also entertaining the possibility of a joint Russian–Japanese construction of underground nuclear power plants in the area of Komsomolsk-na-Amure.[28]

Leading industrialized nations have set up a fund, through the European Bank for Reconstruction and Development, to improve safety standards in nuclear plants throughout Russia and eastern Europe. France and Germany pledged $110 million to this fund.[29] Japan is expected to provide the fund with approximately $5–$10 million.[30] In a related development, the Russian government proposed that Japan annually purchase $100 million worth of uranium left over from the dismantling of nuclear weapons in Russia, but the Japanese government has rejected the request saying that Japan already has an adequate supply for ten years.[31]

These developments point to four urgent needs. First, alternative ways of disposing of nuclear waste must be developed and additional ground storage facilities must be built. This problem boils down to finance. Since transportation of solid radioactive waste on the trans-Siberian railroad is prohibited, it is necessary to build additional storage facilities in Primorye, but the regional government does not have the funds to make this possible.[32] Second, nuclear safety will continue to be a serious problem so long as the political instability in Russia continues. Third, Russia must adopt effective measures to ease the problem of energy shortage in the Russian Far East. Fourth, international cooperation is urgently needed in the energy, technology, financial, and research fields.

ENVIRONMENTAL POLICY DEVELOPMENT

The above description of the environmental situation in the Russian Far East makes it amply clear that the region faces an enormous challenge. The region must strengthen its foundations of economic development but it must do so with a view to protecting the natural environment and human health against the detrimental effects of development. The Russian Far East must meet this challenge on all fronts. It must improve the quality of air, the quality of surface waters, including reservoirs, rivers, lakes, coastal waters, and of course the quality of drinking water.

The challenge is not unique to this region. Indeed, it is facing the entire country. Before the collapse of the Soviet Union, Soviet authorities created a new environmental agency, the State Committee on Environmental Protection (or Goskompriroda), but the Soviet system of central economic planning was inherently predisposed toward industrial growth, to the neglect of environmental protection. Moreover, increasing economic difficulties meant that in practice, the government paid little attention to environmental problems, making virtually no funds available for action.[33]

The Russian Federation has only recently established a basic legal framework for the protection of its environment and natural resources. The Law on the Protection of the Environment, adopted on 19 December 1991, establishes the importance and general principles of environmental protection, giving the Russian Federation Supreme Soviet first priority in determining environmental programs and passing further legislation.[34] The

Russian government is accorded primary responsibility for implementing such programs, and specially designated government agencies have the power to implement specific portions of such programs, such as environmental controls. The law requires regional and local authorities to consult and coordinate with federal authorities and to manage and protect resources under their control.[35]

The legislation establishes certain rights of private citizens and social organizations, such as rights to protest ecological harms, obtain environmental information from official bodies, initiate administrative or judicial proceedings concerning environmental harms, and bring claims for damages against polluters.[36] The law introduces broad regulation of activities affecting the environment, requiring industrial users of natural resources *inter alia* to enter into a use agreement with regional or local authorities and receive a special license. Funds for repair of environmental damage and other activities under the law are to come from an 'Ecological Fund,' to be financed, in part, by fines and damage payments from polluters.[37] The law provides a detailed list of the categories of environmental standards to be promulgated by federal authorities, in areas ranging from radiation to noise pollution.[38] It requires compliance with environmental norms in the construction, expansion, and operation of industrial, transportation, energy, and other facilities.[39] 'Ecological disaster areas' or 'extraordinary ecological situations' can be declared by federal authorities.[40] The law empowers designated authorities to declare various types of nature reserves and privileged areas, including national nature parks and natural monuments, in which environmentally impacting activities are strictly limited.[41]

One of the weakest areas of the law has to do with the role of governmental agencies in monitoring and enforcing compliance with the environmental laws.[42] It provides only a very general provision, merely referring to a number of federal and regional authorities who are to be involved in 'ecological control.' Dispute resolution procedures are provided.[43] Perhaps the most important section of the law deals with liability for ecological harm. It imposes several categories of liability for violations of environmental laws and regulations. It makes individual managers and workers, as well as enterprises, responsible for their actions which are harmful to the environment. For example, enterprise managers and employees may be disciplined for environmental offenses they commit in the course of performing their official duties. 'Administrative responsibility' and associated fines may also be imposed for a variety of environmental offenses, including failure to observe environmental norms and regulations. Criminal liability for environmental harms is also introduced but it is not very specific.[44] The law requires parties causing environmental harm to make full reimbursement for the damage, including the actual costs of restoring the damaged areas, as well as for lost profits and other resulting losses. It also requires such parties to pay compensation for damages done to the environment, human health, or property. Victims, their families, the state prosecutor, and environmental organizations are permitted to bring law suits seeking compensation, as are enterprises and individuals who wish to seek outright termination of a broad range of environmentally hazardous activities.[45]

Although the 1991 law is a landmark legislation, the Russian government has been slow to adopt follow-up and implementing legislation and its effectiveness has yet to be demonstrated. Moreover, the respective roles of federal, regional, and local authorities in establishing the norms, emission and dumping limits, and other environmental standards remain unclear.[46]

Under these circumstances, it is quite understandable that the development of environmental policy at the regional level is still in its early stages and its impact is quite limited. There is no comprehensive environmental policy as such in the territory or in the Russian Federation as a whole. There are only fragments of environmental measures. Development of environmental plans and programs in the region has generally followed progress at the national level. For example, only in 1993 did Primorye adopt a Long-term Program of Nature Preservation and Rational Utilization of Natural Resources up to 2005. On 3 August 1993, the Russian government issued a special decision (no. 532), 'On the Improvement of Efficiency in the Country's Economic Usage of Information and Data about Environmental Pollution.' The decision requires regional environment protection committees to appraise the efficiency of environmental measures of industrial enterprises.[47] In response, Primorskgidromet has begun developing plans for the use of ecological information by industrial enterprises.

Recognizing the importance of natural resource development to the region's economy and its ecological impact, the region must develop a long-term economic plan which balances its developmental needs and environmental requirements. Such a plan must include effective resource conservation and management regimes, including resource restoration programs. Above all else, rational resource development plans and restoration programs must be effectively and consistently implemented. This is particularly critical in the forestry and fishery industries, where developmental interests and short-term financial gains provide more powerful incentives than conservation requirements. Allocation and enforcement authority must be clearly delineated so as to avoid jurisdictional disputes and the resulting failure to carry out resource conservation programs. Not only must the regional and local authorities be financially equipped to carry out these programs, plans must be developed in an open, democratic fashion, with input from all affected parties, including minority populations.

The institutional and legislative foundations of environmental policy are in early stages of development, and the financial, material, scientific, and technological services and agencies of nature conservation are similarly in formative phases. Nevertheless, the various decisions on environmental protection which have been made in the past are of significance. They specify restrictions on the location of production activities and their operation. They are focused on the preservation of ecological balance and restoration of ecosystems, the protection of the environment and the prevention of air, water, and soil pollution, and the rational exploitation and utilization of natural resources.[48] Preferential government credits and tax incentives are provided to encourage enterprises to take nature conservation measures. Laws exist for the protection of various types of resources, including water, air, and forestry. There are state plans for rational utilization of natural resources and environmental protection. The Ministry of Ecology and Natural Resources is responsible for the adoption of environmental codes, regulations, rules, and standards regarding natural resources utilization, environmental protection, and ecological review of economic projects. A number of nature conservation laws and governmental decisions also exist, including laws on mineral resources, on environmental protection, on the protection of natural resources of territorial waters, continental shelf and economic zone, and on the payments and penalties for environmental contamination.[49]

Following progress at the national level, environmental measures are being developed at the regional level as well. For example, in Primorskii Krai, any design project must contain an environmental section and will be evaluated from the standpoint of environmental safety. A project proposal is reviewed by the special-purpose office of the Ministry of Ecology and Natural Resources in Vladivostok. The limits on atmospheric emission and sewage in the surface reservoirs are calculated in terms of maximum allowable limit of emissions (MALE) and maximum allowable limit of sewage (MALS).[50] For enterprises with outdated equipment and processes, however, temporary MALE or MALS is specified until their emissions or sewage are reduced to prescribed levels. Maximum allowable concentrations (MAC) of atmospheric pollutants are used as normative indicators of environmental quality. Included in the air pollution control system are sulfur dioxide, carbon monoxide, nitrogen dioxide, nitric oxide, hydrogen fluoride, and lead and its compounds. Surface water pollution control targets petrochemicals, phenols, synthetic substances, copper, cadmium, and hydrogen ion exponent.[51] Payments are collected for environmental pollution in Primorye, with the amounts credited to the account of the Primorskii Krai Committee of Nature Conservation. The payments are made from the income or other funds of enterprises. Vehicular pollution of the atmosphere is also subject to payments, with the rate of payments depending on the type of fuel, i.e., diesel fuel, leaded gasoline, and unleaded gasoline.[52]

The Far Eastern region must improve its ability to control pollutants at the source. This includes the improvement of equipment to treat and control atmospheric, water, and soil pollutants. Urgently required is the improvement of sewage treatment and discharge facilities, water treatment facilities, and household waste collection and recycling. With the increasing number of automobiles in the region, anti-smog devices must also be installed and properly maintained. Equally important is improved monitoring of radioactive releases into the environment from storage facilities and disposal sites of radioactive waste, as well as the construction of additional storage facilities.

International cooperation is urgently required to arrest the environmental deterioration in the region. However, international cooperation in this field is still very limited and in its early stages. Most notable in this area is the January 1994 agreement between Japan and Russia to cooperate on seventeen environmental conservation projects such as joint studies on acid rain and air pollution. The announcement came at the conclusion of a Japan–Russia joint committee meeting on environmental conservation in Tokyo. This was the first meeting to be held on the basis of the 1991 accord on environmental conservation concluded during the historic summit between Soviet President Mikhail Gorbachev and Japanese Prime Minister Toshiki Kaifu. The joint projects conducted in 1994 and 1995 included joint studies on acid rain, the water quality in Lake Baikal, the environment of the Sea of Japan, and observation of the greenhouse effect in Siberia. The program also included joint observation of methane gas from permafrost regions and exchange of information to prevent air pollution in both countries.[53]

There are some private-level initiatives to develop international cooperation in environmental protection and resource conservation and management. A good example is the cooperation among non-profit organizations from Russia, the United States, and Japan to conduct research on pollution and environmental protection of Lake Baikal. The United States and Japanese participants in the project are contributing equipment and training local members in how to use it. The local Russian participants are monitoring the water quality on a continuing basis and data analysis is being done by all participating groups. They will jointly develop a clean-up plan as well. Information is being shared with the local residents.[54]

CONCLUSIONS

Environmental consciousness is growing in the Russian Far East, but the region's resources and organizational capacity in this area are woefully inadequate. Under these circumstances, international cooperation is not only desirable but essential. Unfortunately, among the current international partners, developmental interests overshadow concerns for environmental protection and resource conservation. Nor is there a strong, sustained commitment of the Russian and Far Eastern governments to environmental protection and resource conservation.

Generally favorable attitudes exist in the region toward international economic and environmental cooperation, particularly among the better educated and the more internationally experienced segments of the population, with the greatest support coming from regional and local administrators. However, there is significant reluctance among those who are supported by state institutions. It should be remembered that cooperative arrangements may not necessarily generate tangible benefits that can be readily and equitably shared between parties with disparate resources and capabilities.

In developing environmental and resource conservation regimes that balance the developmental needs and environmental requirements of the Russian Far East, the Russian government and the regional administrations should adopt 'sustainable development' as the essential goal of the region. In this connection, the recent discussion among the environmental ministers of APEC member countries is particularly instructive.

In March 1994, the environmental ministers of APEC member countries issued an 'APEC Environmental Vision Statement.' The statement included a 'Framework of Principles for Integrating Economy and Environment in APEC'.[55] While discussion of the principles in this framework is beyond the scope of this chapter, let me conclude by offering some ideas, consistent with those principles, which may be considered in developing environmental and resource conservation regimes in the Russian Far East.[56]

First, any foreign participation in industrial or resource development projects should be conditional on the preparation of an environmental impact assessment and a plan for pollution abatement. If Russian parties to international joint ventures lack financial resources or technical capabilities to meet such requirements, the foreign participants should be required to contribute their own resources. Such contributions should be taken into consideration when determining the tax rates, the terms of capital and profit repatriation, and other conditions affecting the joint enterprises in question.[57]

Second, foreign parties planning to engage in industrial or resource development projects should be required to establish their environmental credibility by documenting satisfactory environmental performance in their home countries. If the environmental standards they maintain at home are more stringent than those required of Russian enterprises by local law, then the foreign enterprises should be encouraged to apply the more stringent standards. If the cost of maintaining higher than local standards is prohibitively high, the Russian, regional, and local authorities should provide additional incentives, such as lower taxes, lower rents, higher rates of capital and profit repatriation, etc.[58]

Third, private Russian and foreign lending institutions which provide loans, credits, and other support for environmentally sound developmental projects should receive favorable guarantees and other protection from their respective governments.[59]

Fourth, any foreign enterprise which plans to export or import natural resources from the Russian Far East, either in raw or semi-processed form, should obtain from the regional and local authorities a certificate of environmental worthiness for its resource development operation in the region, as should its local business partners.

Until Russia becomes a member of APEC, international cooperation should be undertaken at the non-governmental level to facilitate Russia's eventual adoption of rules and principles that are consistent with those that will inform and direct the future sustainable development efforts in the APEC countries.[60] Eventually, APEC-consistency may be made a requirement for Russia's membership in the forum.

NOTES

1 An earlier version of this paper was presented at the workshop on 'Trade and Environment in Asia–Pacific: Prospects for Regional Cooperation,' 23–5 September 1994, Honolulu, organized by the Nautilus Institute for Security and Sustainable Development, co-sponsored by the East–West Center, Honolulu and the Monterey Institute of International Studies.
2 *RA Report*, no. 17, July 1994, p. 18.
3 *Utro Rossii*, 9 August 1994, p. 3.
4 *Vladivostok*, 23 August 1994, p. 4.
5 Evgeny E. Jarikov, 'The Current Situation of Environmental Protection in Primorsky Territory,' in *Primorsky Territory: Its Political, Social, and Economic Situation and Environmental Protection*, Vladivostok: Center for Pacific Economic Development and Cooperation; and Monterey, California: Center for East Asian Studies, Monterey Institute of International Studies, 1993, p. 19. The Center for Pacific Economic Development and Cooperation prepared this report for the Center for East Asian Studies.
6 *Ibid.*
7 *Novosti*, 17 August 1994, pp. 1-2.
8 Jarikov, *op. cit.*, pp. 17–18.
9 *Krasnoe znamya*, 27 July 1994, p. 2.
10 Reported by Itar-Tass; cited in *Vladivostok*, 24 June 1994, p. 2.
11 *RA Report*, no. 17, July 1994, p. 167.
12 *Utro Rossii*, 23 July 1994, p.3.
13 A.D. Chernukha, *Medico-ecological and Social Health Factors of Town Population in the Northeast of Russia*, Magadan: The Publishing House, Health Center, 1992.
14 *Ibid.*, p. 24.
15 Chernukha, *op. cit.*, p. 45.
16 *Ibid.*, p. 47.
17 *RA Report*, no. 17, July 1994, p. 166.
18 The United States, France, the United Kingdom, and Japan had dumped low-level radioactive waste in the sea for many years. These countries had opposed a proposal by Denmark to ban all dumping of nuclear materials in the sea. In 1985, however, the advanced western countries, including Japan, decided to temporarily suspend the dumping of nuclear waste into the ocean.
19 'Facts and Problems Related to Radioactive Waste Disposal in Seas Adjacent to the Territory of the Russian Federation (Materials for a Report by the Government Commission on Matters Related to Radioactive Waste Disposal at Sea, Created by Decree No. 613 of the Russian Federation President, 24 October 1992),' Office of the President of the Russian Federation, Moscow, 1993. Translated by Paul Gallager and Elena Bloomstein, Albuquerque, New Mexico.
20 *Hokkaido Shimbun*, 3 November 1994, p. 4.
21 Kyodo, 20 May 1994; cited in *RA Report*, no. 17, July 1994, p. 164.
22 *Hokkaido Shimbun*, 13 November 1994, p. 1.
23 *Japan Times*, 17 April 1994, p. 2.
24 Kyodo, 23 June 1994, *Japan Times*, 17 May 1994, p. 1; cited in *RA Report*, no. 17, July 1994, p. 165.

25 *Christian Science Monitor*, 2 February 1993, p. 7.
26 *Finansovye izvestiya*, 13–19 January 1994, p. 1; cited in *RA Report*, no. 17, July 1994, p. 113.
27 Itar-Tass, 15 February 1994; cited in *RA Report*, no. 17, July 1994, p. 113.
28 Tass, 8 April 1994; cited in *RA Report*, no. 17, July 1994, p. 114.
29 *Christian Science Monitor*, 2 February 1993, p. 7.
30 *Hokkaido Shimbun*, 1 March 1993, p. 1. Earlier, in July 1992, Japan had agreed to come up with a $25 million grant to address the nuclear safety concerns of the former Soviet Union and eastern Europe.
31 *Hokkaido Shimbun*, 26 October 1993, p. 3.
32 A statement by Evgeniy Stomatuk, Chairman of the Committee on Natural Resources of Primorskii Krai Administration; cited in *Krasnoe znamya*, 28 June 1994, p. 1.
33 Brian L. Zimbler, 'Legal Remedies Address a Catastrophic Situation: The Russian Law on Protection of the Environment,' *CIS Environmental Watch*, no. 3, Fall 1992, p. 41. This article provides a summary description of the 1991 Russian Federation legislation.
34 Part I of the Law. The following summary of this law draws from Zimbler.
35 Part I.
36 Part II.
37 Part III.
38 Part IV.
39 Parts VI and VII.
40 Part VIII.
41 Part IX.
42 Part X.
43 Part XII.
44 Part XIII.
45 Part XIV.
46 This problem is pointed out by Zimbler in his discussion of Resolution No. 545, 'On Approving the Procedure for Drawing Up and Approving Ecological Norms for the Emission and Discharge of Pollutants into the Environment and the Limits for the Use of Natural Resources and for Dumping Waste,' adopted by the Russian government on 3 August 1992 (Zimbler, p. 45).
47 *Krasnoe znamya*, 17 August 1994, p. 3.
48 Jarikov, *op. cit.*, p. 24.
49 *Ibid.*
50 MALE is the level of harmful substances in the lower air layer which does not exceed the prescribed levels and MALS is the maximum allowable mass of substances in discharged sewage, with the proviso that the water quality in the control point is ensured. Jarikov, *op. cit.*, pp. 24–5.
51 Jarikov, *op. cit.*, p. 26, Table 6.
52 Jarikov, *op. cit.*, p. 25.
53 *Japan Times*, 29 January 1994, p. 3.
54 *Asahi Shimbun*, 19 July 1992, p. 26.
55 Adopted by APEC ministers responsible for the environment, Vancouver, Canada, 25 March 1994.
56 It should also be noted that the ideas offered below are consistent with the recommendations of APEC's Eminent Persons Group. In August 1994, the group issued a second report calling, *inter alia*, for (1) the sharing of environmental technologies between the environmentally more advanced and less advanced members of APEC, (2) consideration of joint funding of environmentally sound development projects, with more advanced members contributing to the costs of pollution control in less advanced parts of the region, (3) promotion of international acceptance of

the principle of internalizing environmental costs, and (4) the gradual convergence of environmental standards among APEC members. ('Achieving the APEC Vision: Free and Open Trade in the Asia Pacific,' Second Report of the Eminent Persons Group, August 1994, pp. 27–9.)

57 These ideas are consistent with the principles of 'internalization of costs,' 'technology transfer,' and 'financing for sustainable development' of the APEC environmental framework.

58 This recommendation is consistent with the 'technology transfer' and 'financing for sustainable development' principles of the APEC environmental framework.

59 *Ibid.*

60 This is consistent both with the spirit of 'open regionalism' which is guiding the APEC process and with the principle of 'environmental education and information' in the APEC environmental framework.

Part III

Russia, the Russian Far East and the Asia–Pacific neighbors

8 Russia and the United States in Northeast Asia and the Russian Far East

Economics or defense?

Vladimir I. Ivanov

INTRODUCTION

In a geopolitical sense, the Russian Federation has emerged from the wreckage of the former Soviet Union a less European and more Asian country. In scaling down its role as a center of global power, the nation is directing more attention to the regions and countries close to its borders. Northeast Asia holds a promise of long lasting economic dynamism and expanding markets. With the end of communism and bipolar confrontation, how close will Russia's and the Russian Far East's relations with this region be?

Although it is true that ongoing changes in the national and regional political economy are affecting the Russian Far East's economic relations with neighboring countries, a more powerful factor could be the reorganization of political relations in the region, focusing on Russia. The main assumption of this chapter is that a search for solutions in the broader context of US–Russia relations could more effectively help the Russian Far East to overcome its legacy as a hostage to regional and global confrontation. Another assumption based on the experience of the last two years [see p. xxi] is that a new economy in the Russian Far East is emerging, relying predominantly on modest domestic resources.

THE PROBLEM

Northeast Asia is important for Russia in terms of its security and economic interests. The notion of security, however, has expanded considerably. Russia must deal with three world leading economic and military powers. It shares a 2,800 mile-long border with communist China which has a net population growth of close to 16 million people a year. Additionally, the divided Korea is nextdoor to Vladivostok. In addition to reliable defense and efficient diplomacy, the security of Russia depends on its international competitiveness and the dynamics of domestic politics, immigration, and environment, as well as on advances in modern technologies and education. In many of these areas Russia can benefit from cooperation with other countries.

Russia's access to Asia–Pacific markets depends on efforts by the Russian government to support the emerging private sector, ensure preferential economic status for the Russian Far East, and promote the dismantlement of the Cold War barriers to business cooperation in the region. Cooperation with the United States is the key factor. Although it is quite misleading to reduce the prospects of the emerging Russia–US cooperation to narrow geographical limits, the policy of denial of normal contacts between the United States and the Russian Far East was among the limiting factors in the past. Now, when the choice is made between 'guns and growth,'[1] trans-Pacific cooperation with the United States is desirable and possible on the basis of common values and mutual interests.[2] The problem is that this set of interests has not been formulated. Moreover, on the US side, there is little appreciation of the fact that the Asia–Pacific region already competes with OECD economies of Europe for Russian customers and that by the year 2000, it may attract as much as 35–40 per cent of Russian trade.

Russian industries penetrate the Northeast Asian markets with a broad range of goods and commodities, from timber and scrap metal to sophisticated helicopters and advanced technologies. The Russian Far East, with its mineral and energy resources and marine and forest treasures, is now open for international commerce. Its sea ports and transcontinental transport links serve western Russia and other CIS economies. The combination of the short distances to Northeast Asian markets, the resources of the Russian Far East and Siberia, and the industrial and technological base of the nation creates a promise of a synergistic economic effect that could contribute to the transformation of the region and to economic growth in Russia. However, an open and systematic businesslike relationship with Washington is a distant goal in Northeast Asia, quite possibly a mirage. This must not be taken as a complaint. With the gaps and complexities in the US foreign policy decision-making process, the conceptual mismatches in the area of Northeast Asia, of which the Russian Far East is considered a part, do not come as a surprise. Relations with Russia in the Northeast Asian context could, among other things, be a zone of diplomatic discomfort for the United States. For decades Washington constrained Tokyo in the development of closer relations with Moscow; now, possibly, the roles have changed. The nature of the US–Japan alliance and the Russian–Japanese territorial dispute impede Russia's relations with both superpowers as well as the entire region.

There are of course other problems, including Russian strategic and conventional forces in the North Pacific. Russian strategic nuclear submarines (SSBNs), for example, cannot be easily removed from the list of threats by Washington. According to Tokyo-based defense analysts, even the START 2 treaty offers no relief to Japan; the more Russians concentrate on the protection of fewer submarines, the more threatening Russia's force posture could be for Japan. It is quite possible that from the US–Japan joint security perspective, Russia's reestablished position on the Pacific may increase the risk that Moscow may use the Russian Far East for 'projecting its military power in the region.'

The good news, however, is that the period of direct and irreconcilable conflict between the United States and Russia in the region is over. Russia's national interests are not different from those of other regional states: the security of Russian territory and its defense assets; protection of Russian borders, resources, and the exclusive economic zone; regional stability and democratization; freedom of the sea; access to regional markets; domestic peace; and the smooth functioning of the federation. If such a juxtaposition persists, normal interaction with the United States in Northeast Asia may develop gradually without any grand design. However, there are areas where the interests of Moscow and Washington will continue to overlap with friction. A brief review of recent developments illustrates the existing difficulties as well as the prospects for close cooperation with the United States in the North Pacific.

A FLUID CONCEPTUAL FRAMEWORK

Almost a decade has passed since Moscow began the process of re-evaluating its policy in East Asia. The recent revival of patriotism,[3] predicted by the Russian foreign minister in an almost joking manner in his speech at the Conference on Security and Cooperation in Europe in Stockholm on 14 December 1992,[4] shows the current complexities of this process. None the less, Russia's most important objective in general and in the Asia–Pacific region in particular is to enhance its international economic competitiveness, to develop access to markets, and to participate in regional economic groupings.[5]

Washington has the power to ignore these interests and, in comparison with the approach of the previous administration, the Clinton government does. Early in the 1990s, under the Republican administration, the former Soviet Union received some recognition in the context of the 'emerging architecture' of East Asia and the Pacific.[6] It was described as a power similar to the United States, with interests in Asia as well as in Europe.[7] Ironically, the reluctance to treat Russia as a regional power in the Pacific became more visible after the dissolution of the USSR. In early 1993, Lonnie S. Keene of the US Department of State Policy Planning staff, while describing the United States' security and political posture in Asia, did not even mention the Russian Federation.[8] Assistant Secretary of State Winston Lord, in his confirmation hearings, followed exactly the same line in describing Asia. He barely mentioned Russia in the context of a 'global partnership' with Japan, pointed to the Russia–Japan territorial dispute, and to the chance to 'engage Russia, China, and others inside and outside Northeast Asia' in the area of security.[9] The US General Accounting Office in its December 1993 report on the Asia–Pacific region does not seem to identify Russia in the regional context either. But it points to the opportunity for the United States, China, Japan, and Russia to forge multilateral cooperation in preventing arms races, competing alignments, and efforts by one power or group of powers to dominate the region.[10]

At the same time, Russia, as part of Northeast Asia, became conspicuously absent from conceptual and academic deliberations. The report *America's Role in Asia*, produced by the Asia Foundation, as well as the relevant sections of the Heritage Foundation's publication on US foreign and defense policy,[11] and other sources do not mention Russia or the Russian Far East as a part of Northeast Asia. The 1993 White House report *National Security Strategy of the United States* states: 'More than anything else our encouragement of private trade and investment will help these [CIS and East European] countries integrate themselves into the free market economic system'; closer political relationships between the two countries are expected to be the result of a 'wide variety of exchange programs and other initiatives.'[12] However, in the chapter 'How We Can Influence The Future. Regionally . . .,' in the section where the US agenda for Asia is formulated, there is no mention of Russia.[13] The Presidential Report to Congress, 'A Strategic Framework for the Asian Pacific Rim,' does not name Russia in the section 'Sources of East Asian and Pacific Regional Instability,' but indicates that:

> the residual power projection capability of Russian naval and air forces – stationed close to our Northeast Asian allies – in Siberia and Russian Northeast Asia remains a major concern. In addition, Russia retains a formidable nuclear arsenal which must still be factored in our strategic calculus.[14]

Former Secretary of Defense Dick Cheney in his report 'Defense Strategy for the 1990s: The Regional Defense Strategy' does not mention Russia, only 'the Soviet annexation of the Northern Territories of Japan,'[15] and Admiral Charles Larson, former Commander-in-Chief of the US Pacific Command, put the Russian Far East in one line with North Korea as a source of instability.[16] Russia was not even mentioned in President Clinton's address in Seattle during the Asia Pacific Economic Cooperation (APEC) summit meeting.

The point of this is that even with improved relations with Washington, Russia remains in relative isolation in the region, although the rapid expansion of trade across the Chinese border and strong Korean interests make its discriminatory exclusion more difficult.[17] It is not surprising that Russia does not fit US criteria for being an important regional entity, because too little time separates these two former adversaries in the region where their interests once collided. To some degree, Moscow has to blame its foreign policy for this state of affairs. At the 1993 Clinton–Yeltsin Vancouver Summit, the only issues in the Joint Statement relevant to the prospects for Russia–US interaction in the North Pacific were the Sea of Okhotsk fishery, living marine resources, and ecosystems.[18] Not surprisingly, for American politicians and the public, the status of Russia in the Pacific remains one of irrelevance.

The APEC process is among the symbols of positive developments in the region. The concept of regional economic cooperation may be an attractive blueprint of a future regional order based on regional needs, private sector activities, and the interests of the local elites, not only on the policies of central bureaucracies.[19] Russia, however, does not belong to this grouping despite the fact that Northeast Asia is quite important for Russia in terms of trade with Japan, Korea, Taiwan, and China. The Clinton administration's inability or hesitation to clarify its position on Russian membership in APEC probably illustrates the current conceptual stalemate and conflict of interests in America's Asian policy. The cost of supporting and promoting Russia's membership in the APEC forum could be relatively high, and in terms of trade and economic connections, Russia is not important for the United States at present and is unlikely to be so in the future. Under these circumstances, it is unlikely that Washington will press ahead with the creation of an economic and diplomatic environment to encourage Russian interaction with the region. Moreover, defense contracts signed by Russian arms exporters in the region, including increased competition in arms sales to ASEAN countries, e.g., Malaysia, can be interpreted as affecting the interests of the United States as well as 'undesirable' arms and technology transfers to China and India. Moreover, broader access to the regional markets for Russian-made military hardware provides additional resources for the survival of the US 'public enemy number one,' the Russian military-industrial complex.

What Russia can contribute to Asia–Pacific cooperation is probably not the main factor in the decision-making process in Washington. Whether to help Russia develop closer relations with Pacific Asia depends more on Washington's general policy and attitudes toward Moscow, and, possibly, Tokyo. In the opinion of Americans, it is quite conceivable that in the context of specific relations with Japan, cooperative attitudes toward Russia on the Pacific can hurt the broader US interests in the region. The stability of the alliance and exclusive bilateral relations with Tokyo are naturally perceived to be far more important for the United States both globally and regionally than experimentation with changes in its relationship with Russia.

Russia's status in the region is changing. It has improved relationships with the countries of the North Pacific that were, for decades, considered adversaries. Despite unresolved problems, dialogue with Japan is constructive and much broader than at any time before. Experience has been gradually accumulated in dealing simultaneously with South and North Korea. Political disengagement from North Korea has removed another obstacle for cooperation with the United States in Asia. Russia is redefining its role in the region and is interested in stability, cooperation, and the opening of markets. Its efforts have been reciprocated through official and non-governmental channels: summit meetings have taken place in Tokyo, Seoul, Beijing, Washington, Vancouver, and Moscow, the Russian foreign minister was invited to participate in the ASEAN Post-Ministerial Conference, and formal contacts have been established in the framework of the Pacific Economic Cooperation Council, the Pacific Basin Economic Council, and the Council for Security and Cooperation in the Asia–Pacific.

RUSSIAN TRADE AND NORTHEAST ASIA

Russia's standing in Northeast Asia depends on its inner strength but the Russian success at home also depends on access to the Asian and other foreign markets. Realistically speaking, this is more important for the future of the Russian economic transformation than membership in APEC. There is, of course, an alternative: Russia can join the activities of APEC working groups. Technically, however, attendance at working groups by Russian experts must be paid for, and without formal membership it is unlikely that the Russian government will be responsive to such initiatives.

Currently, the view in the United States and other countries is that Russia and the Russian Far East have not reached an 'adequate level' of economic ties with the Asia–Pacific region to enter APEC. Indeed, trade is one of the indicators of Russia's changing economic involvement in regional affairs. The fact is that Northeast Asia's economic value to Russia has grown considerably even under conditions of severe foreign exchange crises. This development contributes to a major reorientation of Russian foreign trade. In 1993, two-way foreign trade of the Russian Federation was $70 billion, less than half of its trade in 1990. This amount is less than the annual US foreign trade deficit but is comparable with the trade figures for Indonesia today and China five years ago. The volume of intra-CIS trade has declined dramatically, leading to a decrease in domestic production, as well as economic and social disruptions, but, at the same time, releasing additional resources for export to Asia.[20]

Earlier, in 1989–90, reorientation began when the trade with former CMEA countries collapsed. For Russia, the volume of exports to CMEA markets dropped from $34.8 billion in 1990 to $7.9 billion in 1992, a rapid decline of these countries' share in Russian exports from 43 to 20 per cent. The imports from CMEA states also declined from $34.7 billion (41.9 per cent of the total Russian imports) in 1990 to $5.3 billion (14.5 per cent of imports) in 1992. Russia's government-subsidized economic contacts with Mongolia, North Korea, and Vietnam declined sharply as well. For example, trade with Vietnam in 1993 was only one-tenth of the 1989 volume, and trade with North Korea less than a quarter of the level registered in 1988.

Despite the absolute drop in Russian exports from $71.1 billion in 1990 to $43.0 billion in 1993, the decline of exports to OECD countries was on a smaller scale ($30.2 billion in 1990 and $24.4 billion in 1992). As a result, the OECD share (mostly European countries) of Russian exports increased to 61 per cent as compared to 37.4 per cent for the former Soviet Union. On the import side, the share of OECD goods also rapidly increased, from 31.9 per cent to 61.7 per cent, although in absolute terms there was a considerable decline, from $32.4 billion in 1990 to $22.7 billion in 1992.

Germany remained Russia's leading European trading partner, absorbing $5.8 billion of Russian exports and providing $6.6 billion worth of its imports in 1993. As far as trade with non-European OECD countries was concerned,

Russian exports to Japan in 1993 were $2.1 billion, and $2 billion to the United States. Russia's imports from these two largest world economies were $1.5 billion from each. In recent years, non-payment by Russia has led to major reductions in trade with Japan; it dropped from the $6 billion peak in 1989–90 to $3 billion in 1992–93. It shows some signs of recovery, but it could take several years before Russia can regain its traditional share of Japanese imports at 1.5 per cent. Canada's exports to Russia have dropped by half, and Australian exports have almost dried up.

China, on the other hand, is becoming Russia's leading trading partner with two-way officially registered trade reaching $7.7 billion in 1993. In 1992, China took over Japan's position as Russia's largest trading partner in East Asia. Similar developments are taking place in the PRCs relations with the Russian Far East where China leads in cross-border and barter trade, its value estimated at $2.5 billion in 1993. Many new links have been established among the neighboring areas of Russia and northeastern China. According to an agreement signed in January 1994, there are twenty-one border check points to facilitate this flow of trade and people. A dynamic sector of Russia–China trade is large co-production projects, research, and development links. Russia is involved in many projects in China and has become its fifth largest foreign investor.[21]

Russia has opened a consulate office in Hong Kong and the Hong Kong Trade Development Council will establish an office in Moscow. Agreements have been reached to open semi-official offices in Moscow and Taipei, as well as to develop contacts between St Petersburg, Vladivostok and Taipei. In 1993, Russia's bilateral trade with Taiwan reached $700–900 million, and trade with South Korea exceeded $1.6 billion. As markets for Russian products, these two economies together now are at least as important as Japan.

Although Russia's foreign trade has shrunk and become dramatically reoriented away from formerly heavily subsidized ideological and political allies towards new partners, in absolute terms the bilateral trade with the Asia–Pacific region reached the 1988–89 trading levels of the Soviet Union. Moreover, in relative terms the share of Northeast Asian economies has doubled for Russian exports and imports; the share of the Asia–Pacific region as a whole absorbed approximately one-third of Russian trade. Northeast Asia is emerging as the most promising and second most important direction for Russia's trade and economic relations after European OECD countries. Russia's overall trade with the four economies of Northeast Asia (China, Japan, South Korea, and Taiwan) is likely to double in the next few years and the share of Northeast Asia in Russia's foreign trade may reach one-third of the total, with the Asia–Pacific attracting 40–45 per cent of Russian trade.

THE RUSSIAN FAR EAST

After being a major military outpost for nearly a century and 'a laboratory for metropolitan experiments,'[22] the Pacific coast of Russia is increasing its role as a gateway for commerce, trade, and investment. Vladivostok and Khabarovsk are becoming centers for business contact with Northeast Asia and North America. They are now linked by direct air routes with all neighboring states and territories. These two cities are ideally located for region-wide business activities and, with improvements in their infrastructure, could compete with other major cities in Northeast Asia in hosting the business offices of Russian and international companies operating in the region.

After the dissolution of the Soviet Union, the relative economic importance of the eastern regions of Russia and their contribution to the Russian economy and exports grew. The Russian Far East's share of the national population is approximately 5.3 per cent. After the loss of port facilities on the Baltic and Black Seas, the Russian Pacific ports (with total capacities of more than 70 million tons a year) became even more important.[23] Four major sea ports (Vostochniy, Vladivostok, Nakhodka, and Vanino) handle approximately the same volume of foreign cargo as the three largest ports in European Russia (St Petersburg, Novorossiysk, and Murmansk). Port Vostochniy's estimated capacity is significantly larger than its current annual turnover of 10–11 million tons. With the loss of facilities in the Baltic states and in the Ukrainian border on the Black Sea, the role of Pacific Ocean-based fishing represents 70–80 per cent of this industry's total capacity.

The economy of the Russian Far East can benefit more from possible comparative advantage from the export of natural resources, manufactured goods and services, transportation of foreign cargo, tourism, and telecommunications, etc. For the economy of the region, the 'transit role' is becoming important and the Russian Far East is emerging as a base for re-export operations, particularly related to trade with China.[24] Currently, the Russian Far East continues to contribute to domestic and export trade by supplying timber and fish, non-ferrous metals, furs, gold, and diamonds, transport links and some manufactured goods, including, until recently, nuclear-powered submarines and military aircraft. The Russian Far East's estimated exports to the Asia–Pacific countries are now about $1.5–2.0 billion annually, or twice as much as in 1989.

Investment in production is becoming the key issue. Both resource-based and manufacturing industries, originally tuned for arms production, need new investment. In the long-term perspective, the Far Eastern economy cannot improve its qualitative characteristics without the infusion of capital from either the rest of Russia, overseas, or from both. The role of the Russian government and local authorities in creating a hospitable investment environment is important. New opportunities for the Russian Far East may be opened up as a result of growing energy consumption in Northeast Asia. Japan alone is expected to utilize about 60 million tons of natural gas by 2010. By the year 2000, 15–20 billion cubic meters of Sakhalin gas could be tapped and another 25–30 billion by 2015. It is believed that 10–15 billion cubic meters will be exportable. The resources of the Yakutia gas fields are several times larger and could make Russia a new leading source of energy supply to Northeast Asia. South Korea is looking to the Russian Far East to meet its long-term natural gas demand by tapping Yakutia gas fields through the construction of 5,000 kilometers of pipelines passing through North Korea. A feasibility study for this plan is being supported by $20 million pledged by Moscow and Seoul. As far as Sakhalin's oil resources are concerned, Lunskoe's reserves are estimated at 52 million tons of oil, of which 7 million would be recoverable with current Russian technology. With western equipment and know-how involved, the project would be profitable. Exxon Corp., Mobil Corp., and Texaco, Inc., have won by tender the right to survey and to invest $484 million in the development of the southeastern section of the Sakhalin continental shelf covering Yuzhno-Lunskoe, Kirinskoe, and Veninskoe condensed gas deposits (Sakhalin-3). These deposits are conservatively estimated as containing 100 billion cubic meters of gas and 50–100 million tons of condensed gas. According to preliminary estimates, the fields off Sakhalin Island could produce up to 100 million tons of oil and 400 billion cubic meters of gas. Recently, Marathon Oil, Mitsui, and McDermott International initiated an oil drilling feasibility study off the coast of Sakhalin; Royal Dutch/Shell and Mitsubishi have joined these activities, thus forming the MMMSM international consortium to develop the Sakhalin-2 project (Lunskoe and Piltun-Astokshkoe fields). Magadan and Chukotka authorities have expressed their interest in foreign participation to explore the continental shelf off their coast. In Chukotka, a number of wells have good prospects for natural gas.

The future of Russia's economic interaction with Northeast Asia looks brighter than a few years ago. The area under the control of the Moscow-based bureaucracy is shrinking. The private sector is emerging, and even state-owned enterprises enjoy much greater freedom of operation, both domestically and internationally. On one hand, natural resources constitute the backbone of Russia's exports; on the other, an aerospace industry is emerging as a competitive force capable of capturing and developing market opportunities in the region. What is going to happen with the 'middle' is hard to predict. There are, however, some limited positive developments in this 'gray area' that affect the export performance of Russia. China, for example, imports Russian cars, aircraft, transport equipment, and machine tools. Russia is involved in the Yimin and Suizhong thermo-power plants projects and is planning to build a nuclear power plant in China. China is interested in Russian industrial equipment, military hardware, technology, training, and weapons system designs. Taiwan is enthusiastically looking for technological cooperation with Russia and is attempting to develop access to sources of advanced technology, new materials, and the cadres of experts in various fields. For South Korea, squeezed between the rising cost of its labor and the competition of China and ASEAN, relations with Russia are associated with the strategic need to achieve a breakthrough in advanced technologies. Samsung plans to produce the next generation of digital video and disc recorders using laser technology developed by Russian scientists.

Hyundai is interested in co-production of Russian passenger aircraft. Daewoo plans to assemble Russian helicopters. Lucky-Goldstar wants to import Russian heavy helicopters and has agreed to market them in Korea and other countries. South Korean private businesses and government agencies want to secure access to the Russian aerospace, electronics, new materials, and precision machine-tool building industries.

The US business community is awakening to the trade and investment possibilities offered by Russia and the Russian Far East. Some American experts describe the Far East as one of the most dynamic spots in the former Soviet Union in which to do business.[25] The mosaic of contracts includes Boeing's decision to open a research center in Moscow, the sale of California's raisins to Russian bakeries in St Petersburg, the development of economic contacts between the Russian Far East and Alaska, and the export of Russian-made motorcycles to a dealer in Seattle. Seattle-based Weyerhauser Co. has been involved in a reforestation project with support provided by the USAID. It hopes to start logging, mill, and market wood products in partnership with Russian companies. Boise Cascade and other lumber mills and paper producers in Washington and Oregon are looking to Russian Far East timber resources as a long-term raw material base. Russian specialists study forest management in California. American experts help Russian farmers to increase the productivity of their land under severe climatic conditions and share techniques of setting up private farms. Peace Corps volunteers work with some Russian enterprises and offices. Joint ventures in the fishing industry have been created, but others have been liquidated.[26]

McDermott International Inc. plans to form a joint venture with the Amur Shipbuilding plant, the largest shipyard in the Russian Far East, located in Komsomolsk-na-Amure. One joint venture plans involvement in marine construction projects in oil and gas fields development; another will be in the area of shipbuilding and related services for both domestic and international markets. Nimir-Petrosakh, a joint venture with a Dallas-based company, started refining Sakhalin oil at a $70 million modern refinery and plans to export to Japan and Korea. Development specialists from Alaska have helped the Sakhalin administrators develop an investment plan for the island.[27] Seattle shipyards have overhauled and converted nineteen Russian fishing vessels for use by fishing joint-ventures. Russian–American Interscrap, the only joint company of its kind on the Russian Pacific, is shipping scrap metal to Russian and South Korean steel mills. Seattle-based Mid-Com Communications Inc. will invest $15 million in Daltelecom to build a 200,000 line capacity network to link Khabarovsk, the Kamchatka Peninsula, and Blagoveschensk.[28]

Ironically, among the obstacles to closer US relations with Russia, both in Europe and in Asia, is the traditional antipathy between US government and business. US business cannot compete effectively against other foreign companies without up-front tax reductions with respect to its activities in Russia.

In 1992, the US government was involved in a number of anti-dumping actions against the Russian Federation on such products as uranium, fer-rosilicon, urea, and titanium sponge. Washington, according to the views expressed by American businessmen, has a major role to play in eliminating barriers to doing business in Russia and in reducing the risks that now pre-clude substantial investment. Without continued political and financial support provided by the government and even-footing with European and Asian companies, American business cannot pursue opportunities in Russia.[29]

The Jackson–Vanic amendment, which links US trade initiatives to Russian immigration policies, is still in effect, despite President Clinton's commit-ments given at the Vancouver summit and the G-7 Tokyo meeting to reassess this law. Under the US interpretation of the COCOM, Washington would retain its veto over the sales of fiber optics for use inside the 2,800 mile-wide nuclear 'exclusion zone' in Siberia and the Russian Far East, where most Russian intercontinental ballistic missiles are based even after the deactiva-tion of COCOM regulations. This approach, based on strategic security concerns, threatens to undermine a project to link fifty cities in Russia with 50,000 kilometers of fiber optic cables. On the other hand, US Secretary of Commerce Ron Brown announced that US OPIC (Overseas Private Investment Corporation) had committed $125 million in loan guarantees to US West International, the joint stock company chosen by the Russian side as the American participant in Roscom to implement the project.

Only recently has the United States repealed the Stevenson Amendment which placed a $300 million limit on ExIm Bank credit and guarantees. The American business community expects that Congress will exert 'healthy pres-sure on the ExIm Bank and OPIC in providing financial assistance to US companies pursuing transactions in the Russian Federation. Suggestions include lowering the standard for ExIm Bank financing and permitting OPIC to take equity positions.'[30] There are, however, many other impediments to further increases in trade and economic relations between Russia, the Asia–Pacific region, and North America. Some of them, such as infrastruc-ture, require a long-term approach. Other outstanding issues, for example the investment environment, transcend pure economic requirements. The viabil-ity of many economic projects that can effectively link Russia with the region depend on domestic political stability and long-term prospects for peace in Northeast Asia.

DEFENSE INTERESTS AND THE UNITED STATES

Russian relations with the Asia–Pacific region and the United States in East Asia may remain underdeveloped because of the conflict between defense and economics. The status quo in US and Russian military postures in Northeast Asia complicates Russia's closer economic relations with Northeast Asia and directly affects the future of the Russian Far East. The 'spontaneous disarmament,'[31] which affects Russia and the United States,[32] is so far not based on strong political leadership but directed chiefly by events as well as by the interests of the military.[33] Surprisingly, the constituency within the US bureaucracy with the most influence that is most interested in developing contacts with Moscow and the Russian Far East is the Pacific Command and, probably, the Department of Defense.

Although Russia does not fit the immediate regional economic interests of the United States and Japan, it continues to be a source of security concern.[34] The perceived military threat posed by Moscow in the Far East has not been eliminated completely even with the end of the Cold War.[35] The technical capability of Russian strategic forces is in conflict with America's deeply-rooted sense of insulation from external threats. 'The only country capable of destroying the United States' is the central point made whenever US–Russia relations are discussed. The 'capable to destroy' syndrome reflects the real attitudes of many Americans toward Russia and its remaining military strength, as presented by scholars,[36] politicians,[37] and defense analysts.[38] Negative perceptions of the Russian military power, even if it is considerably reduced, will continue to affect the security and possibly the economic prospects of the Russian Far East as a factor in the projection of this power to the Asia–Pacific region.[39] For example, for the United States, the presence of Soviet SSBNs in the North Pacific and their modernization used to be a major justification for increased US military activities in the area, as well as the rationale for cooperation with the Japanese Maritime Self-Defense Force. Finally, the US emphasis on SSBN targeting has reinforced Moscow's commitment to protect the Sea of Okhotsk and other areas in the North Pacific, including strategic passages in the area of the disputed territories.

It is symptomatic that the new military doctrine of Russia names no country as a source of threat to Russia, and only major powers and neighboring states are mentioned as the main elements of Russia's external security interests, including the United States, Japan, and China. Among potential sources of military threat to Russian security, the military doctrine mentions:

1   territorial claims against the Russian Federation;
2   potential for local wars and military conflicts close to Russian borders;
3   the use of nuclear weapons, including 'unauthorized use';
4   the proliferation of weapons of mass destruction and the means of their delivery, and advanced military technologies that can change the balance of forces;
5   the erosion of strategic stability as a result of quantitative and qualitative military build-up; and
6   enlargement of military blocs and alliances threatening the military security of the Russian Federation.

The doctrine also reflects a dramatic shift away from the era of numerical superiority in manpower and armor toward an era of qualitative and technological indices of combat potential.[40] An important change has taken place in understanding the main points of discussion about 'defensive' defense posture, as was discussed in the late 1980s.[41] The new doctrine does not attempt to mask the possibility of offensive operations in cases of aggression or conflict, and focuses on active and instant response to external threats. There is a clear indication that Russia will maintain some of its troops in forward deployment modes close to the potential sources of conflict or the sources of threat. The most visible innovation is the doctrine's provision regarding the possibility of resorting to nuclear weapons, which mirrors the US approach (the use of nuclear weapons is justifiable if security or strategic assets are threatened by conventional forces of a nuclear weapon power or by the country closely associated with such a power).

A closer look at the Russian military doctrine indicates that the role of strategic nuclear forces deployed in the North Pacific may prevent further changes in Russia's regional defense posture and therefore in US–Russian reconciliation in Northeast Asia. Under START 2, Russian SSBNs in the North Pacific are becoming less numerous and more vulnerable. It is easier to target a smaller number of platforms, especially if they are on non-alert status. The new military doctrine indicates that not only nuclear strikes, including those against Russian strategic forces, but also use of advanced long-range conventional weapons against 'strategically important' targets such as nuclear power and chemical plants, early warning systems, and command and control centers could lead to a nuclear retaliation.

Characterized as the least lethal of strategic forces, hence second strike delivery systems, SSBNs could also be considered as more difficult to defend from advanced conventional munitions (ACM), or 'smart weapons.'[42] In the published text of the new military doctrine nothing is said about this problem, but the ACM issue is treated with great attention. It is definitely a new element in the Russian security environment; it is highly likely that Moscow is concerned about the possible intent of the United States to speed up the process of converting its strategic forces to conventional weapons, particularly the ASW (Anti Submarine Warfare).[43] Japan and the United States are the principal countries that can use technological advances and economic abilities to develop and deploy future generations of strategic, high-precision, conventional weapons to offset the residual nuclear threats that provide the justification for Russia to develop 'strategic non-nuclear weapons'(SNNW).[44]

STRATEGIC GAMES AND JAPAN

During the Cold War, strategic and political realities imposed rigid limits on Russia's economic contacts with Japan and the surrounding region. From the new Russian standpoint, the future of the US–Japan security alliance is associated with the hope that Japan's role will not extend to the creation of offensive or nuclear military capabilities, and that Russia will not be a target of the security treaty.[45] Obviously, this is related to the future of the Russian

Far East and its maritime territories including the Kamchatka Peninsula, Sakhalin, and the Kurile Islands.

Japanese defense analysts agree that the return of the disputed territories to Japan will drastically redress the strategic balance in the Northwestern Pacific and as long as the Sea of Okhotsk remains a sensitive area for Russia, the Kuriles provide valuable protection against ASW.[46] Although a Russia–Japan conflict is remote and unlikely, a scenario resulting from the increase of tensions between Japan and Russia, including those over the Northern Territories, cannot be entirely ruled out. For example, in 1993 alone, the border with Japan in the waters around the disputed islands was violated more than 7,500 times by Japanese fishing boats. According to US experts, at some point in the future, the Japanese may feel that they can forcibly retake the islands without provoking a major Russian response.[47] From their standpoint, Hokkaido could serve as a spring-board for assault operations against the Russian Far East, particularly the disputed territories, which could be easily occupied considering US–Japan superiority in manpower, armaments, and infrastructure.[48]

Some Russian sources indicate that the nature, scale, and areas of military exercises and everyday military routine on the part of the United States and Japan indicate that a possible offensive operation against the Russian Far East would be launched from the area to the west of the Sangar (Tsugaru) Strait. According to Russian military and naval commanders, both the disputed islands and the Russian Far East coastline are on the list of potential targets. Another major source of concern is a blockade of the La Perouse (Soya) Strait, which would disrupt sea lines of communication between the Russian mainland, Sakhalin Island, and the Kamchatka Peninsula, thus splitting the Russian Pacific Fleet. Indeed, according to a report carried by the Japanese newspaper *Mainichi* in US–Japan joint exercises since 1985, simulated strikes against the Russian Pacific coast, including the Kuriles and Sakhalin Island have been conducted.[49]

The hope of Russian military leadership is that the changing nature of Russian–American relations will lead to a new relationship and new agreements on remaining conventional and strategic arsenals. However, in the opinion of Japanese analysts, it is very unlikely that even better agreements alone will lead to the withdrawal of nuclear weapons from the North Pacific.[50] Geography complicates the overall picture. From the perspective of Japanese military and defense analysts, 'the more defensive the Soviet maritime strategy becomes on the Asia–Pacific front, the more intensive their presence becomes in the region adjacent to Japan.'[51] Further, with regard to the problem of justification of the Soviet military forces 'on defensive grounds,' it is pointed out that these forces 'have little to defend other than themselves, especially along the Pacific rim.'[52]

Despite this, strategic sea-based nuclear forces in the North Pacific continue to demand modernization of the Russian Pacific Fleet.[53] The Japanese Ministry of Foreign Affairs' argument on the territorial dispute with Russia, for example, serves as a justification not to lower guard.[54] At the same time, from Tokyo's perspective, proposals for maritime arms control and confidence building may challenge US–Japanese maritime superiority in the North Pacific, because, in the opinion of the Japanese, the more emphasis Moscow places on retaliatory second-strike deterrence and high survivability systems, such as SLBMs, the more intensive Russian naval presence is likely to be in the areas close to Russian (and Japanese) shores. According to Shigeki Nishimura, it appears to be a 'no way out' situation if Russian strategic platforms are not redeployed.[55] The 'SSBN bastion' concept is seen by the Japanese as defensive in terms of nuclear strategy, but, as long as it incorporates Japanese territory 'this strategy can never be acceptable.'[56] Russian conventional forces deployed in the Far East are perceived as posing a potential threat to Japan's security[57] even with the end of the Cold War.[58] From Japan's perspective, Russia's military posture in the North Pacific is changing too slowly and Russia, according to Makio Miyagawa, deputy director of the Russia Division of the Japanese Ministry of Foreign Affairs:

> retains an awesome military machine equipped with a vast armory of nuclear weapons . . . the results of Soviet 'power diplomacy' remain even today, possibly constituting another area where dangers could be reduced through the appropriate use of [Japanese] economic strength.[59]

Russian relations with Japan demonstrate that although military power under the control of Moscow has ceased to be a destabilizing factor, it continues to be a disorienting force in the long term.[60] Whether the United States is willing and able to correct the situation is unclear. It seems that the US Consulate General office now located in Vladivostok represents a symbolic link between European and Asia–Pacific policies. To our regret, at present, this link appears to be more a technical than a conceptual phenomenon with Pacific Russia and the Russian Far East missing from both the inter-agency politics of the Washington Beltway and those aspects of diplomatic dialogue with Tokyo that are hidden from public eyes. The status quo in the US–Japanese alliance posture toward Russia and the Russian Far East has the potential to aggravate exactly the same problems that the United States is attempting to solve through the G-7 today and is slowly preparing to confront beyond the year 2000.

CONCLUSIONS

The reluctance of Washington to deal with Russia as a part of the Asia–Pacific region is definitely counterproductive to Moscow's interests. However, the existing situation can be explained. A source of relief, if not a solution, might be found in the fact that US interests in Asia at present are not well defined and are driven by inertia; eventually, a reorientation of US policy in the region may result in recognition of Russia as an Asia–Pacific power to be engaged in the affairs of the region. The power of the former

Soviet Union guaranteed US involvement in Northeast Asia and served as a principal factor of regional discipline during the Cold War years. Russia, which is looking for other endeavors, radiates uncertainty. For the Cold War generation strategists still dominating Washington's foreign policy hierarchy, the Russian Pacific probably appears either too small and 'unimportant' as compared with China, too 'unmanageable' as compared with Japan and South Korea, or simply not to be trusted.[61] The residual military standoff prevents government structures from closer and more constructive interactions and, most of all, impedes economic contacts. The nature of US–Japan relations makes Russia an unwelcome partner in this part of the world.

However, the declining profile of Russia in Washington's negative priorities list for Asia is important.[62] In the context of crises unfolding in US–North Korea relations, Secretary of Defense William Perry mentioned that Washington, in its efforts to build an international coalition through the United Nations, was 'working closely with South Korea and Japan, and consulting with Russia, China, and others that have a stake in preserving regional stability and preventing nuclear proliferation.'[63] The United States' 'commonality of strategic interests' with the Russian Federation was also emphasized by Deputy Secretary of State Strobe Talbott in March 1994.[64] However, revealing a probable lack of communication in the same agency, Assistant Secretary of State Winston Lord, speaking on the US policy toward Asia immediately after Talbott, did not mention Russia except in connection with the ASEAN Post-Ministerial Conference.[65]

The strategy of 'cooperative engagement' proposed by Admiral Charles Larson has helped to develop military-to-military relations and facilitated, after seven years of waiting, Tokyo's decision to open limited military-to-military contacts with Moscow.[66] The Russian Pacific Fleet and other forces now participate in military programs including exercises, port visits, training programs and senior exchange visits. In concert with these developments, some initial attempts to conceptualize relations with Russia in Asia were made by former defense under-secretary Paul D. Wolfowitz. He has proposed concentrating more attention on threat prevention, regional resilience (comprehensive security), avoidance of arms build-ups, and cooperative relationships including those with Russia whose security interests, in his opinion, coincide with those of other democracies.[67]

NOTES

1 John Hardt, 'Introduction. Soviet Siberia: A Power-to-Be?' in Rodger Swearingen (ed.), *Siberia and the Soviet Far East: Strategic Dimensions in Multinational Perspective*, Stanford: Hoover Institution Press, 1990, p. xxxi.
2 Foreign Minister Andrei Kozyrev in the first draft of Russia's foreign policy concept, released in November 1992, made a reference to the relations with the United States in the context of the Asia–Pacific region and proposed their close cooperation. *Konceptciya Vneshnei Politiki Rossiiskoi Federatcii* (The Foreign Policy Concept of the Russian Federation), p. 38.

3 President Boris Yeltsin's Address to the Federal Assembly, *Rossiiskaya gazeta*, 26 February 1994.

4 Partial text of two speeches delivered by Russian Foreign Minister Andrei Kozyrev to the Conference on Security and Cooperation in Europe, Stockholm, Sweden, 14 December 1992.

5 Andrei Kozyrev's outline of Russia's foreign policy published by *Rossiyskie vesti,* 9 February 1994.

6 Richard Solomon, 'Asian Security in the 1990s: Integration in Economics, Diversity in Defense,' address at the University of California at San Diego, 30 October 1990, *US Department of State Dispatch*, 5 November 1990, pp. 245–7.

7 *Ibid.*, p. 245.

8 Lonnie S. Keene, 'New Dimensions in Political and Military Postures in Asia: Security Dialogue and Preventive Diplomacy' (25 January 1993, p. 17), paper prepared for delivery at the United Nations Office for Disarmament Affairs-sponsored conference, 'National Security and Confidence Building among Nations in the Asia–Pacific Region,' Katmandu, Nepal, 1–3 February 1993, pp. 6–10. To be precise, there is a brief mention of the territorial dispute between Russia and Japan (p. 5), and of Russia as a part of 'a broader consensus on the nuclear issue' on the Korean Peninsula (p. 8).

9 'A New Pacific Community: Ten Goals for American Policy,' Opening Statement at Confirmation Hearings for Ambassador Winston Lord, Assistant Secretary of State-Designate, Bureau of East Asian and Pacific Affairs, 31 March 1993.

10 *Meeting the Challenges of the Asia–Pacific Region: A Context of Doing GAO Work*, Washington, DC: United States General Accounting Office, National Security and International Affairs Division, December 1993, p. 13.

11 *America's Role in Asia, Interests and Policies,* Report of the Working Group convened by the Asia Foundation's Center for Asian Pacific Affairs, Washington, DC, January 1993; Kim R. Holmes (ed.), *A Safe and Prosperous America, A US Foreign and Defense Policy Blueprint*, Washington, DC: The Heritage Foundation, 1993, pp. 24–7.

12 *National Security Strategy of the United States*, Washington, DC: The White House, 1993, pp. 7–8.

13 *Ibid.*, p. 6.

14 'A Strategic Framework for the Asian Pacific Rim,' Report to Congress 1992, Office of the Assistant Secretary of Defense for International Security Affairs (East Asia and Pacific Region), pp. 6 and 10–12.

15 Secretary of Defense Dick Cheney, 'Defense Strategy for the 1990s: The Regional Defense Strategy,' January 1993, p. 22.

16 Admiral Charles R. Larson, 'United States Pacific Command Posture Statement 1993, May 1993, Key Judgments.'

17 Peter Drysdale and Ross Garnaut, 'The Pacific: An Application of a General Theory of Economic Integration,' C. Fred Bergsten and Marcus Noland (eds), *Pacific Dynamism and the International Economics System*, Washington, DC: Institute for International Economics, 1993, p. 218.

18 'Vancouver Declaration,' Joint Statement of the Presidents of the Russian Federation and the United States, The White House, Office of the Press Secretary, 4 April 1993.

19 Ippei Yamazawa, 'New Ideas for Integration,' *Look Japan*, April 1994, p. 15.

20 In 1993, two-way trade within the former Soviet republics was 22,500 billion rubles, including 13,870 billion rubles of Russian exports and 8,621 billion rubles of imports. The export shipments of Russian oil, gas, mineral fuels, and coal accounted for 88 per cent of total exports to the former Soviet states; the volume of supplies has declined by an average of more than 60–70 per cent since 1991.

21 In 1993, officially recorded Russian exports to China reached $3.3 billion and

imports amounted to $4.1 billion (228 per cent increase as compared to 1992). If transactions not accounted for by federal statistics (mainly small commercial operations, barter deals and cross-border commodity flows) are added, the volume of bilateral trade could amount to $10–12 billion.

22　John J. Stephan, 'The Russian Far East,' *Current History*, October 1993, p. 336.

23　See Mark J. Valencia, 'Regional Transportation and Communication in Developing Northeast Asia: Status, Problems, Plans, and Priorities,' *Northeast Asia Study Report*, no. 2, Honolulu: Northeast Asia Economic Forum, August 1994, p. 87.

24　Won Bae Kim (ed.), *Regional Development in Northeast China. An International Perspective*, Honolulu: East-West Center, 1994, pp. 85–90.

25　Trevor J. Gunn, 'Racing to Enter the Russian Far East Market,' *Business America*, 23 August 1993, p. 2.

26　Reportedly, frustration and uncertainty prevailed among those who wanted to invest in the Russian Far East.

27　Jeffrey Lilley, 'Boom-in-Waiting: Sakhalin Fights to Turn its Oil and Gas into a Better Life,' *Far Eastern Economic Review*, 1 September 1994, p. 29.

28　*RA Report*, no. 17 July 1994, p. 89.

29　'Statement of Richard A. Conn, Jr., Partner, Latham & Watkins, Before the Subcommittee on Commerce, Consumer, and Monetary Affairs, Committee on Government Operations, US House of Representatives,' pp. 6, 12–14.

30　*Ibid.*, pp. 15–17.

31　Joshua Handler, 'Denuclearizing and Demilitarizing the Seas,' Jon M. Van Dyke, Durwood Zaelke, and Grant Hewison (eds), *Freedom for the Seas in the 21st Century: Ocean Governance and Environmental Harmony*, Washington, DC: Island Press, 1993, p. 420.

32　The Russian military in the Far East is deeply affected by the crisis. The number of troops has been reduced by almost half since 1987. There is a chronic shortage of fuel to train pilots in the air force. Since 1992, the budget to maintain the Pacific fleet has been reduced. Within one year of the August 1991 attempted coup the time warships spent at sea was halved. In the Russian navy, more than 100 nuclear submarines are being decommissioned; by the year 2000, the navy will have to dispose of around 160 submarines with 300 reactors. Since 1987, as many as forty submarines and thirty large vessels have been removed from the Pacific fleet. In 1992, ship repair facilities in Vladivostok were operating at 20 per cent capacity. The two largest ships in the Russian Pacific fleet, the aircraft-carrying cruisers *Minsk* and *Novorossiisk*, were withdrawn from the fleet which lacked the funding for their scheduled repair and modernization. Other cruisers can be refitted only at the Nikolaev shipyards, which requires negotiations with the Ukrainian government. The construction of nuclear-powered submarines has been halted at Komsomolsk-na-Amure.

33　Captains Moreland, Ota, and Pan'kov, 'Naval Cooperation in the Pacific: Looking to the Future' (February 1993); Captain Second Rank Alexander S. Skaridov, RFN, Commander Daniel D. Thompson, USN, Lieutenant Commander Yang Zhiqun, PLA(N), 'Asian-Pacific Maritime Security: New Possibilities for Naval Cooperation?' (February 1994); Ji Guoxing, 'Maritime Security for the Asia–Pacific Region' (February 1994), all available from Stanford University's Center for International Security and Arms Control, Stanford, California.

34　Gerald L. Curtis (ed.), *The United States, Japan, and Asia: Challenges for US Policy*, New York: Columbia University, The American Assembly, 1994, p. 218.

35　Seizaburo Sato, 'Recent Changes and Possible Future Developments in the Environment Surrounding Japan,' paper presented at the quadrilateral meeting on 'Asian Security Problems: Opportunities for Reducing Tensions among Major Powers,' Tokyo, 2–5 April 1993, p. 7.

36 'Even after the projected reductions under START are carried out, Russia will retain sufficient nuclear forces to destroy any potential enemy, including the United States,' Mark Kraer, 'The Armies of the Post-Soviet States,' *Current History,* vol. 91, no. 567 (October 1992), p. 333.

37 'Much of Russia's nuclear arsenal could be aimed our way at a moment's notice, and Russia is one of the few countries in the world with the potential to again cast itself as our global rival.' Dave McCurdy, 'US Foreign Policy: The Challenges Ahead,' Remarks before the CSIS Policy Forum, Washington, DC, 7 February 1994, p. 3.

38 'Military staffs each side would continue to perform calculations to estimate whether the Other Side (who used to be the Enemy) could somehow launch a first strike without having to fear massive and certain retaliation.' Fred Charles Ikle, 'The Case for a Russian–U.S. Security Co-community,' James E. Goodby and Benoit Morel (eds), *The Limited Partnership: Building a Russian–US Security Community,* Oxford: Oxford University Press, SIPRI, 1993, p. 13.

39 Patrick M. Cronin (ed.), *From Globalism to Regionalism: New Perspectives on US Foreign and Defense Policies,* Washington, DC: National Defense University, 1993, pp. 46–7.

40 Mary C. FitzGerald, 'Russia's New Military Doctrine,' *Naval War College Review,* vol. 46, no. 2, Spring 1993, p. 42.

41 Mikhail Gorbachev has argued in favor of a reorientation away from the traditional offensive emphasis, as evidenced by his concept of a defensive doctrine in which the armed forces must be restructured to be 'sufficient to repel possible aggression, but not sufficient to conduct offensive operations.' See M. Gorbachev, 'The Realities and Guarantees of a Secure World,' *Pravda,* 17 September 1987.

42 Steven E. Miller, 'Russian–US Security Cooperation on the High Seas,' James E. Goodby and Benoit Morel (eds), *The Limited Partnership: Building a Russian–US Security Community,* Oxford: Oxford University Press, SIPRI, 1993, p. 264.

43 Paul H. Nitze, 'Is It Time to Junk Our Nukes? The New World Disorder Makes Them Obsolete,' *Washington Post,* 16 January 1994, p. C1.

44 FitzGerald, *op. cit.,* p. 29. The author analyzes the view of Russian military writers on the problems of military doctrine and defense requirements, including the article by A.A. Danilevich and O.P. Shunin, 'On the Strategic Non-Nuclear Deterrence Forces,' *Voennaya mysl,* no. 2, 1992, pp. 46–54.

45 Shigeki Nishimura, a Colonel in Japan's Ground Self-Defense Force, suggests that: 'it is, in fact, impossible for Japan to maintain an exclusively defensive posture except within the framework of the US–Japan security system, in which the US provides the supplementary offensive capability,' and that 'a separate Japanese defense capability would require nuclear arms.' *Far Eastern Economic Review,* 2 August 1992, p. 23.

46 Noboru Yamaguchi, 'The Future of the US–Japan Security Relations,' Mike Mochizuki *et al., Japan and the United States: Troubled Partners in a Changing World,* Cambridge: Institute for Foreign Policy Analysis, 1991, pp. 51 and 56.

47 John Y. Schrader and James A. Winnefeld, *Understanding the Evolving US Role in Pacific Rim Security: A Scenario-Based Analysis,* prepared for the Commander in Chief, US Pacific Command, Santa Monica: RAND, 1992, pp. 21 and 37–8.

48 *Nezavisimaya gazeta,* 30 July 1992.

49 TASS, 21 February 1994, in FBIS/SOV, 94/36, 23 February 1994, p. 24.

50 Masahide Yamanouchi, 'Japan's Security Policy and Arms Control in North East Asia,' *IIGP Policy Paper,* 60E, October 1991.

51 Yamaguchi, *op. cit.,* pp. 45 and 52.

52 *Ibid.,* p. 53.

53 John Allen Williams, 'Soviet–American Naval Balance and Maritime Strategies,' Donald M. Snow (ed.), *Soviet–American Security Relations in the 1990s,* Lexington, Massachusetts: Lexington Books, 1989, pp. 146–9.

54 Makio Miyagawa, 'The Employment of Economic Strength for Foreign Policy Goals,' *Japan Review of International Affairs*, vol. 6, no. 3, Fall 1992, p. 288.
55 Shigeki Nishimura, 'Transformation of the US–Japan Defense Posture: The New Soviet Challenge,' *IIGP Policy Paper*, 65E, October 1991, p. 18.
56 Yamaguchi, *op. cit.,* p. 52.
57 *Ibid.*, p. 52.
58 Yamanouchi, *op. cit.,* p. 9.
59 Miyagawa.
60 Hardt, *op. cit.,* p. xxx.
61 See Qin Yongchun, 'US–Russian Partnership and its Implications for Northeast Asia,' *The Korean Journal of International Studies*, vol. 24, no. 3, 1993, pp. 289–308.
62 Thomas L. McNaugher, 'U.S. Military Forces in East Asia: The Case for Long-Term Engagement,' Gerald L. Curtis (ed.), *The United States, Japan, and Asia: Challenges for US Policy*, New York: W.W. Norton, 1994, p. 186.
63 Remarks by Secretary of Defense William Perry to the Asia Society on 'US Security Policy in Korea,' National Press Club, Washington, DC, 3 May 1994.
64 Hearing of the Senate Foreign Relations Committee on US Policy Toward Russia, chaired by Senator Claiborn Pell (D-RI). Witness: Strobe Talbott, Deputy Secretary of State, 23 March 1994.
65 Hearings of the East Asian and Pacific Affairs Subcommittee of the Senate Foreign Relations Committee on US Policy Toward Asia, chaired by Senator Charles S. Robb (D-VA). Witness: Winston Lord, Assistant Secretary of State, Washington, DC, 24 March 1994.
66 Charles R. Larson, 'Cooperative Engagement and Economic Security in the Asia–Pacific Region,' Ronald N. Montaperto (ed.), *Cooperative Engagement and Economic Security in the Asia–Pacific Region*, Washington, DC: National Defense University Press, 1993, p. 71.
67 Paul D. Wolfowitz, 'The American Presence in the Pacific After the Cold War,' Montaperto, p. 81.

9   The Russian Far East in Russo–Japanese relations

Nobuo Arai and Tsuyoshi Hasegawa

INTRODUCTION

The political and economic crisis that was set in motion by the advent of *perestroika* and that continued to accelerate with the end of the Soviet Union has had negative consequences throughout Russia. No region in Russia, with the exception of Chechnya, has been harder hit by the crisis than the Russian Far East. And yet, the outside world has paid little attention to the precipitous process of disintegration of the Russian Far East. Hence, the Western world, including Japan, is largely unprepared for the consequences that may result from the economic, political, and ecological catastrophes that this crisis may bring about.

Japan's involvement in the Russian Far East is characterized by the combination of two incongruous elements. On the policy side, Japan was basically indifferent to the plight of the Far East until the collapse of the Soviet Union. When it began to extend aid to Russia, it encountered a number of problems, which made it impossible to initiate active economic assistance to the Far East. At present it has no comprehensive policy toward the Russian Far East. On the practical side, however, Japan is unwittingly becoming a major player in the Far East's integration into the Asia–Pacific region.

This chapter intends to give a brief overview of the political and economic development of the Russian Far East since the advent of *perestroika*, describe how Japan has been involved during the changing stages in the Russian Far East, analyze Japan's policy options with regard to the Russian Far East, and examine the significance of the recent development with regard to the 'Northern Territories.'

FOUR STAGES OF POLITICAL AND ECONOMIC DEVELOPMENT OF THE RUSSIAN FAR EAST

There are four important variables to gauge political and economic developments of the Russian Far East since the advent of *perestroika*:

1 the extent to which the Russian Far East has been integrated with the Asia–Pacific economies;

2   the question of the center–periphery relations in Russia;
3   the extent to which the regional political and/or economic unit, called the Russian Far East, is emerging; and
4   the question of local political/economic dynamics.

Using these variables, we would like to outline briefly the political and economic developments of the Russian Far East in four stages: the first stage: 1986–89; the second stage: 1990–91; the third stage: 1992–93; and the fourth stage: mid-1993 to the present.[1]

The first stage: 1986–89

The new era dawned, or more precisely was imposed from above, on the Soviet Far East by Gorbachev's Vladivostok speech in July 1986. The speech was hailed as Gorbachev's new Asian initiative, but relatively little attention has been paid to the fact that the first half of his speech was devoted to the domestic problems of the Soviet Far East. Gorbachev severely criticized the Soviet Far East's dismal economic performance and told the Far East to become economically self-sufficient without expecting massive subsidies from the center. He also indicated that the only way for the Far East to achieve this would be to seek economic integration into the Asia–Pacific economy.

This was the beginning of Gorbachev's 'Look East' policy. To symbolize this policy, Gorbachev promised that the hitherto closed city of Vladivostok would be opened to foreigners. The Vladivostok speech was followed by a series of measures designed to facilitate the entry of foreigners to the Far East and to give preferential treatment to joint ventures in the Far East in order to entice foreign capital. Asian experts from Moscow flooded the Far East for short visits, encouraging the backward Far Easterners to get on board *perestroika*. In order to be accepted as a member of the Pacific Economic Cooperation Council (PECC), Moscow hastily created a national committee (SOVNAPECC) with Evgenii Primakov as its head. It was indeed an auspicious beginning of a new 'Look East' policy.

Like many of Gorbachev's ideas, the 'Look East' policy began with good intentions, but it encountered many obstacles during its implementation. In many ways, Gorbachev's speech was unfair to the Far East. Its position was reduced to a colonial outpost closed to its natural neighbors which was not of its own choosing, but rather the result of Moscow's conscious policy. Suddenly and without warning the Soviet Far East was rudely awakened from its slumber, and told to open its gates to its Asia–Pacific neighbors and develop its own economic strategy without relying on subsidies and investment from Moscow.

The 'Look East' policy, however, also had a disturbing aspect. The Far East had been denied entry into what Robert Scalapino calls natural economic territory (NET), and forcibly integrated into the Soviet economic space, eight and nine time zones away. For instance, more than 80 to 90 per cent of the products of the Far East's machine industry were delivered to the European parts of the Soviet Union. In return for raw materials exported to European Russia, the Far East received from Moscow everything it needed including energy, machinery, labor, consumer goods, housing, and other social services. Yet another important aspect of this special status of the Far East was that all these transactions had to be carried out through Moscow with the complex maze of the Communist Party hierarchy and the ministerial system. With Moscow successfully exerting its control over the Far East through the policy of 'divide and conquer,' this mechanism ensured that no Far Eastern regional consciousness that cut across various areas within the region would emerge. Gorbachev's Vladivostok speech was a warning that this would change, but, as the Far Easterners suspected, not everything would change, even under *perestroika*.

First, what changed had a disastrous impact on the Far East economy. As Moscow began implementing economic restructuring after 1987, the growth of the Far East, that had been heavily dependent on investment and subsidies from Moscow, came to a sudden halt. The BAM project, which had been the visible symbol of the Soviet commitment to the economic development of Siberia and the Far East, was frozen. As Moscow placed its first priority on investment in heavy industry in the European Soviet Union, the Far East's share of investment dwindled. Second, what did not change prevented the Far East from seeking new ways of organizing its own economy. As the investment and subsidies were drastically reduced, Moscow's control over the Far East remained. The Soviet Far East was told to be self-sufficient without relying on Moscow's help; and yet, Moscow continued to exert its tight control over resources through its ministries.

The Soviet Far East elite was psychologically unprepared to face the new challenge presented by Gorbachev. The Communist Party *nomenklatura* were firmly entrenched in every corner of the political and economic hierarchy in the Far East, resisting every aspect of the 'Look East' policy. Thus, when the Long-Term Economic Plan for the Development of the Far East, Chita, and Buryat Republic to the Year 2000 was presented in 1987, it was more a representative bureaucratic document composed of the entrenched economic *nomenklatura* than a reflection of Gorbachev's *perestroika*.

The Far East thus lagged far behind the call for economic restructuring. Vladivostok, which Gorbachev promised to open in 1986, was never opened during his tenure of office. Changes began from the political sphere, however. By 1989, waves of *glasnost* and democratization had finally reached the Far East. In Yuzhno-Sakhalinsk, there was a political demonstration, which led to the firing of the oblast first secretary. The first secretary of Khabarovsk Krai, Chernyi, was also replaced. The elections to the Congress of People's Deputies in 1989, and more importantly the local elections in the spring of 1990 greatly changed the political landscape of the Far East. Reformists such as Vladimir Kuznetsov and Valentin Fedorov were elected the heads of Primorskii Krai and Sakhalin Oblast respectively. The Russian

Far East was ready to move to the second stage, if not economically, at least politically.

The second stage: 1990–91

The most important characteristic of the second stage is that Far Eastern development was closely connected with the struggle between the Union (Gorbachev) and the Russian Federation (Yeltsin). The Congress of People's Deputies of the Russian Federation declared its sovereignty on 12 June 1990. Yeltsin visited the Far East in August 1990 to mobilize the support of the Far East for his struggle against Moscow. The Far East actively supported Yeltsin in this struggle. Nevertheless, it must be pointed out that Yeltsin and the Far Eastern leaders had different dreams while sleeping in the same bed. The Far Eastern leaders wanted to take away from the Union government the power of control over their own resources, while Yeltsin wanted to maintain control over resources in Moscow, not under the Union government, but rather under the government of the Russian Federation. Thus, the alliance between Yeltsin and the Far Eastern leaders was like a marriage of convenience, and concealed the seeds of discord once their common enemy, the Union government, was destroyed.

Regional assertiveness was most vividly expressed in the regional governments' attempt to create 'free economic zones.' The most typical example of this development was Sakhalin Soviet's passing of the 'Law on the Free Economic Zone,' which declared Sakhalin's control over resources on the islands. It should be stressed that the major objective of the 'free economic zones' in Sakhalin and elsewhere in Russia was not to create a favorable economic environment to induce foreign investment, as in China, but rather to assert control over resources. In this sense, this move was closely related to the 'war of laws' that paralyzed normal political and economic functions of the Soviet Union.

Regional assertiveness also contributed to the emergence of the concept of the 'Far East' as a regional unit. In September 1990, the Far Eastern Association was established. Unlike the SOVNAPECC, which was basically created by Moscow's initiative in the first stage as a device to seek entry of the Soviet Union into the Asia–Pacific economies through the PECC, the Far Eastern Association was created by the regional initiative. The Association was a loose consultative body composed of the representatives of the executive branches of regional governments. The Association, if allowed to develop, had the potential to develop into an important body that was to map out a comprehensive economic strategy encompassing the entire Far East and coordinate local divergence.

In May 1991, a New Concept of the Development of the Far East was adopted by the Far Eastern Association, which consisted of the following three important components: macro-analysis of the current economic conditions of the Far East; a new industrial policy; and a new investment policy to implement this industrial policy. It also envisioned the establishment of the Far Eastern Development Bank, which would realize the convertibility of the ruble by pooling foreign currency earned in the Far East.[2] Significantly Ivan Silaev, the Prime Minister of the Russian Federation, attended the meeting that adopted this document. A new age of Far Eastern development appeared on the horizon with the blessing of Moscow.

The third stage: 1992–93

The political development at the center from the August *coup* to the collapse of the Soviet Union, however, wiped out whatever positive development had emerged in the Far East. Once Yeltsin triumphed in his struggle with Gorbachev, he showed his true color as a staunch centralizer, imposing his own appointed governors in each region, and separated the local soviets from the appointed executive organs.[3] Yeltsin's administrative reform broke the streamlined chain of command between the central ministries and various sections within the executive committee. As a result, there arose considerable confusion and ambiguities about jurisdictions and the chain of command between the central ministries and the local administration. The abolition of the executive committee left the administrative head without an instrument of implementation for his decisions. Taking Khabarovsk as a case, Kathryn Brown describes this confusion as follows:

> No practical arrangement for the division of power has been worked out, nor have the branches of government defined their duties at all levels of government. Decisions are made only hesitantly; and, once made, they are either blocked by another office or left unimplemented.[4]

Yeltsin's administrative reform led to conflict between the local soviets and Yeltsin's appointed governors. The deadly struggle between the executive and the legislature that eventually ended with an explosion in Moscow in October 1993 also had its carbon copy in many localities, especially in the Far East. The Sakhalin Soviet passed a vote of no-confidence against Fedorov, while the Primorskii Soviet rejected Kuznetsov's economic policy. Making concessions to the conservative demands, Yeltsin replaced Fedorov with Krasnoyarov, and Kuznetsov with Nazdratenko.[5] Khabarovsk governor Ishaev fired his reform-minded vice-governor Pavel Minakir, the brain behind the New Concept.

In the meantime, with the implementation of Gaidar's shock therapy, the imposition of the central authority on the region was also restored economically. Gaidar's economic policy doubly hurt the Far East. On the one hand, Gaidar in theory applied his marketization policy universally without any regional differentiation. This meant that the Far East lost the preferential treatment it had enjoyed previously.[6] On the other hand, however, despite the professed universal application of marketization, Yeltsin actually engaged in separate negotiations with various regions for political reasons, often giving preferential concessions to certain regions. As the struggle at the center between Yeltsin and the Parliament intensified, both sides courted the support of the regional leaders.

In these negotiations, the Far East was put in a disadvantageous position. Unlike the Urals and Western Siberia, which respectively used heavy industry and oil as their leverage, the Far East lacked such bargaining chips. For the Far East, the best they came up with were docking fees for the harbors. With the collapse of the Soviet Union, the Far Eastern harbors increased in importance as the entry points to the land bridge to European Russia and other CIS countries. It was over the percentage of the fees to be delivered to the Far East that the Far Eastern authorities and Moscow fought a fierce battle. As a compromise, it was decided to give 10 per cent of income derived from fees to the local authorities, although the regional leaders insisted on the division of fifty–fifty.[7] The Primorskii Soviet's declaration that it seek the status of republic, adopted in July 1993, was not intended to be a 'declaration of independence' from the Russian Federation, but rather aimed to elevate the krai to the republic level by which it hoped to obtain the right to control resources.[8]

Under these circumstances, the economic conditions of the Russian Far East sharply deteriorated. The necessary supply of machinery, energy, and equipment from European Russia were severely disrupted and became prohibitively expensive, while consumer goods and food supplies were drastically reduced. The hyperinflation, reaching 22 per cent a month, together with soaring transportation costs, often eating up 80 per cent of a unit price, hit the Far East hardest. In 1992, industrial production in the Far East fell by 12 per cent compared with 2 per cent in 1991. Especially, the production of consumer goods dropped by 26 per cent.[9] In the first half of 1993, the industrial production further dropped by 16 per cent.[10]

Each oblast and krai was left on its own to survive. The name of the game became a cut-throat struggle to gain as much access to scarce resources as possible in separate negotiations with Moscow. Primorskii Krai undertook the Greater Vladivostok Project, which envisioned the establishment of a large free economic zone centered around Vladivostok. The Russian Supreme Soviet passed a resolution to grant preferential treatment for this project. Sakhalin competed with Vladivostok by pushing the continental shelf development project.[11] With this situation, there was no room for the development of the Far Eastern Association, which quickly ceased to function.

Ironically, it was precisely this situation that led to integration with the Asia–Pacific region. It was not a result of the 'Look East' policy as Gorbachev had envisaged, but rather out of sheer necessity prompted by the need for economic survival. The shortage of consumer goods and food supplies led the Far East to seek active barter trade with China. Despite the strengthening of central control over export and foreign currency control under Gaidar, exports, particularly fish exports, expanded rapidly, as each region sought to earn hard currency quickly. In 1992, the share of the Far East in Russia's trade increased from 12 per cent to 20 per cent.[12] The fastest growing area was joint ventures with the Chinese. Of 450 joint ventures in the Far East in 1993, 17 per cent were Chinese–Russian joint ventures, compared with 21 per cent for US–Russian and 20 per cent for Japanese–Russian joint ventures.[13] As export and joint ventures expanded, however, they did not bring about any modernization of the industrial structure, as raw materials became the main objects of export and joint ventures. Even worse, the exploitative pattern of export and joint ventures caused negative consequences on preservation of resources and the environment.

The fourth stage: mid-1993 to present

The precipitous decline of the Far Eastern economy continued, but the new situation that emerged in the latter half of 1993 cannot be classified as a mere continuation of the third stage. In 1992, heavy industry, predominantly military industry, ceased normal operations while a few aviation enterprises barely survived with the export of military aircraft to China.[14] In the latter half of 1993, the operation of enterprises crucial to the survival of the local economy such as the paper industry in Sakhalin and fish processing industry in Kamchatka and south Kuriles came to a complete halt. The Far Eastern economy completely lost its competitive edge in European Russia. In the meantime, integration with Asia–Pacific neighbors has proceeded with amazing speed, since foodstuffs, energy, and consumer goods are considerably less expensive to procure from Asia than from European Russia. It can be said that the Far East is quickly dropping out of the Russian economic space. The Russian Far East is being integrated into its natural economic territory (NET). As one journalist commented, the Russian Far East is becoming 'Far East without Russia.'[15]

The manner in which the Far Eastern economy is integrated into the Asia–Pacific region and its consequences, however, are not exactly what Gorbachev had envisioned in 1986. Integration is taking place out of necessity, not out of the Russian Far East's own choice. As a result, there are a number of negative consequences, as we will discuss below.

FUTURE PROSPECTS FOR THE RUSSIAN FAR EAST

Strategy for industrial structure

The Russian Far East faces an important crossroads for future industrial structure. Should it seek further integration with the Asia–Pacific region or should it seek reintegration with European Russia? The direction they choose will have direct impact on how the industrial structure is going to be reorganized and where future investment should be concentrated. Take, for instance, the fishing industry. If the primary direction is to seek integration with the Asia–Pacific region, the fishing industry that has been targeted toward relatively inexpensive marine products such as pollack and herring has to be transformed into an industry catering to the Asia–Pacific market, particularly the Japanese market that is interested only in fresh, expensive fish such as crab and shrimp. The new task requires new technology and new investment.

Psychologically gravitated though the Russians are in the Far East, it seems impossible for the Russian Far East to seek reintegration with the domestic market of European Russia. This unnatural integration that once existed was possible only under the centralized command economic structure.[16] As long as the command economy cannot be recreated, the Russian Far East cannot expect to be an effective player in the Russian economic space. And yet, it appears that a decisive breakthrough to a new strategy seeking integration with the Asia–Pacific region has not taken place among the economic and political elite in the Far East.

Divisions of the Far East

One cannot treat the Russian Far East as a unit. The only common features all the regions of the Far East share are that they have all dropped out of the Russian economic space and that they had to seek drastic means for their survival. From the economic point of view, there have emerged basically three sub-units in the Far East:

1   the southern Far East that shares borders with China, i.e., Primorskii Krai, southern Khabarovsk Krai, and Amur Oblast;
2   the Okhotsk rim with fishing monoculture, i.e., Sakhalin, south Kuriles, and Kamchatka; and
3   the northern Far East, which relies on the extraction of diamonds and gold, i.e., Sakha and Magadan.

The strategy for integration with the Asia–Pacific region is different for each sub-unit.

Political prospects

Given the deepening differentiation and conflicts of interest among these sub-units, it is difficult to imagine that an organization similar to the Far Eastern Association that comprises all the sub-units of the region will be created in the near future. Moreover, political conflicts in the Far East will become more complex and more severe.

First, there will be a continuing tug of war between Moscow and the regional leaders for control over resources and the distribution of taxes. This struggle will be compounded by the Far East dropping out of the Russian economic space. Moscow will find it necessary to court the regional leaders' loyalty. This is the reason why Chernomyrdin and Zhirinovsky made their peregrinations to the Far East. Nazdratenko, on his part, citing the geostrategic importance of Primorye, is attempting to exact concessions from Moscow with regard to federal subsidies.[17]

Second, competition among various oblasts and krais will become more severe and often ugly. During the winter of 1993–94, the Primorskii government seized oil in Nakhodka due to be transported to Kamchatka, citing the shortage of energy and electricity within Primorye.[18] Simultaneously, Ishaev blocked the transportation of coal from Vanino to Sakhalin. In retaliation, Krasnoyarov threatened to stop the delivery of natural gas from Sakhalin to Komsomolsk-na-Amure. Nazdratenko recently called for the transfer of jurisdiction over the southern Kuriles from Sakhalin to Primorskii Krai, a dangerous indication that the territorial dispute between Japan and Russia will become part of the local struggle.[19]

Third, political struggles within oblasts and krais will also become complicated with various factions seeking support from various political influences in Moscow and abroad. For instance, Deputy Prime Minister Oleg Soskovets criticized the Federal Committee of Fisheries for not fulfilling the Presidential order for economic development of the Kuriles. This Presidential order instructed the Federal Committee of Fisheries to transfer a substantial portion of income derived from the Japanese fishermen's fees for harvesting seaweed around Kaigara Islands. The Federal Committee of Fisheries made an alliance with the Sakhalin government and protested against Soskovets' recommendation. New stages of fishing negotiations, involving the areas of the 'Northern Territories,' which will be discussed in more detail below, also indicate the emergence of new players within Sakhalin Oblast, this time, Nikolai Pokidin, the head of the South Kurile district government, over the head of the Sakhalin government.

Fourth, a serious gap between economic necessity and political/psychological reaction to this economic necessity is developing among the populace, making the current situation politically volatile and uncertain. When the survival of the region depends on integration with the Asia–Pacific region, and indeed such integration is proceeding with tremendous speed, it becomes clear that the most important agent to make important decisions is the local government. And yet, the interest of the local population in local self-government has sharply declined. In Khabarovsk Krai, only 35 per cent of eligible voters participated in the local elections in March 1994, and in four electoral districts the turnout did not reach 25 per cent. In the Yuzhno-Sakhalinsk electoral district in Sakhalin the turnout was a mere 17.3 per cent.[20] The second election in August did not gain the necessary percentage of voters, either. In Primorskii Krai, Nazdratenko arrested Vladivostok Mayor Viktor Chrepkov and indefinitely postponed the local election. In some parts, local election results reversed the trend of the national election in December 1993. While in December 1993 the southern part of Khabarovsk gave Russia's Choice a victory (18.7 per cent) over Zhirinovsky's Liberal Democratic Party (13.4 per cent), the Yeltsin supporters were completely defeated in the local election. The majority of newly elected local duma deputies were conservative industrial managers.[21]

Finally, forced integration with the Asia–Pacific region has created political and psychological tensions. The flood of often shoddy Chinese goods, merchants, and laborers in the border regions has provoked a sense of Chinese expansion. This is contributing to a rise in nationalism and even xenophobia. A typical example of such anti-Chinese sentiment is expressed by *Krasnaya zvezda*:

> The PRC . . . is invading Russia's economic sphere. The work of the Chinese in impoverished Russia is paid for in decommissioned ships, hardware, and equipment. Chinese workers are filling up Russian enterprises and leading to the growth of unemployment in Russia. Meanwhile, the Chinese, as a result of the demarcation of the border, are grabbing our lands, illegally detaining Russian vessels, and exploiting our territory in their own interests.[21]

Anti-Chinese feelings led Primorskii and Khabarovsk Krais to tighten the control of incoming Chinese by requiring a passport and visa for crossing the borders. This partially explains the reduction of border trade between Russia and China in 1993.[23]

Furthermore, the Far East's dropping out of the Russian economic space has created uneasy political relations with Moscow. Moscow distrusts Far Eastern regional leaders' loyalty, while the latter unabashedly exploit the delicate 'geopolitical situation' of the Far East to extract more concessions from Moscow. This situation makes it impossible for Moscow and the Far East to coordinate a strategy for Far Eastern economic development.

Ecological crisis

Faced with the struggle for survival, all the decisions in this region are made as stop-gap measures without any consideration for their long-term consequences. Foreign capital is intruding into the Far East only to plunder their natural resources without yielding any gains to the majority of the population. Nuclear waste has been dumped in the Sea of Japan. With very few cities in the Far East having adequate sewage treatment facilities, untreated human and industrial wastes are dumped into rivers and oceans. Chronic shortages of energy have led various Far Eastern regional governments to opt for nuclear energy without consideration for safety. According to William Potter, the matter is not whether an accident will occur, but how damaging such an accident will be.[24]

The Russian Far East's integration with the Asia–Pacific Region is proceeding precisely in a way that will damage the industrial and ecological basis of the region. This cannot but provoke xenophobic resentment among the majority of the people.

The military factor

On the surface, the military and security forces that once closely guarded the border from intrusion of insidious forces of capitalism are in decline. The reduction of forces, the decline in the prestige of the army and KGB, a series of explosions at naval depots in Vladivostok, and the scandal involving five sailors who died of malnutrition in Russkii Island off Vladivostok all attest to the sharp decline in the prestige of the armed forces in the Far East.[25] Nevertheless, several points should be stressed in terms of the military's role in domestic politics in the Far East.

First, the military has traditionally played a dominant role in Far Eastern political development as the moving force behind economic development. Military personnel in the Far East number around 326,000, which constitutes about 4 per cent of the entire population of the Far East (7.9 million). A complete reduction of these forces would be equal to the disappearance of the two major cities in the Far East, Blagoveshchensk and Yuzhno-Sakhalinsk.[26] One must remember that soldiers were also employed for economic purposes, particularly construction, in the Russian Far East.

Moreover, industry in the Far East is heavily tilted toward the defense industry. The survival of these enterprises depends on whether they can successfully carry out conversion to civilian production. The record of conversion in the Far East has been dismal with one defense enterprise after another folding. In the industry where about 80 to 90 per cent of their products were delivered to European Russia, the state order was drastically reduced; the government refused to pay for the losses; the cost of transportation skyrocketed; and since they could not pay even the electricity bill, energy companies cut off electricity. They could not expect to enter the Russian market due to the prohibitive transportation costs. Even if they succeeded in making the conversion, it would be difficult to find a domestic market within the Russian Far East, when the population there is only less than 8 million. The only way for their survival is to export arms to the Asia–Pacific market. This explains the recent increase in Russian arms sales to China, which had become Russia's greatest arms importer, surpassing India, as well as to Southeast Asian countries.

Furthermore, the erosion of authority that threatens the very existence of the military has sharpened the sense of crisis among the professional military men. It is difficult to say to what extent the military has been involved in the political process in the Far East. Yet given the predominant role it used to play under the Soviet rule, and given the erosion of military factor and the crisis of the defense industry, it would be surprising if the military had not been involved in the resurgence of the right-wing backlash of the *nomenklatura* in the third and fourth stages outlined above.

In addition, there is emerging a new disturbing element within the military involving the power struggle between the military, headed by Defense Minister Grachev, and the Border Guard under the security forces, headed by General Andrei Nikolaev.[27] The Federal Border Guard Service, which was once subordinate to the KGB, has become independent. Defense Minister Grachev's attempt to incorporate the Border Guard into the Ministry of Defense has failed. Needless to say, the areas in which the Border Guard can demonstrate their existence are located near the waters around the islands disputed with Japan. A series of shooting incidents near the 'Northern Territories,' which will be discussed below, can be understood in this context as well. The more provocative the Border Guard's actions, the more public attention and authority they will gain. In fact, the existence of the independent Border Guard, which is not subordinate to anyone but the President, may lead to independent actions that will predetermine Russia's foreign policy.[28] A danger of the Kwantung Army syndrome is clearly looming.

Thus, despite the seeming disappearance of the military predominance in the Far East, the military threat has not been completely eliminated from the Russian Far East. On the contrary, the military factor is looming ominously as a factor threatening the stability of the region. It should be recognized that the new military threat comes from the danger of the Russian Far East's disintegration rather than the expansion of its military capability.

JAPAN'S INVOLVEMENT IN THE RUSSIAN FAR EAST

Government policy

The Japanese government has no officially recognized policy toward the Russian Far East. Since the advent of *perestroika*, its involvement in the Russian Far East has remained minimal. In fact, in the beginning when Gorbachev enunciated the first 'Look East' policy, Tokyo's reaction was negative. Following the policy of 'inseparability of politics and economics (*seikei fukabun*),' the Japanese government was extremely reluctant to engage in active political and economic interaction with the Soviet Far East as long as the territorial dispute remained unsettled. The Japanese government vetoed the entry of the Soviet Union into PECC and refused to extend credit from the Export–Import Bank.

The second stage of the Russian Far East's development coincided with the new direction of the Japanese government. Departing from the rigid application of the policy of 'inseparability of politics and economics,' the Japanese government began to expand its realm of cooperation with the Soviet Union by adopting a policy of 'expanded equilibrium (*kakudai kinko*).' Rigid obstacles for interactions with the Soviet Union were removed. Nevertheless, the new policy continued to approach the Soviet Union as a whole, without enunciating policy specifically toward the Far East.

After the collapse of the Soviet Union, the Japanese government decided to extend economic aid to Russia in concert with other G-7 nations. With this policy, the Japanese government began to approach the Russian Far East as the primary target of its aid. Nevertheless, the precipitous deterioration of the Russian economic situation, the continuing territorial conflict, and the instability of the Japanese domestic political situation were responsible for the Japanese government's inability to map out its policy toward the Russian Far East. As of early 1996, Japan's bilateral assistance to Russia stood at a mere $381 million, including $162 million in humanitarian assistance and

$149 million in technical aid. Most of the $4.1 billion in loans to Russia was trade guarantee and insurance designed to protect Japanese import–export activities.[29] At present, the Japanese government has no comprehensive policy toward Russia, let alone toward the Russian Far East. Its policy toward the Russian Far East can be characterized at best as 'benign neglect.' It has little appreciation for the deepening economic and political crisis that the Far East is undergoing.

One of the crucial impediments for Japan's economic aid to the Far East is that this region is not entitled to Japan's official development assistance (ODA), since it is a part of the Russian Federation, and the Russian Federation is not defined by the Japanese government as a developing country. But the argument that Japan's hands are tied because of the legal limitation with regard to ODA is not very convincing. A law can be changed, and all that is required for Japan to extend massive economic aid to the Far East is to pass a bill in the Diet so designated. What is lacking is the political will to overcome legal limitations.

There are arguments against applying ODA to the Russian Far East. Allocating money from ODA will mean a shrinkage of assistance to other developing nations. There is also the fear that aid to Russia will go down a 'bottomless pit.' In addition, foreign aid to Russia will provoke nationalist resentment among the proud Russians and the Russian government in Moscow. Therefore, if the government money is to be used for aid for the Russian Far East, a special legislation will be required.

The absence of policy notwithstanding, Japan's involvement in the Russian Far East has been expanding. This gap between awareness and reality makes the current situation precarious.

Foreign trade and joint ventures

Russian–Japanese trade continues to play a minimal part in the total volume of Japan's trade. After reaching $6 billion in 1989, the Russian/Soviet–Japanese trade showed steady decline until 1992 ($5.9 billion in 1990, $5.4 billion in 1991, and $3.5 billion in 1992). These declines were in sharp contrast with the sudden increases in Sino–Russian trade, from $2.9 billion in 1988 to $3.9 billion in 1990, and to $6.6 billion in 1992.[30] In 1993, the total volume of Russian–Japanese trade recovered to $4.2 billion, while Sino–Russian trade dropped to $5.4 billion.[31] This increase in Russian–Japanese trade reflected the implementation of Japanese economic aid, the bulk of which was used for trade insurance.[32] Nevertheless, the share of Russian–Japanese trade in Japan's total trade has been minuscule. Of Japan's total exports, its exports to Russia accounted for 1.12 per cent in 1989, 0.89 per cent in 1990, 0.67 per cent in 1992, 0.42 per cent in 1993, 0.29 in 1994, and 0.26 in 1995. Its imports from Russia constituted only 1.43 per cent of the nation's global imports in 1989, 1.40 per cent in 1990, 1.03 per cent in 1992, 1.15 per cent in 1993, 1.27 in 1994, and 1.42 in 1995.[33]

The minuscule share of Russian–Japanese trade within Japan's total trade does not mean that Japan is insignificant to the Far East. On the contrary, as shown in Chapter 3, Japan is the most important and the most steady trade partner of the Russian Far East.

The Far East's largest export item is food, particularly fish (40.3 per cent of the total exports in 1994); energy, minerals, non-ferrous metals (28.8 per cent); and timber and other forestry products (19.2 per cent). In return, the Far East mainly imports foodstuffs (29.9 per cent of the total foreign imports), non-food consumer goods (22.2 per cent), and industrial machinery and equipment (32.4 per cent).

In Sakhalin, the Japanese domination becomes apparent. Of the 136 joint ventures registered in Sakhalin in 1992, 65 were with Japanese, 28 with US partners and 16 with South Korean participation. Almost 80 per cent of exports, or $73 million, handled by these joint ventures were bound for Japan, while 73 per cent of imports, or $15 million, came from Japan in 1992. More than 90 per cent of exported items were fish and fish products.[34]

Impact of trade

Japan's involvement in trade with the Far East is not necessarily a blessing for this region. Japan is interested primarily in raw materials. The more these raw materials maintain their natural form, whether they are timber from Khabarovsk or fish from Sakhalin and Kamchatka, the more valuable they are for the Japanese buyers. Thus the trade pattern is strengthening a colonial character, not bringing economic benefits to the Russian Far East. Not only does the bilateral trade stimulate no indigenous industrial development or development of infrastructure, it also plunders the Far East's natural resources. Nor does it necessarily increase employment opportunities for the local population. In fact, all the industrial enterprises in the Far East are facing a severe crisis without any benefits from integration into the Asia–Pacific region. For the restructuring of the industrial base in the Far East, conversion of the defense industry has paramount importance. However, Japanese businesses are not involved in joint ventures with the defense industry in this region.

As for trade with China, Russia imports from China mostly consumer goods and foodstuffs, more specifically meat, soybeans, corn, tea, textile goods, thermos flasks, footwear, etc. In return, Russia exports to China mostly steel, chemical fertilizers, cement, lumber, machinery, equipment, automobiles, and airplanes.[35] Steel and cement are presumably the surplus of the defense enterprises that are exported to meet the construction boom in China. On the whole, trade with China is not likely to change the Far East's industrial structure.

Thus, the process of integration of the Russian Far East into the Asia–Pacific region conceals within itself disturbing trends that, if allowed to proceed unchecked, will surely damage the industrial structure of the Far

East with serious, perhaps even explosive, political and social consequences.

From the point of view of the private sector there are basically three factors that trigger foreign investment: resources, inexpensive labor, and new markets. Japanese investment in Siberia and the Soviet Far East during the early 1970s was seeking natural resources. But the structural change in Japan's economy in the wake of the oil shocks and the subsequent changes in international market forces drastically reduced Japan's appetite for energy resources in Siberia. As for the second factor, the cost of labor in Russia is certainly cheap, but Japanese businessmen are skeptical about its efficiency. There does exist a sizable pool of efficient, ambitious engineers and skilled workers, particularly in the defense industry in Vladivostok, Khabarovsk, and Komsomolsk-na-Amure, who can be employed by Japanese electronics and electrical goods manufacturers, but a psychological barrier to employing Russians exists among Japanese businessmen, who are eager and willing to hire local workers and engineers in Southeast Asia. The Russians are, after all, Europeans with blue eyes and white skin.

As for the third factor, there is no true market in Russia. Even if the transition to a market economy were successful, the Russian Far East with a population of less than 8 million would not be an attractive market. Moreover, at present the Russian Far East has not been closely integrated into the existing network of Asia–Pacific markets. Investment in Russia is not the same thing as investment in a new plant in Thailand or Indonesia, for instance. Infrastructure in the Russian Far East is woefully inadequate, and there are many other known problems, such as inadequate legal structures, non-convertibility of the ruble, lack of entrepreneurship, the Mafia, etc. that keep Japanese businessmen away from this region. In addition, facing an unprecedented recession in Japan, Japanese businesses are not eager to expand abroad at the moment.

It follows from this that if economic interactions with the Russian Far East are left solely to the private sector, we can expect very little to improve the current state of affairs. Indeed, the most notable development projects in the region are developed with government promotion, and, often, with public support.

Large development projects

Japan's involvement in large projects has been drastically reduced compared with its heyday in the 1970s. Every year a number of missions are sent to Russia, but Japan's participation in large projects remains minimal.

The Yakutia Natural Gas Project is designed to extract natural gas in Yakutia (Sakha), and was started during the 1970s as a joint project of the Soviet Union, Japan, and the United States. It was divided into two stages, prospecting and development. Although the first stage was completed, the second stage, which envisioned annual shipments of 7.5 million tons of liquefied natural gas (LNG) to Japan and the United States for twenty-five years, has been shelved. In the early 1990s, this project was revived when South Koreans approached the Russian government with a proposal to build a pipeline from Yakutia to South Korea through North Korea. In 1992, it was reported that Tokyo-based Tokyo Juki and the Far East Energy of the United States obtained the right to conduct a feasibility study for building a pipeline from Yakutia to Japan through Sakhalin. Either project will require a massive injection of foreign capital.[36]

The Sakhalin Off-Shore Oil–Gas Projects have had their share of ups and downs. In 1975, SODECO (Sakhalin Oil Development Company) and Japan concluded an agreement for natural gas prospecting. A feasibility study of Chaivo and Odopto was completed, but the project was suspended due to international tensions in the early 1980s. In the meantime, the Soviet Union discovered four additional deposits, and in June 1991 opened for international bidding the development of two of these deposits. In January 1992, Marathon Oil, MacDermott, and Mitsui Trading Co. (3Ms) won the bid for a feasibility study. This bid was challenged by then Governor Fedorov, who insisted on granting the bid to SODECO–Exxon. Eventually a compromise was worked out, and the feasibility study was conducted in 1992 by 3Ms, joined by Shell and Mitsubishi Trading Company (4M1S). The 4M1S project, called Sakhalin 2, is due to start, pending the approval of a product-sharing law by the Duma, while the Sakhalin 1 project is still being negotiated by the Russian government and the consortium consisting of SODECO, Exxon, and SMOG (Sakhalin Marine Oil and Gas).[37]

The fourth Forest Resources Development Project was slated to start in the beginning of 1992, but nothing had happened as of October 1994. According to the agreement concluded in October 1991, the so-called K-S project envisioned Japan importing timber and lumber from Russia in return for export of machinery and equipment for the next five years with the total volume of trade amounting to $1.4 billion. The delay can be blamed only on the Russian side which has changed the organizational structure dealing with this project so often that the Japanese side has found it impossible to implement the plan. Moreover, after the agreement was concluded, the Russian government imposed exorbitantly high export taxes.[38]

The Japanese participation in large projects is in a way a symbolic expression of the Japanese private sector's interest in the Russian Far East. Its degree of participation is considerable in the Sakhalin Off-Shore Projects, when it is prudent to lay claim for the future development in terms of its long-term energy strategy.

TWO ALTERNATIVES FOR JAPAN'S POLICY TOWARD THE RUSSIAN FAR EAST

There are two alternatives for Japan's policy toward the Russian Far East. The first is to continue the current course. This means that the Japanese government will continue to have no comprehensive policy toward the Far East, keeping Japan's involvement in the region within the general framework of its aid to Russia, and leaving it basically to the initiative of the private sector. The second alternative is to craft a more assertive, comprehensive policy toward the Far East. For this to occur, the Japanese government, not the private sector, must take the initiative.

Some of the consequences of the policy options are already implied. Unlike China and South Korea, Japan could have a tremendous impact on the modernization of the industrial structure in the Far East. If Japan decides not to use this influence, the Far East has little possibility of achieving modernization for a long time. With the exception of extractive industries, everything that assures short-term profits will decline and, eventually, even extractive industries will not survive. In the Asia–Pacific region, a large area of poverty will emerge, and a North–South division will be created in the Asia–Pacific region, but this time it will be the North that will remain poor and undeveloped.

In the meantime, the need for survival will push the Russian Far East, particularly Amur, Primorye, and Khabarovsk, into further integration with China. This will inevitably provoke the Russian sense of pride. The Russians will accept integration with the United States most easily, with Japan without enthusiasm, but with China they will have the most serious psychological difficulty. Furthermore, it is well to remember that China cannot be a disinterested bystander in Russian–Japanese relations. It is in a position to compete with the Russian Far East for Japanese capital.

The conservative political forces in the Far East that resent the process of integration with the Asia–Pacific region will increase their cooperation with the military. Where no other Far Eastern regional awareness exists, the military alone still maintains this awareness. The military may flex its muscle to prevent further disintegration of the Far East and, consequently, the Russian Far East may slam its doors shut to the outside once again. The first alternative is, therefore, not an attractive option for Japan.

The second option will require that the Japanese government eliminate the self-imposed barrier to ODA and pass a necessary bill in the Diet allowing for the use of ODA money or its equivalent for the Russian Far East. Direct Japanese aid should be targeted at several changes.

First, it should be aimed at the development of infrastructure, especially construction and repair of airports, harbors, roads, bridges, and telecommunications. The Defense Agency should eliminate anachronistic restrictions over the use of the Chitose Airport for Russian air transportation.[39] The existing military telecommunications and transport system should be effectively used for civilian use.

Second, Japanese assistance should include medical aid. Instead of building hospitals, it might be more helpful to establish a helicopter landing depot in Nemuro for emergency treatment of residents of Sakhalin and the southern Kuriles. In other places in the Far East, aid should focus on pediatrics and obstetrics that require the most urgent help.

Third, Japan should assist the Russian Far East with environmental protection, including the disposal of nuclear wastes. With Japanese aid, regional governments may be able to assist cities in sewage treatment and garbage disposal.

Fourth, Tokyo should extend help in the development of intellectual infrastructure, including primary and secondary education (publication of textbooks), establishment of technological and business information centers, training of Japanese language teachers, etc. It is highly recommended that the Japanese government set up Japanese cultural centers in Khabarovsk, Vladivostok, and Yuzhno-Sakhalinsk to serve as information sources, where the latest publications on Japan and essential newspapers, business journals and technological information are accessible to the residents.[40]

Finally, law-enforcement is an area where Tokyo's assistance will be important. This is the least developed area. Although the Japanese Maritime Safety Agency and the Russian Border Guards have taken a modest step toward cooperation, the recent reckless policy pursued by the latter against Japanese fishermen in the Far Eastern waters may reverse this trend. As far as the Russian Ministry of Internal Affairs, *Ministerstvo Vnutrennikh Del* (MVD), and the Japanese police are concerned, there has not been any cooperation due to the absence of any bilateral agreement on law enforcement. With the Russian mafia and the Japanese *yakuza* becoming more deeply and brazenly involved in illegal commercial activities, including the smuggling of drugs and prostitutes, it is important that both law enforcement agencies increase the realm of cooperation.[41]

In extending direct aid to the Russian Far East, the Japanese government should take into consideration several factors. First, given the local competition and rivalry within the region, the final decision as to where direct aid will be extended should reside on the Japanese side. It is equally crucial to prioritize the targets of aid. For practical purposes, Japan should concentrate on four areas: Vladivostok, Khabarovsk, Yuzhno-Sakhalinsk, and the 'Northern Territories.' Second, Japan should be attentive to the sensitivities of the Russians. It should clearly indicate that a stable Russian Far East, which constitutes a part of the Russian Federation, coincides with Japan's national interests as well and that Japanese economic aid is designed to help the region in its process of transition. Third, first priority should be the creation of favourable conditions for a stable market economy in the Russian Far East. The Japanese government should encourage the private sector to help the conversion of the defense industry. Instead of aiming at direct conversion of defense enterprises, however, it might be more helpful, and in the long run more effective, to train engineers and managers in the defense industry to start small and medium size private enterprises. Fourth, the Japanese government should encourage regional governments in Japan to play an active role in establishing contacts with their counterparts in the Russian Far East. It might even set aside a part of ODA (or its equivalent) for use by regional governments. The Far Eastern governors' conference has been organized with the strong backing of the Japanese Foreign Ministry. This is a positive step.

It is important that a more assertive, comprehensive policy toward the Russian Far East is not left solely to the Japanese Foreign Ministry. If the Japanese government decides to extend large-scale economic aid to the Russian Far East at the taxpayers' expense, it must have appropriate justification to convince the public. In the past, Japanese policy toward Russia has been dominated by the Northern Territories question. It is imperative to relativize this question in the comprehensive framework of Japan's global strategy. Economic development of the Russian Far East, however, must go beyond Russo–Japanese bilateral relations. There should be an Asian organization similar to the European Bank for Reconstruction and Development that approaches the reconstruction of the Russian Far East multilaterally. The establishment of a Far Eastern Development Bank is essential. Moreover, economic integration should be considered in a multilateral framework. For example, if the traditional bilateral vision between Russia and Japan continues to prevail, it will be difficult to envision a large Japanese market for processed fish from the Russian Far East but multilateral marketing efforts will create value-added fish products catered to China and Southeast Asia, particularly when protein other than meat is becoming an important source of food throughout Asia–Pacific. And here, the Japanese fishing industry combined with trading companies could provide the necessary technological and marketing know-how. The same can be said about the wood processing industry.

A multilateral vision will also help cushion the traditional Sino–Russian rivalry. Various Sino–Russian cooperation projects are in the implementation stage. Current cooperation between these countries includes the construction of a 70-mile railway from Jilin Province to Zarubino in Primorskii Krai which was slated for completion by 1995,[42] the building of a 1,820-meter long bridge over the Amur River between Blagoveshchensk and Heihe, creation of a free economic zone and the repair of the Siberian railway bridge over the Amur near Khabarovsk.[43]

Since neither Russia nor China is capable of financing these projects, outside capital must be secured. These projects, when completed, will bring economic and political benefits to Japan. Thus, Japan should seriously entertain the possibility of extending aid to these projects.[44]

Cooperation should go beyond purely economic projects. Arms control dialogue should be initiated immediately with the Russian military. The United States and Japan should establish a mechanism of consultation with the Russian government to discuss various arms control issues. The recent rescue exercise involving the Japanese Maritime Safety Agency and the Russian military is a positive step forward, but this type of confidence-building measure should be vigorously pursued.[45] It is important to go beyond the inertial force of the Cold War and to come up with a new security arrangement so as to create a constructive international role for the Russian military.

The establishment of a nuclear free zone around Japan could be a realistic possibility in the post-Cold War era.

Japan's active involvement in the Russian Far East, however, does not solely depend on Japan's determination. Even if Japan decides to take the initiative for massive aid to the Russian Far East, it would be impossible to implement it without certain conditions maturing on the Russian side. Nevertheless, it will be counterproductive to include various conditions such as political and economic stability, convertibility of the ruble, establishment of infrastructure and legal system, high quality of officials, and elimination of criminal elements as preconditions for Japanese cooperation, since requiring such conditions will be tantamount to doing nothing. Japan's active involvement must take the absence of these conditions for granted.

There is one condition that must be achieved for Japanese cooperation to be effectively implemented. The Federal government in Moscow and the Far Eastern regional leaders must reach an agreement on a general strategy for economic development of the Far East and create a mechanism for implementation of this strategy. Moscow and regional leaders have fought for too long a zero-sum game over the control of resources. Both sides have lost much from this mutually unproductive struggle. It is about time to set aside their differences and reach a *modus vivendi* from which both can gain.

THE 'NORTHERN TERRITORIES' PROBLEM AND THE POKIDIN PROPOSAL

Non-visa visits

Since the adoption of the policy of 'expanded equilibrium' by the Japanese government, the importance of the 'Northern Territories' problem has been somewhat diffused. The Foreign Ministry of Japan no longer insists on the return of the 'Northern Territories' as the prerequisite for Japan's economic aid to Russia. To this extent, therefore, the persistent 'Northern Territories' question no longer serves as an insurmountable obstacle for Japan to initiate massive aid to the Russian Far East.[46]

Nevertheless, the 'Northern Territories' question continues to exist and cast a deadly shadow on bilateral relations. Furthermore, the way the Japanese government and, perhaps more precisely, the Foreign Ministry switched its policy somewhat obscures the significance of the policy change. By adopting the policy of 'expanded equilibrium,' the Foreign Ministry never repudiated the policy of 'inseparability of politics and economics.' Therefore, the demand for the return of the 'Northern Territories' continues to be the foundation of Japan's Russian policy, despite many changes in the government.[47]

Non-visa visits that both sides agreed upon at the Gorbachev–Kaifu summit opened a new page in the territorial dispute between the two countries. More than twenty trips have been exchanged between residents of

Hokkaido and the disputed islands since April 1992, in which altogether more than 1,000 Japanese have participated. Previously the Japanese government took the intransigent position that as long as the disputed islands were illegally occupied by the Russian government, the Japanese government could not do anything to legitimize its possession. This policy made the closest neighbors the most distant by artificially building a wall between them and barring any human contact between the two peoples. In 1988, for instance, when an Ainu group attempted to establish a joint venture company with a fishing kolkhoz for a salmon hatchery in Kunashiri, the Foreign Ministry's ax fell and forced the Ainu to discontinue this project. When *Hokkaido Shimbun* reporters visited the disputed islands with Soviet visas in 1990, the Foreign Ministry retaliated by disqualifying these reporters from its press conferences.

Non-visa visits changed all this. The human contacts between the two peoples are now encouraged with the Foreign Ministry's blessing. The Japanese government has extended altogether 263 million yen in aid to Kunashiri, Etorofu, and Shikotan, mainly in the form of food, medical supplies, and vehicles.[48] The press freely covered these visits. Suddenly, with the warmth that has been generated by such human contacts, the artificially frozen relationship between the two peoples has begun to thaw, albeit slowly. A Japanese Foreign Ministry official is required to accompany the Japanese on board the ship bound to the islands. He gives a formal lecture on the Japanese government's official policy on the 'Northern Territories.' He is obligated to protest the custom declaration before landing on the islands. The length of this protest session is becoming a contest among the Foreign Ministry officials accompanying these trips. But these protests no longer have teeth, degenerating into mere formality. The major objective for the Japanese government to proceed with non-visa visits was to cultivate public opinion among the Russians for the return of the 'Northern Territories.' To this extent, General Nikolaev's judgment that Japan is using non-visa visits as a public relations campaign for the return of the islands is justified.[49] The Russians who visit Japan are motivated primarily by the desire to improve their social and economic conditions. Non-visa visits, however, have surpassed the expectations of the Foreign Ministry, contributing to growing awareness among the Japanese that perhaps Japan's direct aid to the 'Northern Territories' may be the best way for the retrocession of the islands.[50]

Pokidin proposal

On 4 April 1994, the 'mayor' of the South Kurile District, Nikolai Pokidin sent a telex to the Mayor of Nemuro, Oya Kaiji, proposing that the mayor permit Japanese fishermen to operate within the Russian territorial waters off the disputed islands in return for fishing fees. This proposal, that was made over the heads of the Sakhalin government and the Federal Commission of Fisheries, created a chain reaction.[51]

Basically, this is an imitation of the Kaigara [Signal'nyi] Island system by which, since 1959, the Japanese fishermen (limited only to one fishing cooperative) have been allowed to harvest seaweed for three months in the territorial waters around the Kaigara Islands, small islets belonging to the Habomai group, in return for the payment of fees amounting to 120 million yen. Strictly speaking, this would have violated the rigid Foreign Ministry's position that nothing would be allowed to legitimize the Soviet/Russian possession of the disputed islands. Actually, in order to avoid the conflict between fish (in this case seaweed) and territory, the Foreign Ministry has quietly permitted this loophole, taking the position that this is a strictly private agreement. Previously these fees were taken away by Moscow, but since 1992 all the income derived from the fees has been transferred to the South Kurile District and the Kurile District (Etorofu).

The Pokidin proposal was attractive to the fishermen in Nemuro and Rausu. It proposed that the Japanese fishermen be allowed to catch ten kinds of fish including shrimp, crab, scallop, herring, and pike, for year-round operations. The Nemuro fishermen, who have been suffering from a reduction of fishing operations in recent years, reacted to this proposal with enthusiasm, putting pressure on Oya, who, facing a tough reelection in September,[52] could not ignore this pressure. Eight fishing cooperatives in Nemuro got together in June, and came up with a concrete counter-proposal to the Pokidin proposal. They proposed to pay an estimated 4.2 billion yen for the fishing fees. Oya played an important intermediary role among Pokidin, Japanese fishermen, and the Japanese Foreign Ministry. These fees would become funds for 'the improvement of social capital and the welfare of the islanders.'[53] The Nemuro fishermen were now convinced that their cooperation with the South Kurile government over fish would ultimately lead to the return of the 'Northern Territories.'

In the background of the Pokidin proposal, there was a collapse of the economy in the South Kurile District. The islanders have expressed their grievances for years over the neglect by the Federal Government as well as the Sakhalin government of the welfare of the residents. The 'Kurile Problem' has been used by politicians, they have complained, for their political purposes, whether it was Yeltsin or Fedorov or the Japanese government, without consideration for the welfare of the residents on the islands. While both governments bickered about the sovereignty over the islands, economic and social conditions of the islands deteriorated. As far as the islanders were concerned, a series of 'programs' emanating from Moscow, such as the Presidential Decree for the Establishment of a Special Economic Zone in the Kuriles issued by Yeltsin in December 1992 and the 'Federal Program of Socioeconomic Development for the Kurile Islands, Sakhalin Oblast until the Year 2000' approved by the Presidium of the Council of Ministers in December 1993, were all empty promises concocted for the political game.[54]

The Pokidin proposal was followed by a letter from the enterprise manager of Ostrovnoi to Oya, proposing that a portion of the fish caught by the

Japanese fishermen would be delivered to Ostrovnoi, and that the Japanese side would also provide modern equipment for vacuum packing, which would be used to market their canned products to the overseas market. Shikotan completely depends on its fish processing enterprise, Ostrovnoi, which used to have six factories on the island. But in 1993, two factories were completely closed down, and since October 1993 the remaining four factories have stopped operation. As a result people are leaving the island *en masse*. The total population, that numbered around 6,600 three years ago, has now been reduced to below 6,000. The reasons for the drastic decline in the operation of the canning factory are twofold. First, the providers of raw fish for the Shikotan canning factory are not the fishing kolkhozes on the island, but rather enterprises and kolkhozes in Sakhalin. The Sakhalin enterprises and kolkhozes have switched to catching fish such as crab and shrimp that can be sold for foreign currency. Second, even if raw materials are provided, Ostrovnoi would have a hard time marketing them on the Russian market, since the transportation cost has become prohibitively high and the existing wholesale network has been completely destroyed. No information is available for the fishing *kombinat* in Kunashiri, which employed 800 workers in 1992, and the fish processing factory in Kurilsk in Etorofu (700 employees),[55] but we need little imagination to surmise that the situation is more or less the same as Ostrovnoi.

The near collapse of the canning industry is only a part of the collapse of the entire economy of the South Kurile District. The transportation to Sakhalin and the mainland is the crucial lifeline of the islanders. There used to be regular flights by a small propeller airplane, an Antonov 24, from Yuzhno-Sakhalinsk to Yuzhno-Kurilsk in Kunashiri and Kurilsk in Etorofu. Also there was ferry service once in two or three days from Yuzhno-Sakhalinsk.[56] But since July 1991, the lack of funds to repair the runway of the Mendeleev Airport on Kunashiri has forced its closure, while the ferry service from Sakhalin has stopped due to the shortage of fuel. Transport of passengers and cargo from the Burevestnik Airport in Etorofu to Kunashiri has been conducted by helicopter.[57] The islands are thus virtually isolated from the outside world. The prices of goods on the islands have skyrocketed to as much as four times that in Moscow. It is believed, however, that if transportation were running regularly, more people would leave the islands. By 1993, in fact, more than 1,500 people had already left the 'Northern Territories.'[58] More than half of the 6,100 Shikotan residents signed a petition to Yeltsin and Japanese Prime Minister Murayama to provide them with aid for their departure from the island.[59]

It is ironic that the Joint Declaration signed by Yeltsin and Hosokawa in October 1993 set in motion political movements aimed at precluding all possibilities of transferring the disputed islands to Japan. In the South Kurile District, these movements came from two directions. The first was Pokidin himself who advocated strong measures against poaching by Japanese fishing vessels in what the Russians consider their territorial waters off the disputed islands.[60] The second was 'Putina 1994,' a tough campaign engineered by the increasingly militant Border Guard under the aegis of General Nikolaev in Moscow and Major-General Vitalii Sedykh in the Kuriles.[61] Taking advantage of the new law on 'the State Border of the Russian Federation' adopted by the Parliament, the Coast Guard in 1993 launched a trigger-happy policy of shooting suspected poachers in the territorial waters. The decision to shoot now rests with a captain of the Coast Guard patrol ship. 'Before one was punished for shooting,' commented one of the Coast Guard officers, 'but now, one could get a medal for it.'[62] On 14 August, the Russian Coast Guard chased for three hours a Japanese fishing boat fishing squid near Akiyuri Island of the Habomai group, and finally fired on it, wounding the captain of the ship. On the following day, a Japanese ship catching crab near Shibotsu Island, another of the Habomai Islands, was fired upon, and one fisherman was seriously wounded.[63] Finally, another shooting incident on 13 August ended up killing a fisherman, this time a Chinese.[64] Despite the Japanese government's repeated protests, the shooting continued. On 5 October, another Japanese fishing boat was fired upon, and sank off Shikotan Island.[65]

It is unlikely that the Pokidin proposal was coordinated with this militant policy. Nevertheless, 'the north wind' by Nikolaev and 'the sun' provided by Pokidin are contributing to a general consensus in Japan to move the Pokidin proposal to a successful conclusion. The Japanese Ministry of Agriculture and Fishery as well as the Hokkaido Development Agency support Oya's attempt. Governor Takahiro Yokomichi of Hokkaido visited Sakhalin, and conferred with Krasnoyarov in July 1994. Both sides agreed to establish a Sakhalin–Hokkaido Fishery Cooperation Conference.[66] More importantly, the Foreign Ministry also wants to reach a *modus vivendi* over a scaled-down version, while making it clear that this affair should not prejudice the territorial question.[67]

Nevertheless, a number of issues on the Russian side will have to be resolved before the Pokidin proposal can be successfully implemented. Inevitably, the Federal Committee on Fisheries and the Sakhalin government are not happy with it. The former fears the establishment of precedent for foreign vessels operating in the territorial waters. The first deputy chairman of the Federal Commission of Fisheries, Aleksandr Rodin, already expressed opposition to the Pokidin proposal.[68] The Sakhalin government is afraid that all of the proposed commissions would go to the South Kurile District without a penny going to its coffers. Furthermore, the Kurile District, where Etorofu belongs, fears that this district will be left out of the deal. The trigger-happy Coast Guard, intent on shooting not merely actual violators but also suspected violators of the territorial waters, may spoil the delicate negotiations. The most tricky question is how to come to an agreement without touching on the territorial dispute. There are many forces on both sides, more on the Russian side than on the Japanese, that are waiting for the chance to spoil the deal by bringing the territorial issue to the forefront.[69]

Despite all these difficulties, if the Pokidin proposal is successfully implemented, this may serve as another important milestone for Japan's involvement in the 'Northern Territories.' The successful implementation of the Pokidin proposal will serve as a breakthrough for Japan's active involvement in the development of not merely the 'Northern Islands,' but also in other parts of the Russian Far East. As of the summer of 1996, however, the Pokidin Proposal remained that, a proposal, with neither Moscow nor Tokyo being able to offer a proposal acceptable to the other side.

The October 1994 earthquake

The northeastern Hokkaido earthquake of 8.1 magnitude on 4 October 1994 directly hit the 'Northern Islands.' Preliminary reports indicated the damage was extensive. According to First Deputy Governor Nikolay Dolgikh of Sakhalin, more than 60 per cent of residential buildings in Shikotan were completely destroyed without any possibility of being repaired. All diesel generators on Kunashiri and Shikotan ceased functioning, and the water, sewage, and heating systems were also completely destroyed. In Shikotan alone nine were killed in Krabozavotsk, and three in Malokurilsk. Since all bakeries were destroyed, the South Kurile District had to be supplied by bread baked on ocean-going fishing vessels. Due to continuing after-shocks and the failure of electricity supplies, people camped in the open.[70] Newspapers reported that on Shikotan 40 per cent of the buildings belonging to Ostrovnoi were destroyed by the earthquake. Residential buildings were less severely damaged on Kunashiri, but a military hospital in Goryachye Kliuchi on Etorofu collapsed, killing five and wounding twenty, with ten missing.[71] This tragedy was compounded by human neglect. The three seismological centers that existed in the South Kurile District had been forced to stop their operations the previous year due to a lack of funds.[72] It was pointed out that buildings that collapsed were built hastily in violation of the building code. The damage of the earthquake was nothing but the telling evidence of the Russian government's neglect of the islands.

The Japanese government reacted to this tragedy quickly, offering humanitarian aid to the islands, including dispatching a team of special rescue personnel. The government even considered dispatching the Self-Defense Force for this purpose. It was the Russian side, however, that reacted to this offer politically. On 5 October, First Deputy Prime Minister Soskovets expressed the hope that Japanese aid would be effectively utilized not only for the reconstruction of the devastated islands but also for the construction of modern infrastructure, but he insisted it was not Japan's aid, but the Russian government's emergency aid project financed by the Russian government that was to finance the reconstruction of the Russian islands.[73] Despite the initial indication that Soskovets would consider non-visa status for Japan's rescue personnel, the Russian government made clear that Russia needed no Japanese manpower. The Japanese government thus had no choice but to limit its assistance to humanitarian material aid. On 10 October, however, after his long meeting with Ambassador Koji Watanabe, Soskovets leaked the information that the Russian government proposed to use the 'fishing fees' for reconstruction of the infrastructure. The Japanese government was forced to respond that it would not be able to accept the 'fishing fees', which was tantamount to recognizing Russian sovereignty over the disputed islands.[74] Moreover, Soskovets proposed to open the territorial waters around the disputed islands also to the South Koreans, a proposal that was bound to alienate the Japanese government. It was also revealed that during the negotiations with Ambassador Watanabe, Soskovets proposed to turn the 'Northern Territories' into a free economic zone and requested Japan's participation in this project. This proposal was the reactivating of the Program for Economic Development in the Kuriles, which had been approved in December 1993, but remained just a paper plan due to the lack of funds. Despite its initial attitude that the rescue operation should be handled without raising the territorial issue, the Japanese government was thus put into a corner where it had to make a decision on the relations between the humanitarian aid and the territorial question. When it had no comprehensive strategy toward the Russian Far East, it was inevitable that the Foreign Ministry reacted to the Russian government's offensive conservatively: Japan's aid to the victims of the earthquake would be limited to humanitarian emergency aid, and no aid would be extended to the long-term project to reconstruct the infrastructure.[75]

One of the most important consequences of the earthquake was the exodus of residents on the affected islands. The first group of children, handicapped, and pensioners numbering 200 who lost their houses were evacuated to Yuzhno-Sakhalinsk and Tver.[76] The South Kurile Emergency Committee headed by Pokidin decided to cover the travel and moving expenses of those who wanted to move to the mainland or Sakhalin on condition that the Federal government approved this plan. Soskovets' reconstruction program sounded hollow to the islanders who had been repeatedly betrayed by the government's rosy promises.[77] It was reported that more than 10,000 people applied to leave the islands. If all who wished to leave the islands did so, the current population (17,000) of the 'Northern Territories' would be reduced to less than half.[78] It is difficult to speculate how this denudement of the 'Northern Territories' would affect the fate of the territorial dispute. Interestingly, public opinion polls taken in Moscow and Vladivostok in 1994 indicate a substantial increase in the number of Russians who favor the return of the disputed territories to Japan. In Vladivostok, those who favored the return of the islands jumped from 60 per cent in May to 89 per cent after the earthquake, and in Moscow, from 10 per cent in May to 60 per cent.[79] It was perhaps because of the shift in the public opinion that both the Sakhalin government and the Russian government have had to demonstrate their position that Russia must hold on to the disputed territory even more firmly. Governor Krasnoyarov, who has not visited the islands since the earthquake, reiterated that the Kuriles would remain an integral part of the Russian territory.[80] Undoubtedly, Soskovets' political maneuver with regard to the rescue operation was motivated by this political consideration.

CONCLUSIONS

The tragic earthquake gave both Russia and Japan an opportunity to cooperate. They might be able to skirt around all the sticking questions and reach an agreement for the development of the 'Northern Territories.' When General Nikolaev's boys were busy cleaning up the devastated outposts, both governments could reach an agreement on the Pokidin proposal that would be able to stop further shooting incidents. Unfortunately, however, the dark shadow of the territorial dispute stealthily enveloped the approach to the rescue operations.

The fate of the Pokidin proposal and reactions of both governments to the earthquake will indicate the future direction of Russian–Japanese relations. What is tested here is not merely the willingness on the Japanese side to go beyond the territorial dispute and initiate a more active policy toward the Far East, but also the willingness on the Russian side to set aside various differences for mutual gain.

NOTES

1 For a detailed discussion on the first three stages, see Nobuo Arai, 'Roshia Kyokuto Chiiki,' *Kokusai Mondai*, no. 386 (1992), pp. 59–67.
2 *Ibid.*, pp. 63–4.
3 Takafumi Nakai, 'Roshia no Chiho Seiji Kaikaku to Kyokuto no Chiho Gikai Senkyo,' Rotobo, *Chosa Geppo*, no. 4 (1994), p. 57. See also Arai, 'Roshia Kyokuto Chiiki,' pp. 64–5; Kathryn Brown, 'Khabarovsk: Resurrecting the *Nomenklatura*,' RFL/RL, *Research Report*, vol. 1, no. 38 (September 1992); and Akio Komorida, 'Roshia Enkaichiho no Henbo to Hochitsujo no Keisei,' *Horitsu Jiho*, vol. 66, no. 7 (1994), pp. 64–75, and no. 8 (1994), pp. 19–27.
4 Brown, 'Khabarovsk,' *op. cit.*, p. 28.
5 Nakai, 'Roshia no Chiho Seiji Kaikaku,' pp. 57–8.
6 P.A. Minakir, 'Roshia Kyokuto Chiiki no Keizai Genkyo to Enerugii Jijo,' Rotobo, *Chosa Geppo*, no. 2 (1994), p. 49.
7 *Ibid.*
8 Nakai, *op. cit.*, p. 58; *RA Report*, no. 16 (January 1994), pp. 100–1.
9 P.A. Minakir, 'Roshia Kyokuto Keizai no Genjo to Hatten Keikaku,' Rotobo, *Chosa Geppo*, no. 1 (1993), p. 70.
10 *Ibid.*
11 *Ibid.*, p. 75.
12 A.G. Ivanchikov, 'Roshia Kyokuto no Boeki Keizai Kankei,' Rotobo, *Chosa Geppo*, no. 7 (1993), pp. 50–1.
13 Minakir, 'Roshia Kyokuto Keizai,' p. 73.
14 There are altogether thirty-two enterprises under the defense industrial ministries, of which shipbuilding, ship-repair, and aviation are dominant. Most of these enterprises are concentrated in the southern parts of Primorskii and Khabarovsk Krais. In 1992, the state order to the defense industry in the Far East declined by

24 per cent compared with 1989, while the state payments to debts incurred by these enterprises stopped. E.V. Gutkova, 'Roshia Kyokuto Chiiki ni okeru Kikaikogyo no Genjo to Hatten,' Rotobo, *Chosa Geppo*, no. 1 (1994), pp. 21–2.

15 Elena Matveeva, 'Dal'nii Vostok bez Rossii,' *Moskovskie novosti*, no. 42 (1994), p. 21.

16 A.G. Ivanchikov, 'Roshia Kyokuto no Boeki Keizai Kankei,' Rotobo, *Chosa Geppo*, no. 7 (1993), p. 56.

17 For Nazdratenko's objections to Sino-Russian border agreements, see *RA Report*, no. 16 (January 1994), pp. 95–6.

18 *RA Report*, no. 16 (January 1994), p. 66.

19 *Hokkaido Shimbun*, 10 September (evening), 1994.

20 Nakai, *op. cit.*, p. 62.

21 *Ibid.*, p. 63.

22 Quoted in *RA Report*, no. 16 (January 1994), p. 66.

23 *RA Report*, no. 16 (January 1994), p. 96.

24 For more detailed analyses of this question, see a series of excellent papers presented at the Monterey seminar in July 1993, in particular, Tsuneo Akaha, 'US–Russian Fishery Joint Ventures: A Curse in Disguise?'; Evgenii P. Jarikov, 'Primorskii Territory: Modern Social and Economic Situation'; Nobuo Arai, 'Russo-Japanese Fishery Joint Ventures in the Russian Far East'; and William C. Potter, 'The Future of Nuclear Power in the Russian Far East.' All available from the Center for East Asian Studies, Monterey Institute of International Studies.

25 For the conditions of the Pacific Fleet, see *Krasnaya zvezda*, 13 November 1993, quoted in *RA Report*, no. 16 (January 1994), p. 121.

26 Aleksei D. Bogaturov, 'The Soviet Asia–Pacific Doctrine: General Outlines,' Takayuki Ito (ed.), *The World Confronts Perestroika: The Challenge to East Asia*, Sapporo: Slavic Research Center, Hokkaido University, 1992, p. 58. According to Major-General G.G. Ivanov, who attended a two-day Japan–Russian military joint seminar in Tokyo in February 1993, Russia had cut the number of troops in its Far Eastern region by about 120,000 to roughly half of what it was five years earlier. *RA Report*, no. 15 (July 1993), p. 135.

27 'Pogranichnye voiska v sisteme bezopasnosti gosudarstva,' *Rossiiskie vesti*, 4 August 1994.

28 Sergei Agafonov, 'Ne budet deneg, budut zhertvy,' *Izvestiya*, 8 September 1994; 'Sozdana Federal'naya Pogranichnaya Sluzhba,' *Pogranichnik*, no. 1 (January 1994), p. 1.

29 'Wagakuni no Tairo Nikokukan Shien no Gaiyo,' Foreign Ministry of Japan, 1 August 1996.

30 Rotobo, *Chosa Geppo*, no. 10 (1993), p. 3.

31 The trade figures for 1993 are from Rotobo, *Chosa Geppo*, no. 7 (1994), pp. 84–5.

32 Rotobo, *Chosa Geppo*, no. 4 (1994), pp. 1–5.

33 Rotobo, *Chosa Geppo*, no. 4 (1996), p. 5.

34 'Saharin ni okeru Gobengaisha Kigyo no Katsudo Jokyo,' Rotobo, *Chosa Geppo*, no. 7 (1993), pp. 57–60.

35 'Churo Keizai Kankei no Shintenkai,' Rotobo, *Chosa Geppo*, no. 10 (1993), pp. 7–9.

36 Kazuo Ogawa, 'Kitaisareru Kan-Nihonkai Keizaiken Kyoryoku Purojekuto,' Rotobo, *Chosa Geppo*, no. 1 (1994), pp. 3–4.

37 *Ibid.*, pp. 5–6.

38 *Ibid.*, pp. 12–13.

39 *Hokkaido Shimbun*, 26 June 1994.

40 Three new information centers will be established in Moscow, Khabarovsk, and Vladivostok in the near future.

41 It is important to note that Lieutenant-General V. Butenko of the Federal Border

Guard visited Japan in 1992 to discuss possibilities of cooperation. *Vestnik granitsy*, nos. 2–3 (1995), p. 5. The 'Putina 94' campaign and the accompanying change of policy of the Border Guard made this cooperation difficult.

42 Kiichi Mochizuki, 'Roshia Kyokuto Zarubino-ko Kakuju Keikaku,' Rotobo, *Chosa Geppo*, no. 9 (1993), pp. 1–14.

43 *RA Report*, no. 16 (January 1994), p. 90. This bridge has not been repaired since its construction in 1916.

44 'Churo Keizai Kankei no Shintenkai,' Rotobo, *Chosa Geppo*, no. 10 (1993), p. 18; Kazuo Ogawa, *op. cit.,* pp. 10–12.

45 *Hokkaido Shimbun*, 11 September 1994.

46 The Japanese government was reportedly prepared to extend $200 million in credits for building a Moscow–Khabarovsk communication line, but no final agreement had been reached due to the absence of a mechanism through which this aid could be extended. *RA Report*, no. 16 (January 1994), p. 32.

47 See Prime Minister Tomiichi Murayama's statement in the Diet that the new relationship with Russia should not change Japan's basic position on the Northern Territories. *Hokkaido Shimbun*, 7 October 1994.

48 *RA Report*, no. 16 (January 1994), p. 39. A Russian source quotes $1.5 million. Both Nikolai Pokidin, administrative head of the South Kurile District, and Gennadii Dolin, administrative head of the Kurile District, criticize Japanese aid. Pokidin complains that Japanese aid to his district consisted of food and unnecessary consumer goods such as parts of television sets and video cameras, but no medical equipment or medical supplies. 'We don't need them, and we did not request them,' he states. Dolin received medical equipment, but he would rather see economic cooperation than humanitarian aid. V. Bantin, 'Kuril'skie bogiachki,' *Sovetskii Sakhalin*, 19 January 1994.

49 'Pogranichnye voiska v sisteme bezopasnosti gosudarstva,' *Russkie vesti*, 4 August 1994. It may be added that this cannot be otherwise. Japanese economic aid cannot be separated from its national interests, and as long as Japan stands for the return of the Northern Territories, Japanese aid to the disputed islands is always motivated by this policy.

50 Hokkaido Institute for the Future Advancement, NIRA Research Report, no. 930022, *Hoppo Yonto Shorai Koso ni kansuru Kisochosa*, Sapporo: Hokkaido Mirai Sogo Kenkyujo, 1993, pp. 23–4; *RA Report*, no. 16 (January 1994), p. 45.

51 Sergei Agafonov, 'Mer Kunashira postavil v tupik Tokio,' *Izvestiya*, 8 April 1994.

52 Oya was re-elected in September 1994.

53 *Asahi Shimbun*, 24 June (evening), and 25 June 1994; P. Ochcrov, 'Ostalos' preodelet' bar'ery', *Sovetskii Sakhalin*, 2 July 1994.

54 For the former, see *RA Report*, no. 16 (January 1994), p. 66; for the Presidential decree, see NIRA Research Report, *Hoppo Yonto Shorai Koso*, pp. 61–3.

55 Oleg Bondarenko, *Neizvestnye Kurily: ser'eznyi razmyshleniia o statuse Kuri'skikh ostrovov*, Moscow: 1992, p. 145; its Japanese translation, *Hoppo Yonto Henkan no Susume*, Tokyo: NHK Shuppan, 1994, pp. 175–6.

56 Bondarenko, *Neizvestnye Kurily*, pp. 127–8; *Hoppo Yonto Henkan no Susume*, pp. 154–5; NIRA Research Report, *Hoppo Yonto*, p. 55.

57 NIRA Research Report, *Hoppo Yonto*, pp. 57–8.

58 V. Bantin, 'Kuril'skie bogiachki,' *Sovetskii Sakhalin*, 19 January 1994.

59 *Hokkaido Shimbun*, 17 August 1994.

60 *Sovetskii Sakhalin*, 27 January 1994. According to Pokidin, Japanese poachers catch 50 tons of crab a year, while Russian fishermen catch only 5 tons. He voiced the concern that before long all the ocean resources would be completely depleted.

61 For the background of 'Putina 1994,' see Stepan Pesh, 'Zapretnyi paltus: yaponskie brakon'ery stanut rybolovami posle uregulirovaniia spora o 'severnykh territoriiakh,' *Novoe vremia*, no. 35, 1994, pp. 24–5; Sergei Agafonov, 'Ne budet

deneg, budut zhertvy,' *Izvestiya*, 8 September 1994.

62 M. Kuzevanova, 'U yaponskikh brakon'erov net vykhodnykh,' *Sovetskii Sakhalin*, 23 March 1994; Sergei Avdeed, 'Yapontsy beznakazanno khozyainichayut v Rossiiskikh vodakh,' *Komsomolskaya pravda*, 2 April 1994; an interview with Vice-Admiral of the Coast Guard, Nikolai Gurinov in *Komsomolskaya Pravda*, 8 September 1994; Gennadii Charodeev, 'Yaponskikh brakon'erov u Yuzhnykh Kuril ne smogli ostanovit' dazhe pulemety pogranichnikov,' *Izvestiya*, 1 September 1994.

63 *Asahi Shimbun*, 16, 17 and 24 August 1994; *Hokkaido Shimbun*, 17 August 1994; Gennadii Charodeev, 'Poterav terpenie, morksie pogranichniki perekhodyat na yazyk pulemetov,' *Izvestiya*, 17 August 1994; Natal'ya Barabash, 'Shkhuna prodolzhala udaliat'sya v storonu Yaponskogo morya,' *Komsomolskaya pravda*, 17 August 1994.

64 *Hokkaido Shimbun*, 14 September 1994.

65 *Hokkaido Shimbun*, 6 October 1994; *Asahi Shimbun*, 6 October 1994.

66 *Hokkaido Shimbun*, 12 July 1994.

67 *Asahi Shimbun*, 12, 25 and 27 August 1994; *Hokkaido Shimbun*, 17 July, 19, 20 and 28 August 1994; Vyacheslav Bantin, 'Rybku s'est',' *Ekho planety*, no. 35 (1994); p. 17; Elena Matveeva, 'Kurilskaya rybalka dlya rybakov Khokaido,' *Moskovskie novosti*, 1 August 1994; Vasiliy Golovnin, '"Putina-94" daet resultati,' *Ekho planety*, no. 26 (1994), p. 10; Ev. Averin, 'Rybku s'est' i printsip sobliusti,' *Sovetskii Sakhalin*, 22 June 1994. For a discerning commentary on the relationship between fish and territory, see Valerii Natarov, 'Pryanik dlya yaponskikh rybakov,' *Literaturnaya gazeta*, 25 May 1994.

68 *Hokkaido Shimbun*, 24 August 1994.

69 It has been reported that preliminary talks have already been deadlocked because of the territorial dispute. *Hokkaido Shimbun*, 7 October 1994.

70 Based on Arai's interview with N. Dolgikh on 5 October 1994.

71 *Hokkaido Shimbun*, 6 and 10 October 1994.

72 *Hokkaido Shimbun*, 7 October 1994.

73 *Asahi Shimbun*, 6 and 7 October 1994; *Hokkaido Shimbun*, 6 and 7 October 1994.

74 *Asahi Shimbun*, 11 October 1994; *Nihon Keizai Shimbun*, 11 October 1994; *Hokkaido Shimbun*, 13 October 1994.

75 *Hokkaido Shimbun*, 11 and 13 October 1994.

76 *Hokkaido Shimbun*, 9 October 1994.

77 *Hokkaido Shimbun*, 10 October 1994.

78 *Hokkaido Shimbun*, 11 October 1994; *Asahi Shimbun*, 11 October 1994.

79 *Asahi Shimbun*, 9 October 1994.

80 *Hokkaido Shimbun*, 13 October 1994.

10 Russo–Chinese normalization from an international perspective
Coping with the pressures of change

James Clay Moltz

INTRODUCTION

For decades, each side of the Russo–Chinese border has lived in considerable isolation from the other. Local populations were taught to mistrust their neighbors and, during the late 1960s, even to expect imminent military attack. After a slow process of border normalization from 1986–91, the borders were suddenly opened fully in 1992 after the signing of the Agreement on Trade and Economic Ties (which created most-favored nation trade status between the two countries).[1] In the two years that followed, both sides received a rude awakening to the difficulties of sharing an economic space while trying to maintain regional political and social harmony.

The population of the Russian Far East, much smaller and economically more developed, suffered from the massive influx of Chinese peasants and traders, amidst the trauma of dealing with political, economic, and social revolution at home. But their reaction was initially one of pleasure, as they welcomed Chinese consumer goods. By late 1993, however, it had soured to one of opposition. Loose Russian border controls led to numerous incidents in which shoddy Chinese goods (and even contaminated food) came across the border into Russian markets. These events created press sensations and met with Russian indignation at being 'tricked' by Chinese traders. More threatening, however, was the large number of undocumented Chinese (especially Chinese-Koreans) who began to settle in Russian Far Eastern cities. As a recent newspaper report from Vladivostok notes: 'The public in the Russian Far East has been alarmed by the quiet expansionism of China into our region . . .'[2] Russian regional leaders also began to raise complaints to Moscow about what they saw as an unfair redrawing of the local borders between the two sides as part of the negotiations that followed the 1991 bilateral border agreement.

On the Chinese side, initial optimism has been tempered by a new perception of racist treatment by at least a portion of the Russian population, intimidation by Russian guards at border crossings, and an increasingly hostile business environment in Russian cities. The recent economic downturn in northeast China (due to the decline of state-controlled heavy industries) has put further stress on this region and raised incentives among enterprise leaders and government officials to look elsewhere for more reliable partners.

If not properly managed, these current tensions could lead to the disruption of this promising political and economic opening, causing the two sides to lapse again into the hostility that has characterized so many previous periods. As Stephen Blank cautions, 'Enmity may quickly come to replace amity.'[3] Russian analyst Alexei Voskressenki makes a similar point, noting that: '. . . any considerable destabilizing event in Russia or in China could revive Sino–Russian territorial problems which can lead to a destabilization in the Far East and in Central Asia.'[4] While a return to the Cold War period of relations is unlikely in the near future, a continued failure to achieve the full fruits of cooperation is entirely possible.

This chapter examines the difficulties of opening a region like the Russian Far East in a period of economic, political, and social turmoil. It considers the peculiar history of Russo–Chinese relations, as well as the factors they share with other border regions. Finally, the chapter concludes with a series of policy guidelines for Russian regional decision-makers for dealing with current dilemmas of living along the Chinese border, drawing from the experiences of other countries.

THE OPENING OF BORDERS INTERNATIONALLY

One of the defining trends of the period since the fall of the Berlin Wall has been the dramatic opening of formerly militarized borders, such as those between Eastern and Western Europe. The past two years have also witnessed the further opening of other, less hostile, borders partially blocked by trade barriers and political mistrust, including those between the United States and Mexico and among the states of the European Union (EU). The difficulties of these processes (stemming illegal immigration, smuggling, and domestic discontent) are tempered only by the knowledge of the high costs of keeping such borders closed (increased tariffs, labor costs, and reduced investment opportunities). One African analyst, for example, pinpoints one of the key reasons for the failure of economic development in his region: 'There has to be a concerted effort at converting those borders from their prevailing postures as ramparts into a new function as bridges.'[5]

Thus, while it is tempting to treat the Russo–Chinese border as a unique region facing unique problems, it is fair to say that this area shares certain common features with other international border regions opening to the world market in an era of expanding free trade. Similar to the border regions of the United States facing Mexico, the Russian Far East faces the simultaneous appeal of a huge neighboring market and the security uncertainty of its surging population. The result in the United States – despite the benefits of an enormous $50 billion trade turnover with Mexico and a domestic culture of greater political tolerance – has been the frequent expression of anti-Mexican sentiments by at least a certain portion of the US population, as well as opposition to increased economic ties by a number of self-serving American political figures (including Ross Perot). This suggests that the problem of coping with cross-border relations is not going to be easy in the Russo–Chinese situation. At the same time, the economic success of the North American Free Trade Agreement (NAFTA) suggests that isolationist policies – while perhaps politically popular in the short term – will have self-defeating long-term implications.

Despite these generalizations, the advantages of opening borders do not always seem apparent to regional participants, especially those steeped in long traditions of hostility, as in the Russo–Chinese case. Historically speaking, the Russian Far East has long had an inferiority complex within East Asia, as an underpopulated and underdeveloped border region surrounded by more powerful neighbors. It has been owned previously by China, occupied by Japan and the United States, and has witnessed major military conflicts on its borders during the Second World War, the Chinese revolution, and the Korean War. Its social history has been similarly marked. On the southern side of the border, in northeast China, almost a century of foreign exploitation and decades of communist-inspired propaganda created a similar anti-foreign mentality. Moreover, China's educational system continues to present the Russian seizure of formerly Chinese lands in the Amur and Ussuri river basins as unjust and, perhaps, temporary.[6]

Indeed, historical Russo–Chinese conflicts in the region form a large part of the background necessary to understanding today's problems. Beginning in the mid-1600s, Russian traders and empire-builders met with stiff Chinese opposition as they reached the Pacific Ocean and tried to explore the more hospitable southern territories near the Amur and Ussuri rivers.[7] After several clashes, the dominant Chinese forced the Russians to sign the Treaty of Nerchinsk (1689), which closed the Amur and Ussuri regions to Russian settlement.[8] Peace reigned for almost two centuries as Russian explorers redirected their attention to the northeast regions of the Asian continent and to Alaska. But by the mid-1800s, China's internal problems and the pressure of other foreign adversaries loosened its grip on the Amur and Ussuri regions. Sensing its long-awaited opportunity, Russia set up forts and settlements in the area, in violation of prior treaties. Unable to defend its northern borderlands, a weak and divided China surrendered first the Amur region in the Treaty of Aigun (1858) and then the Ussuri region in the Treaty of Peking (1860).[9] With China self-absorbed by its internal problems, Russia began to settle the region in earnest, aided particularly by the linkages provided to the more populated west by the trans-Siberian railroad. Russians also moved into significant portions of Manchuria, playing a major role in the development of Harbin, despite the loss of strategic ports in the region after the Russo–Japanese War (1904–5). Relations with China declined until 1949, when the Communist Revolution in China offered an unprecedented opportunity for improving relations. But after scarcely a decade of 'brotherly' socialist ties, political differences and strategic conflicts between the two neighbors resulted in a breakdown. Russia's revolution had reached a plateau, and its leaders wanted domestic and international stability above all else; China's revolution had not yet peaked, and its leaders wanted continued social revolution, as well as, militarily, an atomic bomb to wield on the international stage. The Soviet Union could not comply with these desires and unceremoniously pulled out its economic advisors and technical specialists in 1960. This fissure did not heal until the late 1980s, when steady Russian overtures and new Chinese economic pragmatism at last won out over past political disputes.

THE RECENT RAPPROCHEMENT: PROGRESS AND PROBLEMS

Now, after decades of military tension and mutual economic underdevelopment on either side of their shared border, Russia and China have begun a new path in their bilateral and border relations. Since the normalization of relations in 1989, this once highly-fortified border region has been transformed into a dynamic new trading arena. The rapid expansion of Russo–Chinese relations over the past several years caused a dramatic increase in bilateral contacts among government entities, newly private companies, the respective militaries, and individual citizens. The first Chinese consulate in the Russian Far East opened in Khabarovsk in September 1992[10] and has been followed by another in Vladivostok, as well as by several other trading offices. Similar openings at border crossings led to a rapid development of trade, which, even by 1992, totaled $413 million in turnover between China and Primorskii Krai alone.[11] Total bilateral trade surged to a height of almost $8 billion a year in 1993, causing the legacy of the cold war in Russo–Chinese relations from 1960–85 to be seemingly erased.

Yet, in response to high levels of illegal Chinese immigration, Russian authorities were forced in 1994 to institute new controls that made it much more difficult for Chinese citizens to enter the Russian Far East without a visa. Ironically, many of these illegal Chinese were engaged in mutually profitable trade with Russian citizens and enterprises. The result, in tandem with a slight reduction in access to illegal Chinese immigrants, was a dramatic reduction in bilateral trade, which plummeted to $5.1 billion in 1994.[12] These trade levels fell despite the influence of higher trade volume between enterprises located in interior regions and in state-to-state trade (such as arms sales). Ironically, many people on the Russian side do not seem disturbed by these trends, and would seem to prefer it if the many thousands of Chinese now living and working in the region would simply return home. Reeling from the rapid breakdown of old economic safety nets, the heavy toll of several years of high inflation, and a dramatic increase in crime, Russians seem to be in the mood for scapegoating any and all foreign entities. Such attitudes are short-sighted, however, as Chinese trade and investment may be one of the keys to the successful integration of the Russian Far East into the greater Pacific Rim economy.

The attitude of Russian regional leaders has, in an international context, seemed even more strange. In Amur Oblast, Khabarovsk Krai, and Primorskii Krai, regional governors have appealed to Moscow not for help in expanding trade, but for increased domestic subsidies. This behavior, consistent with conservative trends in Russian politics more generally, suggests a return to a belief that the answers to current problems lie in a return to past policies. Indeed, there has been a renewed effort by local government officials to enlist North Korean (rather than Chinese) labor for a number of timber harvesting, construction, and other labor-intensive projects.[13] Apparently, due to the long Russian experience (albeit often negative) with North Korean laborers, these deals are seen as politically 'safer' and 'more reliable' than enlisting nearby Chinese, whose presence could cause social disruptions. Primorskii Krai Governor Yevgeniy Nazdratenko visited North Korea in March 1995. He stated after his trip that: 'Resumption of ties with the DRPK may happen to be very profitable for the Maritime Territory.' Nazdratenko chastised the Yeltsin government for jeopardizing these relations in the past few years and called on Moscow to reorient its policies toward Russia's 'more reliable' Korean neighbor.[14]

The regional press – perhaps drawing on trends in popular sentiment – has tended to fan rather than cool the flames of tension in the Russo–Chinese relationship. Without providing sources, one Russian journalist puts the figure for Chinese immigrants at 5 million for the Far East and Siberia alone.[15] This type of journalism only fuels the fires of racism. Another report quotes a People's Deputy to the Russian Duma as saying: 'At first the [Chinese] colonization of Russian lands will bear an economic character, but then political problems might crop up.'[16] In many reports, the anticipation of an eventual Chinese seizure of the Russian Far East is envisioned, despite the lack of evidence of such intentions (much less capability) on the Chinese side. According to Russian analysts, China is naturally threatening to Russia because of its very dynamism and size, compared to a Russian Far East that is weak and even declining in population.[17] If such trends continue, the argument goes, Russia will simply not be able to defend its interests in the region.

To many Russians, the border dispute appears to be a legitimate complaint. In fairness, slightly more territory is being returned to China than is being returned by China to Russia in the ongoing border demarcation process. While Russians in the region admit that this area was seized by force or coerced from the Chinese in unfair negotiations over a century ago, they point to the case of similar seizures internationally that have never been rectified. One Vladivostok newspaper analyst recently bent American history after the declaration of the Monroe Doctrine in 1823 to his purposes, arguing:

The first victim of this new foreign policy was Mexico, which only recently had achieved independence from the Spanish crown. Regular attacks by American soldiers into its territory began, and in 1848 the government of this country was forced to turn over Texas, New Mexico, a significant part of California including the port of San Francisco – in all more than half of its lands.[18]

He argues that, of course, America has never returned this territory or sought to 'rectify' these seizures. Such arguments represent a common attitude in the region. Moscow, by contrast, has largely tried to appease Beijing, given the Russian government's interest in arms sales and stable political relations. This too has drawn the ire of Russian Far Easterners, who complain about deals struck behind their backs.[19]

Whether Far Easterners are right or wrong on the best approach to the border negotiations, a central question that does not seem to be addressed in the regional debate is what path of relations is likely to be more fruitful in the long run – one towards rapprochement (albeit with certain risks), or one back towards old-style relations and more traditional economic partners (such as North Korea)? For the answers to these questions, it is useful to return again to the international context of these developments.

RETURNING SOME SENSE TO THE CHINESE DISPUTE

Chinese business people have expanded their networks of connections and activities throughout the Asian-Pacific region. Due to its previously closed borders, the Russian Far East has only recently been affected by these dynamics. Past Soviet policies also created suspicions of foreigners, a condition only worsened by the artificial Russification of the Russian Far East under Stalin, which eliminated many ethnic minorities from the region. Where immigration has been more open, such as in Indonesia, Hong Kong, and other countries of Southeast Asia, former mainland Chinese have risen to play leading roles in these business communities. But many Russians fear that with its overwhelming population and shared border with Russia, China could conceivably use its economic representatives to achieve political aims, including even Russian territory. However, several mitigating factors in the Russian situation are worth noting, which, while they do not obviate all of Russia's concerns, suggest that Russia should be able to manage the influx of Chinese successfully.

One key point worth mentioning in this discussion is that Russia is more developed – both in terms of its technological base and its educational level – than China. Where it lags behind is in the development of capitalist business techniques, which China has been developing since the late 1970s. Recent problems of alleged Chinese 'exploitation' of Russians stem largely from this gap. Russia's lack of a modern business infrastructure, including the range of consumer protection laws and regulations that might guard local consumers against shady foreign business practices, allowed Chinese businessmen to get away with dumping low quality products. That is, the lack of Russian customs controls and consumer protection mechanisms provided opportunistic

Chinese traders with an open environment to exploit. This does not excuse the Chinese from responsibility, but it does suggest that Russia may share the blame for these problems. Also, since China's Heilongjiang province is not one of the more economically developed regions of China (at least in terms of market reforms), Russia was dealing with some of the more backward segments of the Chinese business community. Primarily, their wares included low-priced clothing, consumer goods, and food products. This wave of Chinese traders benefited from lax Russian immigration controls and the lack of visa regulations. The fact that Russian consumers had little experience in this area and needed almost everything only worsened the situation. These conditions almost encouraged Chinese traders to dump their products for profit. But new inspection regulations instituted in early 1994 (along with changes in the visa law) have dramatically reduced the problem of illegal trading due to new mechanisms for customs inspections and quality control. While this has resulted in a short-term reduction in overall Russo–Chinese trade, it should lay a better groundwork for more stable long-term economic relations.

As time passes, a growing percentage of Russia's trade with China is moving beyond the limits of the border trade that dominated its early years. Specifically, new orders from Chinese state enterprises and the military for Russian manufactured goods have allowed Russia to build up a large trade surplus with China. Along with Turkey and Iran, China is one of the few countries with a large demand for Russian technologies, particularly in the areas of power generation, military hardware, and machine tools. Additional orders are likely to be forthcoming as the rapidly growing Chinese economy continues to develop. Thus, Russia faces no real choice but to try to live with the difficulties this trade entails. At the same time, however, it will be increasingly important for Russia to think through the consequences of its arms sales and military cooperation, especially in the context of possible future Chinese political instability.

Rather than lapsing into self-defeating, ultra-nationalist policies, therefore, it would seem more expedient for Russian regional leaders to acquire a more realistic understanding of the nature of the Chinese 'invasion.' Far from a government-organized campaign to take over the region, the influx of Chinese is more accurately described as an exodus by opportunistic Chinese peasants looking to improve their economic conditions in an over-heating and inflation-ravaged Chinese economy. China's own ability to control the economic impulses of its population remains highly dubious, as does the center's control on the regions, including northeast China. These points suggest that the 'invasion' is really one of individuals or small family-based groups, not a national movement or an organized state-controlled enterprise. This does not make the reality of undocumented Chinese in Russia any less of a concern, but it does suggest that new, more effective strategies may be possible for dealing with it. One such strategy, not much discussed in the local press, is simply to coopt Chinese by making them Russian citizens. This would both solve the regional labor shortage and create fewer political incentives (if, in fact, they existed in the first place) for acting as 'fifth columns' for Beijing's alleged territorial aspirations.

The opening of the border with China and the influx of illegal aliens has also raised concerns about the possible use of cheap Chinese labor. However, the option of completely closing the border and halting mutual trade and investment is not a realistic choice for Russia. Evidence from the international economy suggests that it is better for a more developed neighbor (Russia) to engage the economy of its lesser developed and more populated neighbor than to attempt to keep the neighbor out and prolong underdevelopment there.[20] These calculations formed the basis for the passage of NAFTA in the United States, despite objections by certain politicians.

Indeed, a more serious threat than current immigration problems is the threat of truly uncontrolled migration if China experiences a sharp decline in its living standards or experiences future political instability.[21] This could cause Russian Far Eastern leaders to wish that they had helped to contribute to regional stability through the construction of more stable economic relations, rather than contributing to cross-border political tensions and impeding economic cooperation.

Ideas abound for international cooperation involving the Russian Far East and northeast China. Since the early 1990s, for example, various schemes have been proposed for the development of the Tumen River area along the Russian–Chinese–North Korean borders.[22] The most prominent among these is the Tumen River Area Development Programme supported by the UN Development Programme (UNDP). The concept is to develop border areas of the three riparian countries, either jointly or separately, in such a way as to complement the developmental needs of the respective countries. In May 1995, representatives of China, Russia, and North Korea initialed the Agreement on the Establishment of the Tumen River Area Development Coordination Committee, and along with Mongolia and South Korea also initialed the Agreement on the Establishment of the Consultative Commission for the Development of the Tumen River Economic Development Area and Northeast Asia and the Memorandum of Understanding on Environmental Principles Governing the Tumen River Economic Development Area and Northeast Asia.[23] Pending ratification by the parties, the agreements will provide a legal foundation upon which to advance international cooperation in the development of the Tumen River Area and Northeast Asia.

From the perspective of the Russian Far East, there are both favorable and disconcerting factors surrounding this scheme.[24] On the favorable side are the geographical location of the Tumen River Basin, some complementary economic conditions of the riparian countries and other countries (including Japan and the United States), the improving political climate in Northeast Asia, and the growing interest in attracting international capital and technology into the border areas of the riparian countries.[25] So far China has been much more enthusiastic about the Tumen River development project than Russia. This is most visibly symbolized by the fact that China has already invested much of its own resources in the construction and improvement of the Hunchun–Tumen rail connection along the Tumen River. But very little infrastructural development has taken place on the Russian side. Russia has several concerns: the political and security implications of the development of the border region, particularly with respect to Russian–Chinese relations,[26] the political uncertainty in North Korea, the environmental impact of development in the border region, and the enormous financial requirements for which domestic supply is woefully inadequate. While recognizing the potential economic benefits of regional economic cooperation in Northeast Asia, including this project, Moscow is preoccupied with the more immediate task of domestic economic reforms. Moreover, leaders in Moscow and in the Far East do not necessarily see eye to eye with respect to international economic cooperation. Moscow has been particularly sensitive to any schemes that might compromise its control over the Far Eastern territories.

CONCLUSIONS

Many Russian economists continue to maintain that improved relations with China are the key to the Russian Far East's successful integration into the Pacific Rim economy. In the past year, the Yeltsin government seems to be getting this message, spurred on largely by the growing size of Russo–Chinese trade and the importance of Russia's surplus for the overall Russian trade balance. But aid from Moscow alone can solve neither the dilemmas of regional development nor the current difficulties in relations with China. Rather than falling back into isolation policies, the experience of other similar border areas internationally suggests that Russian regional leaders would be better served by resisting the temptation to blame the Chinese. A more forward-looking policy would be to create policies that would enable Chinese enterprises and labor to play a positive role in Far Eastern development strategies, while at the same time using the necessary administrative controls to both limit potential illegal Chinese activities and to provide guarantees so that Chinese workers and businesses can fill niches not provided for by Russian sources. Of course, China need not be granted special favors over other regional actors, such as South Korea, Japan, or the United States. At the same time, however, the Chinese should not be discriminated against simply because of racist scapegoating and Russia's own economic and legislative inefficiencies. The economic potential of the huge Chinese market (which dwarfs that of Mexico) should act as a beacon for Russian Far Eastern development. It would be a sad irony if regional political problems were to jeopardize the best chance the Russian Far East has for successful integration into the greater Pacific Rim economy.

NOTES

1 See Vladimir S. Miasnikov, 'Present Issues between Russia and China: Realities and Prospects,' *Sino-Soviet Affairs* (Seoul), vol. 18, no. 2 (Summer 1994), p. 34.
2 Vladimir Rybakov, 'U Kitaya v dozhinikakh?' *Vladivostokskoe vremya*, 7 March 1995, p. 2.
3 Stephen J. Blank, 'The New Russia in the New Asia', Monograph of the Strategic Studies Institute, US Army War College, Carlisle, Penn., 22 July 1994, p. 29.
4 Alexei D. Voskressenski, 'Current Concepts of Sino–Russian Relations and Frontier Problems in Russia and China', *Central Asian Survey*, vol. 13, no. 3, 1994, p. 378.
5 A.I. Asiwaju (Nigerian academic and government advisor), 'Borders and Borderlands as Linchpins for Regional Integration in Africa: Lessons of the European Experience,' *Journal of Borderlands Studies*, vol. 8, no. 1 (Spring 1993).
6 Information from Sinologists from the Institute of Far Eastern Studies (Moscow), provided in comments at the conference on 'Chinese Immigration in the Russian Far East,' 12–13 December 1994, Georgia Tech University, Atlanta, Georgia.
7 For two recent histories of this period, see W. Bruce Lincoln, *The Conquest of a Continent: Siberia and the Russians*, New York: Random House, 1994; and Benson Bobrick, *East of the Sun: The Epic Conquest and Tragic History of Siberia*, New York: Poseiden Press, 1992.
8 A subsequent agreement (Treaty of Kyakhta, 1727) clarified the exact demarcation of the border and established locations for border stations, outposts, and beacons. See Voskressenski, *loc. cit.*
9 China fared somewhat better on its western borders with Russian Central Asia, receiving certain contested territories in the Ili valley from the Treaty of St Petersburg (1881).
10 *RA Report*, no. 14, January 1993, p. 35; Radio Vladivostok, 16 September 1992.
11 *RA Report*, no. 15, July 1993, p. 107; *Finansovye izvestiya*, 26 February 1993, p. 2.
12 ITAR-TASS, 16 April 1995; in FBIS/SOV, 95/075, 19 April 1995, p. 34.
13 Remarks by Alexander Zhebin at the Center for East Asian Studies, University of California, Berkeley, 8 May 1995.
14 On Nazdratenko's trip, see Andrei Polutov, 'Chto privelo Nazdratenko v Pkhen'yan?' *Vladivostok*, 18 March 1995, p. 14.
15 Viktor Ivanov, 'Ves' mir poka ne prevratilsya v Chinatown. No mozhet prevratit'sya,' *Vladivostokoe vremya*, 19 January 1995, p. 5.
16 'Primor'ya!' *Utro Rossii*, 23 February 1995, p. 1.
17 See V. Shabalin and V. Portyakov, 'O sopostavlenii dinamiki rosta ekonomicheskikh potentsialov Rossii i Kitaya,' *Problemy Dal'nego Vostoka*, no. 3, 1993.
18 Ivan Yegorchev, 'Demarkatsiya granits ili peresmotr istorii?' *Utro Rossii*, 18 March 1995, p. 3.
19 Marina Yashina, 'Legko "chertit" grantisy iz Moskvy,' *Vladivostok*, 3 August 1994, p. 3; also, 'Kak v Gosudarstvennoi dume "utochnyaut" russkie granitsy,' *Vladivostok*, 9 February 1995, p. 6.
20 For a study of the economics of free trade versus protectionism on the US–Mexican border, see Raffaele DeVito and Jacob Wambsganss, 'Maquilas and NAFTA: Implications of a Free Trade Microcosm,' *Journal of Borderlands Studies*, vol. 8, no. 2 (Fall 1993), pp. 105–20.
21 I am grateful to Vladimir Portyakov for raising this issue in an interview with him at the Institute of Far Eastern Studies, June 1995, Moscow, Russia. On the demographic forces behind China's population growth, see Jack A. Goldstone, 'The Coming Chinese Collapse,' *Foreign Policy*, no. 99 (Summer 1995), pp. 35–52.
22 For a description of the recent developments surrounding the Tumen River project, see Tsuneo Akaha, 'The United Nations, Korea, and Northeast Asia: The Tumen

River Project and International Cooperation,' paper presented at the Min-Sok Forum 'The UN and Korea,' 27 June 1995, San Francisco, California.

23 Correspondence with Michael Underdown, Programme Manager, Tumen River Area Development Programme, 27 June 1995. See also *Guo Ji Shang Bao*, 2 June 1995, p. 1.

24 For a critical assessment of Russia's participation in the Tumen River development project, see Anna V. Shkuropat, *The Emergence of Pacific Russia: A Prymorsky Perspective*, Princeton, NJ: Princeton University Program on US–Japan Relations, 1995, pp. 80–7.

25 Examples include the declaration by China of Hunchun as a Special Economic Zone (SEZ), Russia's establishment of a Free Economic Zone (FEZ) in Nakhodka, and North Korea's declaration of the Rajin-Sombong area as a 'free trade zone.'

26 In addition to the issues discussed above, China's interest in developing transportation access to the Sea of Japan via the Tumen River development has obvious economic and security implications for the Russian Far East.

11 Russia's Far East in contemporary Russian–Korean relations

Vladimir F. Li

THE RADICAL ECONOMIC REFORM AND THE RUSSIAN FAR EAST

The Russian Far East occupies a special place in the geo-political area of the Asian-Pacific region due to a number of factors. The region boasts vast natural resources, especially timber, coal, gas and non-ferrous metals. Currently, the Far East's share in Russia's overall production of diamonds is 98 per cent, tin 80 per cent, gold 50 per cent, tungsten 14 per cent, coal 13 per cent, lead and zinc 10 per cent. More than 20 per cent of Russia's hydropower resources, as well as vast biological marine reserves are also concentrated in the region.[1] The harbors, which never freeze, and the fertile land found in this maritime territory offer a unique environment for civilized life. Anyone who has visited it at least once, however, is well aware that the Soviet totalitarian system's reliance on non-economic coercion has deformed the development of productive forces in Russia's wealthiest region. In 1992 and 1993 alone, Khabarovsk Krai, Sakhalin Oblast, and the Republic of Sakha (Yakutia) were forced to cover 50 to 70 per cent of their budgetary expenditures with subsidies from the Russian Treasury.[2] Through the years of Soviet totalitarianism an extremely ugly economic structure developed here. Nearly two-thirds of the production potential of the manufacturing industry is devoted to the military-industrial complex.

The deep and protracted crisis which affected the entire Russian economy with the disintegration of the USSR moved to the forefront the issue of survival and rapid revival of the Russian Far East through the mobilization of Russia's internal resources and the development of an international division of labor in the Asia–Pacific region. In this respect, Russia's Far East is counting on the accelerated development of relations with its nearest neighbors – South Korea and North Korea. The Russian President's April 1992 decree 'On social and economic development of the Far Eastern territories' and a number of government resolutions pertaining to the Primorskii and Khabarovsk territories, the Sakhalin region, and the Kurile Islands have been a tremendous benefit to the region. These include the right to be a key participant in setting up free economic zones, privileges to market some export products (up to 30 per cent), and permission to attract foreign investors.

RELATIONS WITH NORTH KOREA

What is behind the Far East's special interest in establishing business connections with the Korean peninsula? It is worth recalling that the modern history of Korea's independence began in the autumn of 1945 when the Soviet and American armed forces liberated the Korean peninsula from Japanese colonial occupation. The decolonization of Korea, however, did not bring peace and good fortune to the peninsula. A tragic period related to the Cold War and the Soviet–American global rivalry. Between June 1950 and July 1953 the fratricidal war swept the peninsula bringing huge casualties and destruction.[3] After signing an armistice, the Soviet leadership continued to strengthen North Korea's military–strategic potential in every way possible and did not recognize South Korea for many years, although South Korea had declared independence in 1948.

The futility of the Kremlin's long-standing orientation to Pyongyang was obvious earlier, but became especially pronounced during the years of Soviet *perestroika*. The unofficial summit meeting between the USSR President Mikhail Gorbachev and South Korean President Rho Tae Woo took place in June 1990 in San Francisco. On 30 September 1990, the Soviet Union and the Republic of Korea signed the declaration on the establishment of diplomatic relations.[4] Since that time Moscow has become, at least for now, the only self-proclaimed superpower to maintain official relations with both states of the Korean peninsula. This major diplomatic feat has undoubtedly strengthened both the position of the former USSR and the Republic of Korea. At the same time, it has marked a turning point in the radical realignment of the major powers in the Asia–Pacific region.

The political and business partnership between Moscow and Seoul has considerably dwarfed the importance of the Soviet (now Russian)–North Korean military–political and economic alliance, which was based on the 6 July 1961 alliance treaty signed by Nikita Kruschev and Kim Il Sun.[5] After the collapse of the USSR, Russia, as its successor, denounced Article 1 of the treaty which provided for each side's obligation to render immediate 'military and other aid by all available means' in case of 'armed attack' by a third party. The Pyongyang leadership reacted strongly to this action by Moscow – an action which had been taken largely due to pressure from Seoul. It is precisely since that time that North Korea has stepped up efforts to develop its own nuclear arms, a move which has sharply threatened the delicate balance of forces on the Korean peninsula and in the region as a whole.

The process of diversifying economic, scientific, and technical relations is very painful for both North Korea and the Russian Federation. The following analysis of statistical data confirms this.

Over the past two or three decades when Soviet–Chinese and Soviet–Japanese relations were locked in crisis, North Korea was the USSR's key foreign partner in East Asia. In the 1980s the USSR's exports to North Korea covered 70 to 80 per cent of Soviet imports of magnetite clinker,

50–75 per cent of cement, 20 per cent of pig iron, 75 per cent of lime, as well as 15 per cent of starch, 13 per cent of rice, and 18 per cent of sports footwear.[6] The bulk of these deliveries (up to two-thirds) were dispatched to the regions of Siberia and the Far East. On the basis of the Soviet–North Korean scientific and technical agreement of 14 October 1957, extensive geological and geographical prospecting for minerals was carried out in the northeastern part of North Korea and the northeastern part of the Primorskii territory. This helped enrich the data concerning the nature of the Pacific ore belt.[7] According to Russian specialists, this joint research contains unique information on the deposits of a number of minerals which could be developed through Russian–Korean business cooperation. However, under conditions of stagnant Russian–North Korean relations the unique research is lying idle at the Russian Academy of Sciences' Far Eastern branch in Vladivostok.

Currently, the Russian Far East economy is suffering from curtailed business relations with North Korea in such labor-intensive sectors as the timber industry. It is worth recalling that in the former USSR the slave labor in timber-cutting and its initial processing and export were performed by hundreds of thousands of convicts, Gulag prisoners. Shutting down many of these concentration camps during the years of post-totalitarian liberalization caused a sharp reduction in timber production, including in the East Russian region, as well as an acute shortage of timber for both export and domestic needs.

Poor road conditions in the Far East and Siberia mainly affected lumbering during severe winters, which Russians, working on contracts in the European part of the country, cannot always endure. The Soviet–North Korean agreement on joint development of timber resources of the Khabarovsk territory and the Amur region, signed on 30 July 1957, helped solve the problem. Thanks to this agreement, which was extended in 1960, 1967, 1972 and 1981, the North Korean side largely contributed to reactivating the dying timber industry of the Far East. By the mid-1980s the North Koreans had already created ten large forestry plants in the Khabarovsk territory with an annual output of 5 million cubic meters of timber. Moreover, five North Korean timber enterprises with an annual capacity of 2.4 million cubic meters were set up in the Amur region. By then North Koreans had procured over 60 million cubic meters of commercial timber in the Far East, as well as some 3 million cubic meters of wood chips of which the Soviet side exported almost the full amount to Japan and other East Asian countries. In turn, this cooperation allowed North Korea to meet nearly 60 per cent of its requirements for timber.[8]

However, since the late 1980s and early 1990s cooperation between North Korea and the Soviet Union (Russia) has encountered many problems. North Korean lumber workers, taking advantage of the inaction of the Russian administration, irrationally cut down the best coniferous forest tracts, went back on their commitments for tree planting in the areas of cutting, inflicted grave damage on the region's environment, and produced low-quality timber products. Cases of mass violations of human rights in the closed settlements of North Korean workers have also become public knowledge. All this has led, particularly since the collapse of the Soviet Union, to further curtailment of timber-cutting cooperation between North Korea and Russia. This, in turn, has aggravated the crisis in the timber industry of Russia's Far East. The slave labor of tens of thousands of North Korean workers used to give the Russian Far East up to 3 million cubic meters of timber a year. The decline of this business threatens devastating losses (exports included), which Russia so far has been unable to rectify even with painstaking effort.

RELATIONS WITH SOUTH KOREA

The strategic course of post-totalitarian Russia to establish business relations with Seoul is largely dictated by objective requirements of the Russian economy, especially of the Far Eastern economic region. Russia hopes, on the basis of a mutually-beneficial cooperation, to involve South Korea in its projects to overhaul the economy of the Far East. The initial trade and economic transactions gave cause for optimism. In exchange for raw cotton Russia received high-quality steel and industrial equipment for its Far Eastern enterprises. The ports of Nakhodka and Pusan established direct overseas freight and passenger traffic. The Russian vessels registered at the Far Eastern steamship company began to regularly call at South Korean ports for repair. In December 1990, the two countries signed an agreement on scientific and technical cooperation. In January 1991, Seoul pledged a $3 billion loan for the Soviet Union for a term of three years, including $1.5 billion to pay for commodities purchased by the Soviet side. As a result, in 1991 the trade turnover between the two countries exceeded $1.2 billion compared to $888 million in 1990.[9]

Russian–South Korean cooperation has noticeably reanimated the life of the Russian Far East. By 1991, twenty-three Russian–South Korean joint ventures had been set up, of which thirteen were located in the Far Eastern economic region, nine in Moscow and one in St Petersburg. In 1992, twenty-six offices of large and medium-sized South Korean firms began operating, including eight in the Russian Far East.[10]

On 19 November 1992, during President Yeltsin's visit to South Korea, the two countries signed a treaty on guidelines in relations between the Russian Federation and the Republic of Korea, creating a more extensive international and legal basis for mutually-beneficial cooperation. During the visit the sides stated the similarity of their positions regarding the joint development of productive forces in the Russian Far East. The largest cooperative projects between the two countries are related to Russia's Far East. These projects include the joint development of Yakut coal, the transportation of Siberian gas and oil, the reconstruction of the port of Nakhodka, and South Korean involvement in the conversion projects of forty-five defense plants of the

Primorskii territory and the Khabarovsk region.[11] Direct exchanges between military agencies of the Russian Federation and the Republic of Korea are being established, signalling the mutual recognition of a military-strategic role in the Asia–Pacific region. To promote scientific and technical cooperation with Russia, the South Korean government approved in 1992 six basic areas of cooperation, including aeronautics and space research; communications; transport and ground equipment; shipbuilding and naval equipment; chemical production, and supersonic materials. In November 1992, a standing Russian–Korean joint commission on economic, scientific and technical cooperation was set up in Seoul, involving businessmen and experts of the Russian Far East. In January 1993, a consortium among South Korean Tey, Lucky Goldstar, Samsung, and others began to discuss the construction project of a gigantic 5,000 kilometer gas pipeline connecting Yakutia, Sakha, North Korea, and South Korea, valued at US$22 billion. The participants spoke in favor of the search for new international sources to finance the project.

The breakthrough in Russian–South Korean relations, despite Pyongyang's extremely negative reaction, is becoming an important factor in stabilizing the security situation in Asia–Pacific. The dialog between Pyongyang and Seoul picked up, but the sudden death of Kim Il Sun prevented the inter-Korean summit meeting slated for late August 1994. The Russian–South Korean rapprochement does not run counter to the strategic interests of any of the Asia–Pacific states.

THE TWO KOREAS' STRATEGIC AND ECONOMIC SIGNIFICANCE

Contradictions between the perspectives of the United States, Russia, China, and Japan on the Korean peninsula hamper considerably the comprehensive involvement of South and North Korea in the economic and social revival of Eastern Siberia and the Russian Far East. The United States, while favorably assessing the prospects of Korea's reunification from the economic point of view, has poor regard for it from the military-strategic position. If the two parts of Korea were to reunite, the issue of the withdrawal of the US armed forces from the peninsula would inevitably surface. Outwardly, China offers a favorable assessment of various sorts of confederative ideas such as 'one state, two systems' on the Korean peninsula. This would provide Beijing with an additional counterbalance to Japan's potential claims in Eastern Asia. Moreover, this idea is similar to China's position on Taiwan. At the same time, Beijing cannot but fear the possibility that a unified Korea, where Seoul's dominance would be inevitable, would noticeably weaken China's influence on North Korea, with all of the subsequent consequences for China's foreign policy in East Asia.

In the current situation, it appears that Russia is more interested in a peaceful reunification of Korea. Moscow would get a strong business partner to offset Japan and acquire realistic means of strengthening peace and stability in the region. At the same time, post-totalitarian Russia is interested in a long coexistence of North and South Korea. It is precisely unforced cooperation and integration of production potentials of the South and the North that will create an entirely new system of international cooperation in the Asia–Pacific region.

The latest reports of the State Bank of the Republic of Korea indirectly confirm this premise. According to 1992 figures, South Korea produced 5.3 million tons of rice while North Korea harvested 4.2 million tons. Electric power production in the South reached 24.1 million kw, in the North 7.1 million kw, a total of 31.2 million kw. South Korea produced 42.6 million tons of cement and North Korea 4.7 million tons, 47.3 million tons together. However, there are industries where North Koreans dominate. Coal production in South Korea amounted to 11.9 million tons but in North Korea 29.2 million tons, a total of 41.4 million tons on the entire peninsula; iron ore production in North Korea totalled 5.7 million tons, to South Korea's 0.2 million tons, totalling 6 million tons. North Korea's foreign debt ran at $9.7 billion in 1992 and South Korea's at $42.8 billion, or $52.5 billion in total.[12] These statistics, given all their conventional and relative nature, indicate that a unified Korea may become one of the leading chains in Asia–Pacific integration, occupying a stable place among the ten most advanced post-industrial economies. In roughly three decades, moreover, the total number of Koreans will exceed 100 million people.[13]

The above figures indicate that a new sub-regional center of force may be formed on the Korean peninsula which will not be inferior to the Russian Far Eastern economic region in its economic parameters. It does not follow from this observation, however, that the two Koreas may monopolize international cooperation and integration concerning the development of the productive forces in the Far Eastern economic region. South and North Korea, in view of the huge financial burden required to restore state integrity which, according to some estimates, is running at $1.2 trillion,[14] will hardly be able to fully respond to the challenges of accelerated modernization facing the Far Eastern economic region and the Asian part of post-totalitarian Russia.

CONCLUSIONS: FUTURE RELATIONS WITH NORTH AND SOUTH KOREA

The above discussion leads to the conclusion that there is a need to find new approaches to the problems and prospects of the Russian Federation's interaction with the two states on the Korean peninsula. First, the current geo-political situation in the Asia–Pacific region is characterized by an extremely fragile balance of strategic forces, the violation of which is fraught with devastating dangers not only of a regional but of a global nature. Especially dangerous in this respect is the threat of North Korea's withdrawal from the Nuclear Nonproliferation Treaty (NPT) and a sharp rise in the confrontation between North and South Korea.[15] In this situation more and more Russian international affairs analysts tend to think that essential conditions for unforced restoration of the integrity of a single Korean state have not ripened yet in the current geo-political environment. A complete failure of various political illusions about Korea's reunification patterned on West Germany's recent absorption of the eastern part of the country is quite obvious. Therefore, there are serious grounds to believe that in the coming years Moscow will favor the concept and policy of a long-term peaceful coexistence and economic cooperation between North and South Korea in order to lay the groundwork for restoring Korean democratic unity.[16]

Second, Russian academic and business circles are more inclined to think that Russian–North Korean business ties should be substantially depoliticized and revived. As was noted above, the mutually beneficial relations between Russia and North Korea were largely curtailed after 1991. Meanwhile, North Korea's hard currency debt to Russia exceeds $3 billion. The Russian side is unable to write off this huge debt, although most of it resulted from Soviet arms deliveries to Pyongyang. Russia is convinced that North Korea has the potential to meet its foreign obligations.[17]

Third, it was noted above that Russian–South Korean relations have been developing intensely in recent years. The initial euphoria has now been replaced with disappointment and pessimism, however. The grandiose 'projects of the century' often get stuck on the stage of technical developments through the fault of both the Russian and South Korean sides. Russian academic and business circles are more and more convinced that the Republic of Korea has, by many times, overestimated potential opportunities of capital investment in Russia's economy (up to $10 billion by the year 2000). It is unlikely that private South Korean businesses, even with state support, will be capable of independently realizing large-scale projects to develop Yakutia's coal and gas, or build major transport, industrial, and other facilities. With acute labor shortages, extremely poor infrastructure and an underdeveloped social sphere, investments will take quite a long time to recoup. Therefore, reality dictates the need for radical diversification of Russian–Korean business cooperation. Russia's business-minded political elements tend more and more to think that the industrial development of the natural resources of the Russian Far East could be more effective on the transnational basis involving private and state investment not only from the Republic of Korea but also from Taiwan, Japan, the United States, Singapore, and other countries.[18]

Fourth, it is impossible to ignore the fact that Russia's cooperation with South and North Korea in the Russian Far East is currently primarily geared towards the development of raw material industries of the region, e.g., coal, timber, gas, and non-ferrous metals. This does not quite correspond to the long-term economic and social development strategy of the Russian Far East. Russia's Eastern part can integrate into the future Asia–Pacific community as a full-fledged partner, as a highly-developed industrial and technological complex, rather than a mineral and raw materials appendage. In this connection, the region has an acute need to develop, on the basis of manufacturing industry's conversion, a large auto maker which would not entail an intensive development of related industries, infrastructure and social sphere.[19] Challenging almost an absolute monopoly of the car-making giant in the city of Togliatti on the Volga River, a modern auto maker in the Far East could intensively promote the creation of a free market economy in Russia. Moreover, the issue of environmental protection features prominently in business relations between the Russian Far East, the two Korean states, and other East Asian nations. The scales of timber-cutting without reforestation works are such that in approximately forty years forest tracts may disappear completely.[20]

Fifth and finally, we have already noted above that the political instability in Russia and the insufficient influence of the state in the process of national reproduction constitute one of the fundamental problems which hampers an intensive flow of private foreign investment in the Russian economy. Life has shown that foreign investors mistrust Russia's attempts to insure foreign investments. This premise suggests that it is of primary importance to form a transnational insurance fund in the Asia–Pacific region.[21] It is precisely this kind of fund that can guard investors against entrepreneurial risks in post-totalitarian Russia, guarantee a complete replacement of capital invested in the development of the Russian economy. There can be no doubt that the creation of such a fund, acting independently or in cooperation with the International Monetary Fund and the Asian Development Bank, would generate a keen interest from business circles not only of the two Korean states, but also of Japan, the United States, Taiwan, and other economies of the Asia–Pacific region.[22]

The post-confrontation Russian–Korean cooperation effected for the sake of progress and stability has a serious future not of itself, but within the context of general processes of the economic, political and strategic integration in the Asia–Pacific region.

NOTES

1 *International Relations in the Pacific*, Moscow: Nauka, 1979, pp. 143–6; V. Andrianov, 'Russian Far East: Relationships with the Center,' *Problems of the Far East* (Moscow), no. 6 (1993), p. 3.
2 *Problems of the Far East* (Moscow), no. 6 (1993), p. 4.
3 'Russian Far East,' *Problems of the Far East* (Moscow), nos. 1–3 (1992), pp. 45–7. In the war 9 million Koreans were killed or wounded. See, Kim Chull-Baum (ed.), *The Truth About the Korean War*, Seoul: Publ. Co., 1991, pp. 41–2.
4 G. Toloraya, S. Diikov, and G. Voitolovsky, *The Republic of Korea*, Moscow: Mezhdunarodnye otnosheniya, 1991, pp. 35–6.
5 Treaty of Friendship, Cooperation, and Mutual Assistance between the Union of Soviet Socialist Republics and the Democratic People's Republic of Korea (signed in Moscow on 6 July 1961). See Byun Dae-Ho, *North Korea's Foreign Policy*, Seoul: Research Center for Peace, 1991, pp. 249–51.
6 N. Bazhanova, *DPRK's Foreign Economic Relations*, Moscow: Nauka, 1993, pp. 87–9.

7 *Ibid.*, p. 88.
8 *Ibid.*, p. 89.
9 *Democratic People's Republic of Korea*, Moscow: Politizdat, 1985, p. 186.
10 *Ekonomicheskaya gazeta* (Moscow), no. 33 (1980), p. 80.
11 L. Anosova and G. Matveeva, *South Korea: A Glance from Russia*, Moscow: Nauka, 1994, p. 228.
12 See The Bank of Korea, *Annual Report, 1993*, Seoul: The Bank of Korea, 1993; Gill-Chin Lim (ed.), *Korea into the Future: Peace, Unity and Progress*, East Lansing: Michigan State University and Hanyang University, 1994, pp. 44–5.
13 These statistics are quite conventional. The Korean peninsula also is one of the most militarized regions in the Asia–Pacific region. The feverish arms race stepped up when North Korea's per capita income was seven times lower than in South Korea, the GNP was ten times lower than in the southern part of the country. (*Izvestia*, 12 July 1994.)
14 *ITAR-TASS Bulletin*, 21 February 1994.
15 See Kim Dae-Jung, *Korea Reunification*, Cambridge: Cambridge University Press, 1993, pp. 7–23. The most authoritative documentary evidence of the development of nuclear arms is the KGB report No. 363-K submitted to Mikhail Gorbachev in February 1990. It reads, *inter alia*, 'According to available data the DPRK's Nuclear Research Center situated in the city of Janben, Pyongan-pukdo province, has completed the development of the first nuclear explosive device . . . The State Security Committee is taking measures to verify the data. KGB Chairman V. Kryuchkov.' (Quoted in *Izvestia*, 24 June 1994).
16 *ITAR-TASS Atlas* (Moscow), no. 41, 12 November 1993, pp. 17–18.
17 *Izvestia*, 12 July 1994. Analysts of Korean affairs cite other more realistic estimates. Some estimate that to bring North Korea's economy up to South Korea's level, $250–400 billion will be required (*Kompas*, 24 August 1994, p. 61).
18 V. Denisov, 'Nuclear Safety of the Korean Peninsula,' *Mezhdunarodnaya zhizn*, no. 5 (1994), pp. 23–31. The UN-approved project aimed at creating a free economic zone in the basin of the Tumen River at the junction of the three countries – Russia, China, and North Korea – may serve as an example of multilateral international cooperation in the development of natural resources and the Russian Far East economy. To launch the project, it is planned to invest some $30 billion of the Asian-Pacific nations' capital, including Japan, the United States, South Korea, in the coming 15–20 years (P. Korkunov, 'On the "Tumenchiang" Free Economic Zone Project,' *Problems of the Far East*, no. 3 (1994), p. 14). As of October 1994, South Korea and China are the most promising participants in this project. Their mutual gross turnover in 1994 was expected to reach $13 billion. South Korean capital is quite integrated into China's economy through the creation of modern industrial enterprises. In 1993 alone South Korean investment in China amounted to $590 million (*ITAR-TASS Bulletin*, 26 August 1994).
19 'Reforms in Russia and in the Republic of Korea,' international workshop, Moscow State University 1994, Moscow.
20 *Novaya yezhednevnaya gazeta*, Moscow 1994.
21 In 1993, the turnover of inter-Korean trade did not exceed $200 million. Such large corporations of South Korea as Samsung, Hyundai, and Lucky Goldstar have begun business operations in North Korea but they limit their activity to insignificant investments (*Izvestia*, 12 July 1994).
22 N. Petrakov, 'The Situation of the Russian Economy,' a report presented at the international workshop on this topic, Moscow, 1994. According to Russian economists' estimates, in the late 1980s, indicators of the export efficiency, i.e., the difference between the costs of per unit of production and export proceeds, in the Russian Far East were: 189 per cent for fuel, mineral raw materials, and metals, 142 per cent for machinery and equipment, 212 per cent for metal-working

machine tools, and 250 per cent for power equipment. This means that, despite the depressive and even crisis state of the Russian economy, industrial processing is much more effective than raw material production and its export to international markets. Hence, the economic expediency of deep diversification of Russia's foreign economic ties, especially in the Far Eastern region.

12 The Russian Far East and Northeast Asia

Security cooperation and regional integration

Robert A. Manning

INTRODUCTION

Is there a relationship between measures that enhance security and stability in Northeast Asia and efforts to integrate the Russian Far East into the dynamism of the Asia–Pacific economies? Obviously, a stable security environment is a vital underpinning for sustained economic growth. But, more broadly, can a new logic of geoeconomics – the imperatives flowing from the character of the unprecedented Information Age economic interdependence – transcend the burden of lingering suspicions and latent rivalries that hold the potential to disrupt the Pacific Rim's economic dynamism?

This paper employs the larger notion of 'comprehensive security,' defining security expansively to include issues beyond traditional politico-military factors that are part of the gestalt of stability, and addresses a number of cross-cutting issues where economic and traditional security concerns, such as maritime safety, nuclear cooperation, and arms sales, intersect. It also argues that patterns of cooperative security behavior may have a synergistic effect on economic issues by helping to improve overall bilateral relationships, the sub-regional security environment, and/or by reducing perceived risk for foreign direct investment. This paper is premised on the assumption that Russia continues in the direction of economic privatization and a pluralist, rule-of-law political system, and in the security realm, on the continuity of the US–Japan security alliance.

Based on that premise, there appear to be a range of issues, including cooperative action in regard to traditional security concerns on the principal security challenge to the region and the sub-region – the North Korean nuclear threat and the process of reunification of the Korean Peninsula – that hold varying degrees of promise for new Russian engagement in Northeast Asia. The Russian proposal in March 1994 for an international conference on the Korean nuclear problem appeared a rather transparent advertisement for recognition that Russia is a great power with important interests in the region.

As a Eurasian power, the Soviet Union was a defining factor in the security equation in Northeast Asia throughout the Cold War. However, beyond the security guarantees and subsidies it provided to allied Asian Communist regimes, it was marginal in the economic realm and decidedly Eurocentric in mind-set. Like its predecessor, Russia is also a significant factor in the sub-regional security equation, albeit of a lesser magnitude in military terms. But where the USSR's relationship to the dynamic Asia–Pacific economies was defined primarily in the negative as a threat, Russia is pursuing a course of positive engagement and is increasingly viewed as a real or potential partner. This trend began in the late 1980s with the new policy towards East Asia pursued by then Soviet President Mikhail Gorbachev. It has continued, although with a lower profile, with the same goal of enhancing Moscow's economic and political engagements in the region.

THE KOREAN CATALYST

The strategic fulcrum of the Pacific is Northeast Asia, where the interests of the four major powers – the US, Japan, China, and Russia – and the two Koreas are joined. It is relations amongst these states (which include three of the five declared nuclear powers and the world's three largest economies), particularly US–Japanese, Sino–Japanese, and Sino–American relations, that are the key determinants of Asia–Pacific security and stability, and of the possibilities of cooperative approaches to it. While examining the dynamics of bilateral relations among these major powers is outside the mandate of this chapter, clearly the interests of the four major powers overlap on the Korean Peninsula. The recently negotiated US–North Korea nuclear agreement, if fully implemented, is likely to result in an acceleration of the North–South reconciliation process. This may catalyze new possibilities for sub-regional cooperation. Managing the external aspects of the Korean question strongly suggests a role for the surrounding major powers in the process as well as giving impetus to economic prospects such as schemes to develop the Tumen River basin and the Sea of Japan rim. It is the range of possibilities that may be opened up following a resolution of the nuclear problem in particular that I seek to explore.

Even upon resolution of the nuclear issue, the principal – and immediate – source of tension most likely to result in instability and/or conflict remains the heavily-armed standoff on the Korean Peninsula. The most urgent issue is the North Korean nuclear weapons program, but the longer term concern is the process of Korean reunification. Though the implications for the global proliferation regime of the North Korea nuclear problem are beyond the scope of this paper, it has both global proliferation and regional security aspects.

In regional terms, the nuclear issue is inextricably bound up in the question of Korean reunification. The scenarios for reunification run the spectrum from implosion and Romania-type collapse to explosion and a second Korean war. How reunification occurs is likely to have major implications for the regional balance, particularly for the future of US military presence in the region. All four major powers and South Korea seek both to achieve a de-nuclearized Korean Peninsula and to avoid a second Korean war accompanied by a destabilizing collapse of North Korea.

In pondering Korean scenarios, the starting point is the best case scenario, a 'soft landing' for North Korea. This is the preferred choice of both North and South Korea as well as the four majors powers. Such a scenario rests on the realization of a negotiated termination of North Korea's nuclear weapons program. This, in turn, rests on the willingness of the leadership in Pyongyang to pursue Chinese-type economic reforms and, essentially, trade its nuclear program for economic and political engagement with the international community in a step-by-step reciprocal confidence-building process. The theory behind the 'soft landing' approach is that foreign trade, aid, and investment would cushion and begin to refurbish the failing North Korean economy such that a gradual, peaceful reunification process could result with help from a magnanimous ROK. While not inconceivable, fears of the Pyongyang leadership that even a controlled opening would lead to an undermining of its political control suggest that such an outcome is rather unlikely.

An implosion scenario would involve large flows of refugees from North Korea across the DMZ (demilitarized zone) to South Korea, to the ethnic-Korean areas of China, and to Japan. While it might be peaceful, collapse of the regime, or a struggle between North Korean factions, could also involve military force, and would be destabilizing to Northeast Asia in general, as well as to South Korea, which would bear the primary responsibility for a reunification by *force majeure*. An explosion would be the worst-case scenario in which a desperate North Korea would launch a suicidal assault on the South, hoping to seize Seoul, and then pursue peace.

In the case of either implosion or explosion, the result would be rapid unification by absorption. Such an outcome would resolve the nuclear issue (although, in the worst case this could lead to a Ukraine-type problem of inherited nuclear capability). This could have a palliative effect on the subregional Northeast Asian nuclear arms race, the specter of which has been greatly exaggerated by many analysts. Korean nuclear proliferation has not been a factor in Chinese nuclear modernization plans. Furthermore, Japan, which has lived with the threat of hundreds of Chinese bombs, will not abandon its Constitution or pacifist political culture, especially not in the short-term, because Pyongyang proliferates. North Korea, however, provides a convenient political rationale for Japanese development of hi-tech dual use capabilities (from the accumulation of plutonium to the H-2 rocket) and defensive systems designed with China in mind. As it muddles towards a democratic transformation, Russia has become a secondary factor in the equation. However, Russia's still sizeable military force, military/technological ties to China and its relationships and borders with North Korea, China, and the Sea of Japan continue to guarantee Moscow's role as a player in regard to the Korean Peninsula.

A NORTHEAST ASIAN AGENDA

In spite of lingering security concerns in Northeast Asia, no formal cooperative political framework or multilateral process has been initiated. This reflects in part the weight of the sub-region's checkered history, and in part the solidity of US–Japan and US–ROK bilateral alliances. However, there is an urgency in the current political environment which suggests that the situation may be ripe for developing a new Northeast Asian political framework. Such a framework, along with APEC and the ASEAN Regional Forum, could evolve into a component of the emerging Asia–Pacific architecture, which is comprised of overlapping or multi-layered mechanisms.

As the crisis over the nuclear issue has unfolded, momentum towards such a sub-regional framework has begun to evolve. Formally, South Korea has proposed – in former President Roh Tae Woo's September 1992 UN speech and in Foreign Minister Han Sung Joo's October 1993 speech to the Asia Society in Hong Kong, as well as Han's tabled proposal at the 1994 initial ASEAN Regional Forum (ARF) meeting – a forum among the two Koreas and the four major powers.[1] All parties, with the possible exception of North Korea, have some measure of interest in the idea. Former Secretary of State James A. Baker III raised the idea in a *Foreign Affairs* essay.[2] Such a Northeast Asian initiative is also a logical follow-up to Seoul's Nordpolitik which has fulfilled its objectives. Moreover, the prospect of the smallest power taking the lead would give the initiative a special credibility.

A forum for Northeast Asia has compelling logic. As discussed above, the interests of the four major powers (the United States, Japan, China, Russia) overlap: all support a denuclearized Korean Peninsula, all would prefer a 'soft landing' for North Korea, all have an interest in minimizing the turmoil resulting from Korean reunification, and all have an interest in expanding economic growth in the region. Korea has a strong interest in harmony among the major powers to whom, historically, its security has been hostage. Thus, it would be possible to build on a 'form follows function' basis. South Korean, US, Russian, and Japanese officials have all expressed an interest in some form of a Northeast Asian political entity.

Beyond Korea, there are a host of issues particular to the sub-region around which Northeast Asian interests converge. In this regard, a sub-regional political framework should adopt a 'comprehensive' notion of security, including the range of issues beyond traditional military concerns (marine resources, environment, piracy, nuclear safety, narcotics trafficking, refugee flows, and perhaps peacekeeping) in defining the parameters of any forum.

Equally important is carefully structuring an agenda to keep contentious bilateral issues, particularly territorial disputes such as the Northern Territories or the Senkaku Islands, outside the scope of any such forum. Clear parameters must be set so that none of the participants – particularly China or Japan – will fear that the forum could be used to 'gang up' on any one member over issues in dispute.

Moreover, the magnitude and immediacy of the Korean crisis shows that limiting participation to essential players would increase chances of success. For this reason, a separate Northeast Asia forum, either apart from or as a subset of the ASEAN Regional Forum, may be suggested. There are some processes already under way, such as the Northeast Asia Economic Forum.[3]

Informally, the diplomacy surrounding the North Korean nuclear issue over the past three years has begun to build a sense of a security community and of the associative interests which are prerequisites for any such mechanism to be effective. US-led efforts to end North Korea's nuclear weapons program and achieve a denuclearized peninsula have involved intense consultation and coordination with South Korea as well as Japan at the Assistant Secretary level. Over the three years, this has evolved into trilateral coordinating efforts toward North Korea. The United States has also worked closely with Russia, and has increasingly engaged China on this issue. This pattern is a key building block to new multilateral efforts.

Beyond the nuclear issue, however, there is the important agenda of managing the transition on the Korean Peninsula. That three of the four major powers in the area are Permanent Members of the UN Security Council gives sub-regional consensus reached by a consultative mechanism a potentially global impact. The Korean question will ultimately be resolved by Koreans through the North–South dialogue which has already produced the framework for reconciliation and arms control signed in December 1991.

While Korea is not analogous to Germany and the '2+4' process in legal/political terms, there is an important role for outside powers in managing the external aspects of North–South reconciliation. If the Koreas turn the armistice into a peace treaty, achieve a denuclearized peninsula, and reach arms reduction agreements, there is a role for outside powers in endorsing, respecting, and/or guaranteeing the outcomes of such developments. Since the United States and China are signatories to the armistice, they should, at the very least, have a notary role to play in the realization of a peace treaty between North and South Korea. Russia remains formally a treaty ally of North Korea.

In regard to security issues, since three of the four regional powers are also members of the nuclear club, if the agreement for a denuclearized peninsula is implemented, they could provide more specific security assurances or a no-first-use pledge. The rich arms control experience of the United States and Russia could facilitate Conventional Forces in Europe (CFE)-type negotiations possible in the joint military commission created under the North-South reconciliation accord.

If North Korea collapses, managing the fallout would be primarily a Northeast Asian problem. In terms of risk management, there is logic in multilateral consultations to coordinate efforts among the four powers and Seoul to manage such a crisis. Such a collapse would produce refugee flows to China, Japan, and Russia as well as to South Korea – not to mention the desperate military action which may occur in an implosion scenario. If the current nuclear crisis is not resolved and North Korea continues on what is likely to be a suicidal trajectory, a five-power forum – or perhaps five plus an empty chair should North Korea change course – makes sense as a preventive diplomatic mechanism.

Beyond Korea, there is an equally important sub-regional agenda which could serve to mitigate concerns about China and Japan, and help integrate Russia into the region (Moscow should also be invited to join APEC). A Northeast Asia political security consultative mechanism would embed both China and Japan in a multilateral framework that could foster an atmosphere conducive to overcoming traditional fears, building trust and confidence, and creating a larger context for addressing both Russo–Japanese issues and Sino–Japanese relations. These will be a major determinant of stability in the Pacific in the twenty-first century. Over the longer term, in the event of the withdrawal of US troops in Korea, such a political framework could help anchor the United States in the region.

NUCLEAR COOPERATION

There is one vital non-military security issue which bridges the Korea issue and the broader Northeast Asia agenda: nuclear safety in Japanese plutonium reprocessing. Japan's reprocessing program and its transport and stockpiling of plutonium has set off alarm bells across Asia. The program is of questionable economic rationale. Most estimates suggest that the glut of enriched uranium and plutonium and the general economics of energy render commercial breeder reactors inviable until the mid-twenty-first century. Plans drafted in the late 1970s by Japan, Germany, France, and Britain have been overtaken by economic reality. Thus far, only Germany has begun to retreat from its nuclear agenda. Burning MOX fuel in power reactors might be six to ten times more expensive than uranium according to some estimates, but some studies suggest it may not be quite that costly. The start-up date for Japan's large breeder reactor has already been put back several times, and is now scheduled for the year 2030. Its cost is now estimated in the $12 billion range, which makes Japanese utility companies increasingly reluctant to participate. Additionally, the Japanese public are not particularly anxious to have 70 to 80 tons of plutonium stored in their country.

South Korea is already more dependent on nuclear power than Japan, and a reunified Korea, due in part to fears of Japan, might have an interest in reprocessing. Some in the South Korean scientific/technical and political elite already favor reprocessing. If reprocessing is necessary – and market forces suggest it may not be – it could be done on a regional basis with all facilities and plutonium under IAEA custodianship as originally envisioned in the agency's charter with equal access, as necessary, by all in Northeast Asia. Given the Clinton Administration's new proliferation initiative to focus on excess plutonium stockpiles and place stockpiles from dismantled weapons under IAEA safeguards, a Northeast Asian forum could also explore a ban on enriched uranium and plutonium production. Such an initiative would be a major confidence-building measure, melting latent suspicions about Japan, bolstering the global non-proliferation regime, and preempting a post-Korean reunification arms race. The issue could be part of a sub-regional energy development agenda. The plans of a multinational consortium, the Korea Energy Development Organization, to supply light water reactors to North Korea as part of the US–DPRK nuclear agreement could be the initial phase of such an agenda.

A wide range of issues under the rubric of nuclear cooperation could be the agenda for a Pacific counterpart to EURATOM, perhaps an ASIATOM, which would function as an element of regional institution building to manage sub-regional nuclear cooperation. Such a mechanism might pursue cooperation not only on reprocessing, but on safeguards, management of spent fuel (an issue which has already generated tension between Russia and Japan), and cooperative efforts to enhance nuclear safety. As civil use of nuclear power is only in its infancy outside Northeast Asia and Taiwan, ASI-ATOM might begin as a sub-regional enterprise and expand if and when countries in Southeast Asia move to nuclear energy. Certainly Russia, or at least the Russian Far East, would be an important participant in such a venture. Since 1991, Japanese nuclear officials have raised the possibility of helping Russia build MOX fuel reactors which would not only supply energy for the Russian Far East, but also enhance security by using the surplus plutonium from dismantled Russian nuclear weapons.

Such a nuclear, if non-military, confidence building measure (CBM) could, in turn, foster a political climate amenable to military transparency (defense spending, doctrinal talks, maritime safety) discussions which should be prominent features of the Northeast Asia agenda. Such discussions could be held between militaries in tandem with political talks. Expanding military-to-military dialogue can be an important tool in reducing the risks of miscalculation, if not for building trust and confidence. Japan has already initiated bilateral military talks with China, providing a precedent on which to build. Russian military deployments and activities would be an important item for discussion. In addition, arms sales and missile proliferation should be part of this agenda.

MARITIME COOPERATION

There is also a Northeast Asian dimension to environmental concerns. Acid rain from China is falling in South Korea and Japan. Moreover, management of marine resources in and around the Sea of Japan lends itself to cooperative action. These problems require collaborative sub-regional solutions, such as pooling resources to monitor pollution, and are part of larger maritime cooperation agendas that should be pursued in a Northeast Asian framework. Issues such as piracy, refugee flows, illegal narcotics trafficking, unlicensed fishing, monitoring marine pollution, and creating a database and sharing information on shipping and sea lane safety offer a rich agenda for modest initiatives.

Perhaps the easiest topic for discussion might be search and rescue/maritime safety cooperation. This would entail multilateral planning and mechanisms to share real time information in response to emergencies. Recent clashes between the Russian military and Japanese fishing boats, or reports of piracy in the East China Sea, are vivid examples in which maritime cooperation might play a preventive role. Building on such endeavors, maritime cooperation could expand to sharing maritime surveillance intelligence or responsibilities for monitoring various areas. Russia and Japan already have an incidents-at-sea agreement which could become multilateral.

One issue that may best lend itself to trilateral cooperation is the Cold War legacy in the Sea of Okhotsk. While the START 1 and START 2 agreements will reduce Russian employments of SSBNs in the area, the continued deployments of Russian strategic weapons and the continued US response of aggressive submarine patrolling practices reflect bureaucratic inertia on both sides. A trialogue or a US–Russian initiative to curb these outmoded realities in close consultation with Japan should be considered.

SEA OF JAPAN CONCEPT

The cumulative effect of confidence-building measures along the lines of those outlined above would likely create a synergy of economic initiatives under discussion in Northeast Asia in the Sea of Japan concept. The logic of the Sea of Japan concept is that there is a complementarity between Russian and Mongolian natural resources, Chinese and North Korean labor and light industry, and Japanese and South Korean capital and technology that is capable of producing a growth cluster, similar to those we have witnessed elsewhere in East Asia. China and Mongolia are interested in an outlet to the Sea of Japan, and there is some interest among localities in western Japan: Niigata Prefecture has allocated 3 billion yen to set up an Economic Research Institute for Northeast Asia.

In the Russian Far East, the beginnings of sub-regional cooperation in the form of joint ventures and joint infrastructure development are unfolding. In Khabarovsk, there are some 250 joint ventures, from manufacturing to restaurants, operating, thirty-nine of which are South Korean.[4] China and Russia have begun construction on a railway between Hunchun and Kraskino, and have agreed on the lease of Zarubino Port. Japan's Ministry of International Trade and Industry (MITI) is funding preliminary studies on the development of Primorskii Krai. There is also growing interest in the proliferation of free trade zones from Vladivostok to the Rajin-Sonbong zone in North Korea's Tumen River region, where the borders of China, Russia, and North Korea converge.

While the grandiose plans for a $30-billion Tumen River development project by the United Nations Development Program (UNDP) are unlikely to be pursued, there is some initial small-scale infrastructure development underway. This free trade region would comprise the Russian Far East, northeast China (Heilongjiang, Liaoning, and Jilin provinces), North Korea, South Korea, Mongolia, and Japan. Although the Tumen River scheme is likely to remain largely a pipedream for at least the rest of this decade, some modest infrastructure improvements, such as the Chinese development of Chongjin port will occur, but not until Japan, and perhaps South Korea, are prepared to finance such a large-scale scheme will it have any chance of being realized. North Korea's behavior in regard to this project may offer a useful window into Pyongyang's thinking. North Korea's only designated 'zone of free trade and economy' thus far is the 600 square kilometers which encompass the Rajin and Sonbong areas, a coastal area in the Tumen region in the isolated northeast corner of the country.

NORTHERN TERRITORIES

What, if any, relation would any of these economic developments or confidence-building measures have on the enduring legacy of enmity between Russia and Japan over the Northern Territories dispute? Devising solutions to the Russo–Japanese territorial dispute has become a veritable cottage industry; the missing ingredient has not been failure to devise the right formula, but rather the political will of both sides in the face of assertive nationalism in both Russia and Japan. Only when the mutual agenda of Russia and Japan reaches the point that both Moscow and Tokyo realize that their mutual interests are best served by getting the Northern Territories issue sorted out will one or more of the many proposed options be adopted.

In retrospect, the solution proposed by then Soviet People's Deputy Boris Yeltsin during his January 1990 visit to Japan appears to be less far-fetched than it was judged at the time. Yeltsin said:

> It should be a step-by-step policy which, on the one hand, would create a sense of confidence among the Japanese people that the territorial issue is not standing still and which, on the other hand, would put our people in a position to form an opinion in favor of compromise.

Yeltsin suggested a multi-phased process beginning with Russia acknowledging the problem, and then turning all four islands into a free-enterprise zone for Japan, demilitarizing the islands, signing a peace treaty to formally end the Second World War, and finally allowing the next generation of politicians to choose a final denouement within a fifteen to twenty year time frame. Options for these would include: a joint protectorate, free international status, and the transfer of the islands to Japan. A variation could perhaps include an Okinawa-type resolution acknowledging sovereignty and agreeing on a timetable to implement it. In any case, a negotiated resolution of the issue is more likely to be a reflection of a new sense of normalcy in Russo–Japanese relations than a catalyst for it.

CONCLUSIONS

In the near term, issues relating to the Korean question and to proliferation give an urgency to the six Northeast Asian governments' need to begin proactively meeting these challenges. Until and unless North Korea meets its international obligations in regard to its nuclear activities, the sixth chair in any forum should remain empty. None the less, there is advantage in building on the above-mentioned pattern of trilateral diplomacy and establishing a mechanism to manage the risks ahead on the Korean Peninsula, and to begin a dialogue on the broader sub-regional questions sketched above. Steps in such a direction can create a habit of dialogue and new patterns of cooperation that foster a security environment with a burgeoning sense of shared interests.

Over the longer term, a Northeast Asian political framework can be an important factor in ameliorating the latent suspicions and rivalries that lie just beneath the surface in Sino–Japanese, Korean–Japanese, and Russo–Japanese relations. For the United States, a forum which focuses on issues of common concern could facilitate its search for a new equilibrium in Sino–American relations. By enmeshing all of the key players in a broader institutional framework, a Northeast Asian political forum could create a healthy interface with efforts to redefine the respective bilateral relationships as well. A still larger question is whether the logic of geoeconomics can create a new strategic calculus, redefining perceptions of interests and concepts of security sufficiently to generate new organizational forms of political cooperation. Such efforts can have an important impact on the definition of Russia's post-Cold War role in the Asia–Pacific and the fostering of a broader sense of economic and political partnership, particularly between the Russian Far East and Northeast Asia.

NOTES

1 Han Sung Joo, 'Korea and China in the Asia–Pacific,' speech to the Asia Society, Hong Kong, 27 October 1993.
2 James A. Baker, III, 'America in Asia: Emerging Architecture for a Pacific Community,' *Foreign Affairs*, Winter 1991/1992, p. 3.
3 A non-governmental forum among individual researchers and institutions in Northeast Asian countries concerning regional economic cooperation, established in 1991. The secretariat is located in Honolulu, Hawaii.
4 Michael Spector, 'A Russian Outpost Now Happily Embraces Asia,' *The New York Times*, 14 August 1994, p. A12.

13 Conclusion

Tsuneo Akaha

Several conclusions emerge from the foregoing analyses. Some of them reflect convergence of views and others represent important differences of opinion.

Domestically, Russia and the Russian Far East have so much to do, politically, economically, legally, and socially. Moscow currently lacks a coherent, comprehensive, and long-term view regarding the Russian Far East's role in Russian policy towards Asia–Pacific. This is because Moscow's geographical and temporal horizon is constrained by the political uncertainty at the national level. The political turmoil in Moscow has retarded and distorted economic reforms, the slow and painful process of economic transformation has threatened political instability and social dislocations, and preoccupations with immediate security issues, such as the Chechen crisis, have diverted Moscow's attention.

Fortunately, there are some indications that the economic and social costs of reform the Russian people have so far paid may have been worthwhile. As one analyst put it:

> The new political institutions function. Strikes are rare, and no serious social unrest is on the horizon. Incredibly, most of the Russian economy, measured by either employment or output, has been privatized in just two years. Russia has already become a market economy . . . In short, Russia has undergone fundamental changes and appears to be on the right track.[1]

However, many dangers still remain: high inflation, ruble instability, manufacturing decline, regional income gaps, growing public and private debts, credit instability in the nascent banking industry, wide-spread capital shortage, fraudulent management and stock practices, monopolistic enterprises, fragile and incomplete institutions of civil and commercial law, fiscal shortfall, incomplete taxation, weakening social safety net, politicization of federal–regional relationship, and regional fiscal imbalances.[2]

Regional developments are an integral part of the twists and turns of Russia's political and economic reforms. Given the widespread feeling among the Far Eastern communities of the historical neglect, and even exploitation, by Moscow, the Russian government must allay fears of 'more of the same' in the new Russia. The democratization process in Russia must include an open discussion of this region's role as part of Russian policy in the Asia–Pacific region. Moscow must encourage active participation by regional leaders in the national debate. Ultimately, a federalist union must be forged with a politically sustainable balance between the national and regional powers.

Moscow should view the Russian Far East's close economic ties with Asia–Pacific countries, particularly with the Northeast Asian neighbors, as being in its own interest. Not only will such development make economic sense for the development of the Far Eastern region, it will also reduce Moscow's burden. Moscow should support the formation of indigenous foundations of economic development in this and other regions, including infrastructure, investment capital, modern technology, efficient public and corporate management, skilled labor, and scientific and environmental expertise. Also needed are political, legal, and social institutions to support the region's economic foundations. Unless the region develops a degree of self-sufficiency in these basic ingredients of economic development, it will remain a net burden on Moscow.

Given the importance of the defense sector in the Russian Far East, the process of civilian conversion is both important and difficult. Moscow and the Far Eastern leaders should make military–civilian conversion a top policy priority and seek international cooperation. Russia's growing arms export to Asian countries may serve the short-term interests of its capital-short defense industry, but they may come to haunt Russia if they retard or, even worse, reverse the slowly improving political relations among the Asia–Pacific countries. Northeast Asia is an already heavily armed region. China alone has 2.93 million men in uniform, while North Korea has 1.128 million, South Korea 533,000, Taiwan 376,000, and Japan 239,000. Japan's defense budget, the largest in the region, stands at $53.8 billion, South Korea is second with $14.4 billion in defense spending, followed by Taiwan with $11.3 billion, China with $7.5 billion, and North Korea with $2.2 billion.[3] Moscow should review its weapons and weapons technology exports in terms of their long-term impacts on the region's security environment.

Successful reduction of the economic burden of the military–industrial complex in the Russian Far East and in Russia as a whole will depend on the development of civilian industries and reduction of international tension. Conversion must make a strategic sense for Russia and be based on a stable national consensus concerning economic priorities.

Strategically, conversion must proceed at such a pace as not to threaten Russia's national security. This means the process must be linked to security cooperation and confidence-building measures involving Russia and its major foreign policy partners. In Asia–Pacific, Russia's conversion efforts must proceed in tandem with the development of bilateral and multilateral security consultations and confidence and security building measures (CSBMs). Efforts in this area, unfortunately, are just beginning.[4]

Economically, conversion will be a long-term and painful process. It creates winners and losers in the domestic economy, not to mention politics. The Russian government must make difficult decisions as to how to reallocate the nation's increasingly constrained resources. Clearly, the development of a long-term national industrial policy is in order. The policy must spell out which civilian industries will receive focused capital investments and political support and which industries, including the superfluous defense industry, will receive substantially lower priorities than in the past. Obviously, Moscow must demonstrate a strong political will and exercise effective leadership in forging a national consensus on the nation's future economic priorities. Currently, however, such conditions are largely absent.

The development of a national industrial policy raises equally difficult questions about the role of government in economic development. Whether the subject is raised as a question of preference or of reality, this is a formidable question. The history of Russia, before and during the Soviet era, is fraught with state-dictated or controlled economic development (or underdevelopment). In the absence of a healthy private sector and a civil society to support it, Russia today faces a fundamental dilemma over the role of government in economic development. Some argue that until market forces are sufficiently strong to sustain economic development, the state (Moscow) should implement a selective industrial policy with a focus on the development of strategic and basic industries. In this, 'industrial targeting' model, reminiscent of the Japanese postwar economic recovery and growth, protection of some key industries in the initial stages of market development is deemed not only unavoidable but perhaps even desirable from the point of view of orderly transition and political stability. Opponents argue that the government's heavy-handed control of economic reform will stifle budding entrepreneurial developments and perpetuate the inefficient bureaucratic management of the national economy. As well, critics of the state-directed development model assert that domestic industries should be exposed as quickly as possible to the international market disciplines in terms of efficient and price-competitive production.

An additional, equally difficult question for the Russian Far East is whether industrial production should be geared toward export to the rest of Russia or to the international market. Those that emphasize the region's geographical location, i.e., its proximity to the burgeoning Asia–Pacific economies, argue in favor of export-oriented development strategy and point to the recent trends toward trade expansion as supporting development in this direction. They also point to Japan and other East Asian countries as successful models that the Russian Far East could emulate. Their argument is based on the fact that the internal (regional) market in the sparsely populated Russian Far East is very small. Supporters of this view argue that even if Russia as a whole continues the current path toward a market economy, the distance to the more populated European Russia will be a major handicap for Far Eastern producers. However, trade enthusiasts should keep in mind that in terms of export competitiveness the Russian Far East is starting near the bottom of the Asia–Pacific trade system. As such, they should be aware of the real danger that export-driven development might force the region to become a perpetual exporter of primary commodities and importer of manufactured products. Will the Russian Far East's historical dependency on Moscow be replaced with a future dependency on the Asia–Pacific? This is not a rhetorical but a real question facing the region.

Specific reform measures that are urgently required include inflation control and reduction of public, quasi-public, and private sector debts. Moscow should also do all it can to establish Russia's international credit-worthiness by following marketization policies consistently and persistently and making debt payments a top priority. Convertibility of the ruble should be established as quickly as feasible. Moscow should develop an effective legal infrastructure for sound domestic and international business. Equally urgent is sweeping privatization of land and resource ownership. However, privatization should be a democratic and de-politicized process, with effective public oversight. These conditions are largely lacking at present.

Moscow and regional governments should develop a politically sustainable policy to restore inter-regional economic ties as quickly as possible. Obstacles to trade and investment between the country's regions should be removed as quickly as possible. Moscow and regional governments should provide the basic public goods, including national security, public safety, legal, transportation, and communication infrastructure, social welfare, environmental protection, and resource conservation. If domestic capital and expertise are inadequate, the international community should provide technical support, humanitarian aid, and intellectual assistance.

The Russian Far East will most likely continue its reliance on natural resources exploitation for its near-to-mid-term economic development. Moscow and the Russian Far East should take advantage of the complementarity that currently exists between their economies and those of the neighboring countries of Asia–Pacific, with the former as resource exporters and the latter as suppliers of consumer goods and labor. Effective resource conservation measures must be developed and faithfully implemented with a view toward sustainable development. Environmentally sound resource management will help sustain the region's comparative advantage in the international trade in natural resources. Resource processing and semi-manufacturing industries must also be developed. In the longer term, however, Russia must make concerted efforts to diversify the region's economy to include technology-based manufacturing.

Internationally, Russia and the Russian Far East should work closely with Asian-Pacific organizations and institutions in order to build the international community's confidence in Russia as a credible and legitimate partner in the Asia–Pacific economic community. Moscow should make the utmost effort to satisfy the basic requirements for membership in APEC, including development of a market economy and promotion of economic ties with the current members of the region-based grouping. When Russia does join the group, Moscow should include representatives of the Russian Far East in its delegation.

In developing complementary economic relations with the neighboring countries, Russia and China should develop a politically and socially sustainable regime for transborder trade and commerce.[5] Initially the two countries should promote transborder investment in labor-intensive, small to medium enterprises. Care must be taken to control the quality of production and environmental impact, so as to avoid the potentially harmful effects of quality-related complaints on both sides. Equally important will be the development of balanced and mutually beneficial relations between the neighboring communities across the border. Moreover, Russia and China should develop a politically sustainable regime for the cross-border movement of people. Particularly important will be the elimination of the enduring suspicion among the Far Eastern population that China may have territorial interests in Russia. China should not assume that all Russians welcome a Chinese presence any more than a Japanese, Korean, or US presence in the Russian Far East.

Moscow and Beijing should carefully evaluate their current weapons and weapons technology trade policies in terms of their long-term impact on Asia–Pacific security. The two countries should promote military–civilian conversion to reduce the reliance on exports/imports of weapons and weapons technology. In the absence of an established framework of multilateral security consultations, bilateral arms deals are bound to raise neighbors' suspicions about the military and political ends of such transactions.

The Russians and Japanese should continue to make progress simultaneously on the political and economic issues between the two countries. Legacies of the conflict-ridden history between the two peoples will take a long time to disappear, if they have any chance of disappearing at all, and the development of a relationship built on mutual trust and confidence will require sustained, long-term efforts on both sides. Moscow and Tokyo must make the utmost effort to educate their respective peoples to the global importance of normalizing their bilateral relations. As geographical neighbors, Russia and Japan must develop a friendly and cooperative relationship that is based on broad domestic support and the long-term interests of the two peoples. This means, among other things, that Moscow must be genuine in its desire to resolve the territorial dispute and the issue of Japanese prisoners of war. Tokyo must not be seen as taking advantage of the current vulnerabilities of Russia in seeking a resolution to these issues. Japan's growing flexibility in its policy towards Russia must be further broadened to include expanded economic cooperation, technical exchange, and cultural contacts. Russia must make it unequivocally clear that it is committed to the promotion of better relations with Japan based on effective implementation of its international legal obligations.

Sustainable development is another area in which Russia and the Russian

Far East must make their own efforts and also seek international cooperation. Environmental protection should be given a high priority through all
phases of development. This is true even in the current times of economic
difficulty, because the protection of the natural and human environment will
help maintain a healthy and productive population. Environmental neglect
will generate anti-development, anti-market, and anti-foreign sentiments,
which are obviously detrimental to the development of a market economy
and cooperative international relations. Foreign participation in resource
exploitation and industrial development in the Russian Far East has already
generated some anti-foreign sentiments among the local communities
because the foreign presence has been associated with the destruction of
their environment and resource base. The United States and Japan, in particular, should actively and visibly share their experience and expertise in
economic development and environmental protection with Russia. The
United States and Japan should take a leading role in multilateralizing the
currently bilateral economic and environmental cooperation. The two countries should invest in the capacity building of domestic and international
nongovernmental groups and organizations involved in resource conservation and environmental protection.

The United States and Japan should also cooperate with the other G7
member countries and other regional institutions, e.g., the Asian
Development Bank (ADB), the APEC forum, the Pacific Economic
Cooperation Council (PECC), and the Pacific Basin Economic Council
(PBEC) in assisting Russia's efforts to develop a market economy which will
satisfy the requirements of public and private capital assistance. The United
States and Japan should also cooperate with the other Asia–Pacific countries
in removing barriers to trade and investment in the Russian Far East.

The United States should develop a coherent, consistent, and visible Asia
policy, in which the Russian Far East is defined as an area of priority in
US–Russian relations. So far, Washington's policy toward Moscow has been
characterized by a European bias. In his speech at the annual meeting of
PBEC in Washington DC in May 1996, President Clinton mentioned Russia
but once and only in passing. In contrast, almost one-third of the entire
speech was dedicated to discussing US policy toward China. Apparently,
China is an economic power in the Asia–Pacific but Russia is not. It would be
short-sighted, however, if the increasingly aggressive US economic policy
toward the Asia–Pacific falls short of promoting closer economic ties with
Russia. To ignore the potential of Russia, more precisely the Russian Far
East, as an economic partner in the Asia–Pacific would be to push it back
into the role it had played during the prewar and Cold War decades, that of
a heavily fortified frontier, a source of volatile tension, a neglected region of
frozen economic opportunities.

Japan, China, and South Korea should welcome US initiatives to promote
multilateral dialogue in Northeast Asian economic cooperation. At the same
time, Japan, China, and South Korea should actively seek US participation in

bilateral and multilateral discussions and projects involving the Russian Far East so as to counter the European bias in Washington's Russian policy.

The United States and Russia should make further efforts to place their nascent 'partnership' on a firmer ground and accelerate cooperation in regional security, including in Asia–Pacific.[6] The two countries should lead the development of multilateral security consultations involving Japan, Korea, and China, the three countries of Northeast Asia that have virtually no experience in multilateral security cooperation. Although formal security cooperation in Northeast Asia will likely continue its bilateral character, cooperation should be gradually multilateralized. The United States, Japan, China, and South Korea should engage Russia in confidence-building measures, including promotion of military personnel exchange, transparency in defense spending, control of illegal trade in the defense sector, and nonproliferation. They should consult closely on regional security issues, such as North Korea, without further isolating Pyongyang. Pending progress on the nuclear issue in North Korea, Russia and China should develop a balanced relationship with North and South Korea. Japan and the United States should seek normalization of relations with North Korea but at such a pace and in such a way that it will not be detrimental to the interests of South Korea. Quite instructive in this context is the gradual, consensus-based security dialogue that has developed in the ASEAN Regional Forum (ARF) – the process in which the United States, Russia, Japan, China, and South Korea already participate.

North–South Korean reunification will have a major impact on the future of the Russian Far East and its relations with the neighboring countries. Although the realizability and modality of reunification remain uncertain, Russia, the United States, South Korea, and Japan can help in the development of a non-threatening political environment surrounding the Korean peninsula by consulting closely as each of them approaches normalization with North Korea. These countries should encourage and offer opportunities for North Korean participation in scientific, environmental, and cultural exchanges among non-governmental groups. There are a number of areas in which specific experiences and expertise of the international community can be made relevant to the needs of North Korea, such as in marine environmental conservation and resource management.

Russia and South Korea should cooperate in developing a politically sustainable policy of ethnic diversity in the Russian Far East with a focus on the re-integration of ethnic Koreans who were forcibly removed from the region during the Stalinist period. The international community should provide support and encouragement for the struggling Tumen River Area Development Program, but the immediate beneficiaries – the Russian Far East, China, North Korea, and Mongolia – should hold realistic expectations with regard to the scale of the project and the level of international support, including foreign capital participation.

Leaders in Moscow and the Russian Far East should encourage competition among Japanese, Chinese, South Korean, and US businesses in seeking opportunities in the Russian Far East. This will both facilitate market competition and enhance the strategic position of Far Eastern enterprises *vis-à-vis* international partners. Russian business partners must recognize, however, that long-term international participation in the economic development of the Russian Far East cannot be assured unless they offer rational terms and conditions in their business relations. Japan, China, Korea, and the United States have much to offer, bilaterally and multilaterally, in the development of human resources, modern business management, scientific research, and environmental protection.

The politically sound and environmentally sustainable development of the Russian Far East represents a serious challenge to the leadership of the international community. Given the geographical proximity and potential impact, the countries of Northeast Asia have the most to gain from successful development and the most to lose from failure. History has never provided a better opportunity for international peace and cooperation in this part of the world than at the present moment. We shall see whether the leaders of the countries concerned will rise to the occasion.

NOTES

1 Anders Aslund, 'Russia's Success Story,' *Foreign Affairs*, September/October 1994, p. 58.
2 These and other problems facing Russian economic reform were discussed at the 'Symposium on Russian Economic Reform,' 2–3 March 1995, Tokyo, sponsored by the Economic Planning Agency of Japan.
3 These figures are from 1995, except for Taiwan's, which is from 1994. Estimates of China's arms expenditure vary widely. The Institute for International and Strategic Studies, London put it at $28.5 billion in 1994.
4 For recent discussions on the prospects of confidence and security building efforts in Northeast Asia, see Edward A. Olsen, 'Post-Cold War Confidence Building Measures in Northeast Asia,' and Simon Duke, 'Northeast Asia and Regional Security,' *Journal of East Asian Affairs*, vol. 9, no. 2 (Summer/Fall 1995), pp. 252–87 and 323–84, respectively.
5 For an insightful, balanced study of border trade and its implications, see James Clay Moltz, 'Breaking with Moscow: The Rise of Trade and Economic Activity in Former Soviet Border Regions,' Deborah Anne Palmieri (ed.), *Russia and the NIS in the World Economy: East-West Investment, Financing, and Trade*, Westport, Connecticut and London: Praeger, 1994, pp. 97–114.
6 For a call for further deepening of Russian–US partnership, see Andrei Kozyrev, 'The Lagging Partnership,' *Foreign Affairs*, May/June 1994. A skeptical view is found in Zbigniew Brzezinski, 'The Premature Partnership,' *Foreign Affairs*, March/April 1994.

Index

LOVE IN THE MOON

Canéda, whose mother was French, is disgusted when after her brother becomes unexpectedly the Earl of Langstone her French grandmother invites them to visit the family.

Her mother had run away on the eve of her marriage to the *Duc* de Saumac because she had fallen in love but her parents had never spoken to her again.

Because Canéda hated them for hurting her mother who is now dead and she also loathes the *Duc* de Saumac who tried to injure her father, she plans a very subtle revenge on them both and sets out for France in her brother's yacht.

How the revenge on the *Duc* is successful but involves unforeseen circumstances, how her grandparents are very different to what she expected and how love is stronger than hatred is all told in this exciting 282nd book by Barbara Cartland.